ROUGH PASSAGE

Rough Passage

TRUE TALES OF SHIPS AND MEN

By

Dana G. Prescott

THE CAXTON PRINTERS, LTD.
CALDWELL, IDAHO
1958

Library of Congress Catalog Card No. 58-5330

Printed and bound in the United States of America by
The CAXTON PRINTERS, Ltd.
Caldwell, Idaho
81866

TO
THOSE
WHO SAIL
THE
SEVEN SEAS

FOREWORD

It is the fate of most to experience adventure secondhand, and perhaps that is just as well. We must then seek it through books, camera, or stage. But there is little that any participant in true adventure can tell which really gives the whole picture and so it must be seen through the eyes of several. Thus, the reader of such an occurrence is actually seeing more than any individual participant. This is a great advantage and one which allows the fullest appreciation.

True stories of the sea offer some of our finest adventure tales. In this collection Dana Prescott presents a varied, documented picture against the backdrop of the common stage—the sea itself.

In reading these stories, one is mindful of the essential common denominator which is the elemental force of nature as epitomized by the sea. Man in his essential being has always had a definite relationship to the sea. He has learned of its moods and fancies; he has carefully studied its winds and currents; he has brought to it his own efforts in utilizing its forces for a livelihood.

Something of man's primitive past is present in every sea disaster. Combining the struggle for survival with the science of oceanography is a linking of two extremes in man's conquest of the sea. And yet the sea has never been fully conquered. Down through history, the world's flood has had to be used as a partner-force, a helper and a comfort as well as a source of food and a highway of commerce.

Thus, we read of these stories, culled from the great number of similar ones, and realize how much the sea enters into the daily lives of thousands today as much as it did in the past. There can be no complete mastery of the sea. When we think it is conquered, along comes a West Indian hurricane to remind us of the unlimited power, or a *Doria-Stockholm* collision to point to the eternal vigilance which must be exercised at sea.

No anthology can ever be a complete roundup of sea literature; just so, no collection such as ROUGH PASSAGE can represent more than a limited field. However, here is a grouping of yarns which in themselves brings out all the vital qualities of men against the sea. We can sit back and relax as we read them but they will bring us out of ourselves and ignite our inborn love of the sea which is always a part of our heritage.

EDOUARD A. STACKPOLE, *Curator*

MYSTIC SEAPORT
MYSTIC, CONNECTICUT

ACKNOWLEDGMENT

I wish to express here my deepest gratitude to Miss Eleanor Stephens, librarian of the Stillman Library at the Seaport, Mystic, Connecticut, for her unceasing and gracious help offered me in my research work for this volume; to her assistant, Miss Grace Jones, who spent many arduous hours preparing the typescript in its proper final form; and to Mr. Edouard A. Stackpole, the Seaport's able Curator, who "set me right" on many authentic details in these chapters, and who graciously consented to write the Foreword to this book.

D. G. P.

CONTENTS

ROUGH PASSAGE

I

THE SAGA OF THE SKIPPER
WHO STAYED

"S O S . . . GKJY . . . S O S . . . S O S . . . GKJY!"
Out of the terror of a storm-ridden night in the
North Atlantic crackled the urgent call letters of
distress!

It was 5:30 A.M., Sunday morning, January 24,
1926, and the United States liner *President Roose-*
velt, commanded by Captain George Fried, ploughed
eastward through rough seas toward England. Kenneth Upton, the *Roosevelt's* chief radio operator,
lighted up a cigarette and idly twisted the dials
on the 600-band for a silent visit with other tossing ships in one of the severest storms that had
raked the North Atlantic in fifty years. Upton suddenly sat bolt upright as he caught the distress
signal. Quickly he fingered down through his list
of ships' call letters—GKJY, British freighter *An-*
tinoe! Tensely alert, Ken Upton began translating
the dots and dashes as they snapped across nearly
one hundred miles of mountainous seas, telling a
frantic tale of a disabled steering gear, flooded engine room, and stove-in hatches.

For five days the eight-thousand-ton *Antinoe* had
drifted helplessly in the trough of a raging North
Atlantic sea. At four o'clock that Sunday morning,
Captain Harry Tose balanced himself on the bridge

of his wallowing vessel, wondering whether he or his twenty-four officers and crew would ever see England again! It had been touch and go with fifty- to seventy-foot waves smashing at the very vitals of the little freighter—bowled along by ninety-mile-an-hour hurricane winds out of the west. Through all the hideous ordeal Captain Tose marveled at the calm discipline the crew maintained. Below, his four engineers had struggled ceaselessly to keep the pumps going and maintain steam until they were driven, three days before, from the engine room by the inrush of water that doused the stokehold fires. And, now, at 5:30 A.M., Arthur Evans, the *Antinoe's* lone wireless operator, had stuck to his post half the night ceaselessly pounding out, "S O S . . . GKJY . . . S O S . . . S O S . . . GKJY!"

"Give positions, *Antinoe!*" The dots and dashes fairly sparkled from Upton's fast-clicking key. "This is the *President Roosevelt!*"

"Approximate position 47 degrees north latitude, and 38 degrees west longitude!" flashed back Evans. "For God's sake hurry, *Roosevelt!*"

Grabbing the phone, Upton called the bridge. He quickly briefed the bridge on the position and condition of the *Antinoe*. Immediately Captain Fried checked the *Antinoe's* given position against the *Roosevelt's* present bearings. She appeared to be some eighty-five miles away. Further communication with other ships in the vicinity showed the *Roosevelt* closest at hand—with the big Cunarder *Aquatania* the next nearest. But Captain Charles of the *Aquatania* had problems of his own, battling westward—and making no headway—in the teeth of the very gale that had disabled the *Antinoe!*

"I'll go in for the rescue!" Fried wirelessed the *Aquatania's* master in a rapid-fire decision.

"Best of luck!" flashed back the skipper of the big Cunarder.

"Position verified!" tapped out Upton encouragingly to Evans. "We're on our way—will be there in few hours!"

"Thanks—but hurry!" Upton could feel the urgency in Evans' acknowledgment.

The bridge phone buzzed. Upton grabbed the receiver and heard Captain Fried's voice.

"See if you can get more accurate bearings, Mr. Upton," he urged. "We've got to hit 'em on the nose to save 'em!"

Immediately the *Roosevelt's* radio operator set up the direction finder. Then he tapped out a QST to all vessels and shore stations. He told them the *Roosevelt* was rushing to the aid of the *Antinoe*—giving them the approximate positions of both vessels. All shore stations and ships' radios stayed silent, and Upton was in control of all radio communications on both sides of the Atlantic to avoid the possibility of interference. All radio attention was focused on the rescue ship and the ship to be rescued—it was the routine handling of an S O S call. Then Ken Upton went rapidly and certainly about the business of setting up new radio bearings.

By 8:00 A.M. Nelson Smith, second operator, came on duty to relieve his chief. But there was no relief that morning—Smith kept in constant contact with Evans on the *Antinoe,* while Upton stood by the direction finder getting a new bearing every fifteen minutes and accurately establishing bearings between the two ships as if they were in sight of each other.

Meanwhile, Smith pounded out words of encouragement to Evans. The situation aboard the *Antinoe* was desperate, Evans told him. Time and again his weary shipmates would stick their heads in the wireless shack asking pertinent questions, or giving bits of graphic information.

"How many knots is she makin', Sparks?" one would ask.

"God, if she doesn't come into sight soon it's all up!" moaned another.

"Number 3 hatch just let go, Sparks!" came the weary voice of a third. "An' th' water's two feet higher in the hold!"

"Cargo's shifted again, an' she's listin' five more degrees starb'rd!" yelled a fourth man.

"Y' say she *sounds* nearer?" asked a fifth man in an urgent voice.

Following Chief Operator Upton's latest bearings on the radio direction finder, Captain Fried ordered full speed ahead as the *Roosevelt* surged headlong into the rough seas. With legs spread wide to keep his balance, Fried scanned the gray expanse of stormy water with his binoculars, tensely watching for the disabled *Antinoe.* An hour passed—two hours! Still no *Antinoe!* Then, at twelve noon, through a sudden rift in the raging snow squalls, Captain Fried picked up the dim outline of the distressed ship—dead ahead!

"There she is, Bob!" he called to his chief officer, Robert Miller. "And right on th' nose, too!"

"Thank God for that direction finder!" answered Miller reverently.

"Phone the engine room and tell 'em to start pumping oil overside!" ordered Fried. "We'll circle her with a path of oil an' smooth out th' tops of those combers!"

Captain Fried cut the *Roosevelt* to half speed and maneuvered in the lee of the *Antinoe*. He was mentally estimating the situation and making tentative rescue plans in his mind when the bridge phone buzzed loudly. It was Chief Operator Ken Upton.

"Captain Tose—T-O-S-E—the *Antinoe's* skipper, doesn't want to abandon ship immediately," advised Upton over the phone. "Says he's confident weather will soon moderate, then he can reach port. In spite of the flooded stokehold, he says he's able to keep up enough steam for generators—but would we stand by in case matters get worse?"

"Of course we'll stand by!" shot back Fried. "But tell him to show good lights during the night so we can keep him in sight if trouble develops!"

"Aye, sir!" answered Upton and hung up.

At 4:00 P.M. Evans reported that the generators were being shut down to build up steam for the engines. He told Arthur K. Ransom, third radio operator of the *Roosevelt,* then on duty, that if matters worsened on the *Antinoe* the *Roosevelt* would be advised. That was the last radio message from Evans. Ransom called the bridge and reported to Captain Fried.

"Captain Tose is a game skipper, and I can see

his point in wanting to pull his ship out of trouble by himself," observed Fried to his chief officer as he hung up the phone. "But I don't believe he realizes the very real danger he's in!"

"What's up now, Captain?" asked Miller.

"He's cut his generators to save steam for his engines—still thinks he can make it under his own power . . . if the weather should moderate!" Captain Fried shook his head dubiously.

"The fool!" broke in Miller angrily. "Why can't he play it safe an' abandon now while there's a chance!"

"Sometimes we skippers are a stubborn lot," answered Captain Fried in a quiet voice. "We don't give up our ships that easy."

But a few impatient passengers aboard the *Roosevelt* got wind of the fact that the *Antinoe's* skipper refused to abandon ship, and a delegation was sent to Captain Fried to persuade him to continue the voyage.

"If he doesn't want to abandon ship and thinks she's safe," they argued, "then what good can the *Roosevelt* do by waiting around. We've got important appointments and we're in a hurry to get to our destination, Captain Fried!"

Fried smiled at them grimly.

"I know the *Antinoe* is in a worse condition than her master describes," said Fried calmly. "The *Antinoe* needs more help than her captain realizes. If, to avoid delay, I were to leave the ship and go on my way, I would never go to sea again. If I leave the *Antinoe,* I know that the ship will be lost through my failure to stand by when it needs assistance."

Silently the disgruntled delegation left Captain Fried.

Terrific snow squalls swirled blindingly down on the edge of the premature darkness of a wintry North Atlantic night, all but blotting out the *Antinoe's* shadowy hulk with her faintly blinking riding lights. By nine o'clock that Sunday night the fury of the sudden squall had reduced visibility to a half mile, and the stabbing beam of the *Roosevelt's* searchlight failed to pick up the floundering freighter. Then, as suddenly as it had roared out of the west, the snow squall passed. But the *Antinoe* was nowhere to be found in the seething caldron of the stormy sea!

Time and again the powerful searchlight of the *Roosevelt* swept the black expanse of towering combers and sizzling spray—but the hulk of the *Antinoe* and her twenty-five weary men of the sea seemed to have disappeared from the surface of the angry North Atlantic! Captain Fried tensely scanned all points of the compass as he peered through his night glasses. Fearful thoughts raced through his mind. Had he been too late? Where had he slipped up? Would it have been better to have heaved a "messenger line" aboard the *Antinoe* and demanded that Captain Tose abandon ship? A strange, nauseous feeling swept over Fried as he frantically tried to pick up the lost *Antinoe* in his binoculars . . . twenty-five men gone! My God!

"Any luck, Captain?" asked Chief Officer Miller who had just come on the bridge.

"Not yet, Bob," Fried's answer held an ominous meaning.

"Well, we did the best we could," observed Miller. "That squall fouled us up!"

"Not the best we could, Bob," came the captain's weary answer. "There are still twenty-five men out there—hoping!"

"Aye, sir," nodded the chief officer. "But suppose, sir, she's. . . ."

"We can't 'suppose,' Bob—we've got to keep looking—and hoping, too!" There was grim determination in Captain Fried's voice.

Somewhere around midnight faint signals crackled through the earphones of the *Roosevelt's* third operator, Art Ransom. He had taken over from Nelson Smith, the second operator, just moments before. Feverishly Ransom adjusted knobs on the receiver, trying desperately to bring the signals in stronger. But it was no use—the result was the same, just a jumble of dots and dashes jammed together. Suddenly out of the welter of static cracklings and sputterings young Ransom caught faintly the familiar call letters—GKJY!

"Ken! Nelson!" he blurted out jubilantly. "I got th' *Antinoe!* Evans must be on th' air with an emergency set! Somebody call th' skipper!"

Upton and Smith sprang from their bunks on the double. Upton grabbed the bridge phone. Captain Fried answered.

"Th' *Antinoe's* afloat, Captain!" Upton fairly screamed over the phone. "Ransom's catching faint signals from her, now!"

"Thank God!" breathed Fried in relief as he hung up.

"Good news, I hope," Chief Officer Miller spilled out the words expectantly.

"Aye, Bob, good news!" relayed Captain Fried. "At least the *Antinoe* is still afloat!"

Then Fried swung into action. He knew that what must be done must be done quickly! He knew, too, that while the *Antinoe* was afloat somewhere out there in those mountainous seas he had to act fast—angry seas wait for no man, and there were twenty-five seamen's lives at stake!

With a 30° roll—and shipping tons of green sea over her forepeak—the *Roosevelt* plunged forward at full speed, traversing in a concentrated search. All that stormy night Captain Fried stood glued to the bridge windows, vainly peering through his binoculars for a sight of the lost freighter! The gale-ridden night gave way to a dismal dawn of ugly white-plumed combers. Still no sign of the *Antinoe!*

More blinding snow squalls closed in on the *Roosevelt* as she battled the smashing seas. Visibility, zero. Great danger lay ahead should they suddenly come upon the *Antinoe!* It was now 4:00 P.M. Monday. Captain Fried ordered half speed, then left the bridge in charge of Chief Officer Miller and joined his navigating officer, Second Officer Magnus Eriksen, in the chartroom. Carefully they studied the ticklish situation and approximated the positions of both vessels. Then, suddenly, a pale beam from a weak sun shone through a rift in the storm, casting a vague shaft of light through a chartroom port. Without further word Eriksen grabbed his sextant and rushed out to "shoot the sun"—the thing he had waited for days to do. He returned quickly to work out a true course. For several minutes Eriksen bent over the chart table and calculated the *Roosevelt's* position from his sun observation. Then he turned to Captain Fried with a big grin.

"I think we can safely come about and steam on a 135 true course," he beamed. "I—I think we can locate the *Antinoe!*"

"Might be the answer at that," nodded Fried. "God knows we've tried everything else!"

Forty minutes later Captain Fried picked up the *Antinoe* in his binoculars, just off the *Roosevelt's* starboard bow. Fried spotted the wallowing freighter's signal flags. They fitfully spelled out AJ—"I desire to abandon ship, but have not the means!"

"Thank God we made it in time, Bob!" Captain Fried's voice was full of reverence as he spoke to his chief officer. "An' thank God, too, for a little sun—an' Eriksen's accurate calculations!"

"Aye, sir!" grinned Miller.

Passengers and crew members alike voiced their joy and relief as loud cheers rang out along the *Roosevelt's* decks. Immediately more signal flags were hoisted aboard the floundering *Antinoe:* "Water in forward and aft holds, fire and engine room flooded and radio out of commission!"

For a moment the weather seemed to moderate, though the sea still ran high. Captain Fried made a fast survey of the situation. At best it would be a risky operation—an open boat lowered in that

mountainous sea could be an invitation to death!
But Fried had no other choice—twenty-five men's
lives were in his hand! His officers, to a man, all
clambered to take command of the rescue boat.
It made Captain Fried's decision easier.

"Mr. Miller, man and lower a port boat at once!"
ordered Fried. "Call volunteers for the manning
of the boat—I'll maneuver the vessel on the lee
side of the *Antinoe* to give you some protection
from the weather—carry on!"

"Aye, sir!" sang out the chief officer and hurried
to the boat deck.

When Miller called for volunteers nearly the
whole crew rushed up to him—including waiters
and stewards!—begging him to let them go. Quickly
the chief looked them over, then called those who
were to be with him in the rescue boat. Bo'sun's
Mate Ernest Heitman and Master-at-arms Uno
Witanen were the first chosen. Then Master-at-
arms M. Jacobowitz, Seamen Joannes Bauer, Alex
Fugelsang, Cosmo Franelich, and Sam Fisher. Chief
Officer Miller knew all their capabilities—he had
chosen well!

"Bo'sun, clear away Number five boat and prepare for immediate lowering!" ordered Miller grimly. "It's a rough risk, but we've got to make it—
twenty-five men are depending on us!"

But mishap stowed away on the rescue boat.
Failure and death were there, too. A bight of a
line fouled the aft releasing gear and the forward
end of the lifeboat hit the water with a resounding
thwack. Before the after gear could be cleared, the
Roosevelt rolled heavily to port, dangling the life-

boat by the after fall. Men spewed out of the boat and clutched at the grab lines. Working feverishly, the deck crew struggled to release the after fall. Suddenly it freed itself and the boat tossed crazily in the heavy seas. Men managed to scramble over the gun'ls of the pitching lifeboat and break out the oars. But a Lundin boat is an unmanageable thing at best, and in spite of Miller's herculean efforts to steer any sort of course toward the *Antinoe*, the boat spun wildly around in the waves and spume without making headway.

A vicious snow and hail squall struck suddenly as the tiny lifeboat crested a mountainous comber at a dangerous angle. Captain Fried, mindful of the dire possibilities of the situation, shouted lustily for Miller to return—but a roaring blast of wind thrust the words back to him as he stood by helplessly on the bridge and watched the cockleshell boat capsize, tossing the whole crew back into the angry sea! Miraculously the men scrambled aboard the lifeboat, heaving away at the oars in a game attempt to pull across to the *Antinoe*. Miller then caught sight of the captain's frantic gestures ordering the chief officer and crew to pull alongside the *Roosevelt*.

"Get your men aboard, Miller!" roared Fried above the storm.

"Aye, sir!" shouted back the chief officer. "Just wanted to get th' boat by th' davits!"

"Damn th' boat!" thundered Fried. "Get your men aboard!"

Hand over hand the battered crew pulled themselves wearily up the lines and ladders thrown over the ship's side. A dozen willing hands hauled them over the rail to the deck. But death rode by their side! Three of the crewmen slipped and fell back into the pounding seas. With almost superhuman strength, Master-at-arms Uno Witanen managed to get the three back into the pitching boat—then, as the men started up the slippery ladder, he tried to guide the lifeboat under the davits and he, too, lost his balance. Undaunted, Witanen swam around the crazily tossing Lundin boat and grabbed hold of the stern rope as the boat spun by him. Powerfully stroking his way through the rough waters, Uno Witanen tried to direct the lifeboat toward the distressed vessel. He passed within fifty feet of the *Antinoe* as her crew whipped out a line to him—but it fell short by inches, while he and the boat drifted from sight in the thick, blinding snow squall and gathering darkness!

At almost the same instant that Witanen lost his balance, Bo'sun's Mate Ernest Heitman—who was then halfway up the side of the *Roosevelt*—turned sharply to yell at him and missed his footing on the unsteady ladder. Heitman catapulted into the mountainous seas and disappeared astern within five minutes! All night long the *Roosevelt's* searchlight swept the stormy North Atlantic, vainly seeking the lost men—but the sea was empty, and the taut business of rescue must go on . . . the lives of twenty-five seamen aboard the *Antinoe* still hung precariously in the balance!

Urgency demanded action, and time was of the essence. Around twelve noon, Tuesday, January 26, lines shot from the Lyle gun were proving unsuccessful. One line failed to follow the projectile rapidly enough, the second try fell far astern of the wallowing freighter, the third line dropped far short, and the fourth shot carried true, but the line parted when the *Roosevelt* rolled violently to port. Captain Fried shook his head disgustedly—precious hours were being lost!

"Avast firing!" ordered Fried from the bridge. "Clear away and lower a boat—empty—and pay out line enough to let it drift to the *Antinoe*."

Chief Operator Upton who had kept in constant contact with Evans on the *Antinoe* by signal flag and blinker light, signaled frantically: "We're drifting a boat over to you—have crew stand by to board it!"

"We're weak, but we'll try!" signaled back Evans.

As Fried circled the *Roosevelt* around the *Antinoe* he ordered tons of oil pumped overside to help prevent the giant combers from breaking. Then he came in close to the disabled freighter.

The task was a dangerous one, and Fried knew that the handling of so large a ship within a hundred yards of a sinking hulk—in a high-running midwinter sea—must be a calculated risk that would challenge the sharpest seamanship of any shipmaster! Lines, rope ladders, and cargo nets festooned the *Roosevelt's* starboard side like a giant spider's web, giving the rescued men the best possible chance to climb aboard should the "drifting boat" plan succeed. Minutes later the boat was ready—fully equipped with all necessary gear and provisions in case the twenty-five *Antinoe* survivors got aboard —then broke adrift in a sudden snow squall.

As the tiny boat lowered into the heavy swells silent prayers rose in the hearts of the passengers and crewmen who lined the starboard rail of the *Roosevelt.*

Failure dogged the first attempt. The line fouled in the *Roosevelt's* screw and the boat drifted far astern in the murky storm. Another nerve-wracking hour was lost in maneuvering the big liner through the rough seas and back into position for a second try. Again the ship's crew cut the line—but this time the second boat drifted close in toward the *Antinoe's* stern . . . close enough to take off her crew!

There was a tense moment aboard the *Roosevelt.* Captain Fried kept his binoculars glued to the wreck and mumbled a soft prayer. This could be it, he hoped. Then he saw men struggling weakly toward the fantail of the 50° listing *Antinoe,* but they never made it to the freighter's stern rail— and the empty lifeboat drifted beyond their reach!

"Sorry, we couldn't make it," ruefully signaled Evans to Upton. "Men too weak to get to boat . . . no food, no water for three days!"

Captain Fried watched the discouraging situation with moist eyes. While he doggedly tried to think up a more practical plan of rescue the bridge phone buzzed loudly by his side. It was Second Operator Nelson Smith. He told the captain he had a message for him from Mr. Charles H. Rossbottom, general manager of the United States Lines.

"Read it!" ordered Fried.

" 'Hang on and let schedules be damned!' " repeated Smith over the phone. A grim look of determination hardened Captain Fried's eyes.

But it was now 5:00 P.M. Darkness dropped fast over the snow-laden skies of the North Atlantic and Navigating Officer Magnus Eriksen made an entry in the *Roosevelt's* official log: "Ceased rescue work on account of darkness. Continued to maneuver near derelict."

All through a bitter night that was interspersed with snow and hail squalls, driven by gale winds, the *Roosevelt* kept a constant vigil over the hapless *Antinoe*. At midnight Evans sent a terse blinker signal to Chief Operator Upton who had just relieved Second Operator Nelson Smith.

"Help must reach us immediately!" he flashed. "List getting heavier . . . every sea boarding us!"

Upton contacted Captain Fried by phone and gave him Evans' message. Fried turned to Chief Officer Miller who had just come on the bridge from a quick tour topside.

"What's the weather, Bob?" he asked in a tone of preoccupation.

"Moderating winds, Captain, but the seas are still rough—though a hail squall is beating it down, somewhat," answered Miller. "Why?"

"Can we launch a boat with relative safety?" questioned Fried further. "Upton tells me the *Antinoe's* signaled that she's in a bad way!"

"Aye—we can lower a boat, Captain—we've got to!" was the officer's quick answer.

So, by 1:00 A.M., Wednesday, January 27, a boat was readied and lowered in a moderating sea. Again Chief Officer Miller took charge, with Fourth Officer

Frank M. Upton (no relation to the *Roosevelt's* chief radio man, Kenneth Upton) second in command. At the oars were Alfred Wall, deck storekeeper, and five firemen, Charles Diaz, Adolph Albertz, Juan Arenada, John Hahn, and Frank Roberts. But again failure lurked aboard the Lundin boat as its crew pulled across to the helpless *Antinoe* under the powerful beam of the searchlight, and tried to lay the lifeboat alongside. Three times they gamely fought moderately rough seas—three times they narrowly escaped crashing against the side of the careening freighter. For nearly two hours they struggled to keep the lifeboat from broaching to in the heavy seas as sudden gale-driven snow squalls pounced down on them. They lost their boat, but they managed to get back to the *Roosevelt* and scramble up the cargo nets to the deck, drenched to the skin and half frozen!

Captain Fried then ordered the *Roosevelt* hove to until daybreak. But there was no answer from the *Antinoe* when Ken Upton blinkered to Evans, "Can you last until daylight?"

At 8:00 A.M. the weather was still unfavorable, with heavy seas and more snow squalls. Through his binoculars Fried could see that the *Antinoe's* condition was worsening. Immediately he ordered the Lyle gun into action. Time after time lines parted — projectiles fouled, or fell too short, or dropped too far astern of their target. Everything went wrong until an artillery officer among the passengers—a Colonel Clint Calvin Hearn—hit upon the plan of using a spring to allow a line to travel through the air with the projectile.

"Sounds feasible," agreed Captain Fried, "and it might be just the thing to do the trick!"

"I can make a short, stout brass spring," volunteered Chief Engineer John Turner, "reaving it to one end of the projectile, then to the line."

By one o'clock Turner had the spring completed. Tensely the whole ship's company waited as the Lyle gun was loaded and fired. True as an arrow, the projectile and the line sailed across the *Antinoe's* fantail. A heavier line was bent on the heaving line, then bent on the lifeboat's half-mile-long painter. The empty boat was sent adrift, and the *Antinoe's* crew hauled it hand over hand toward their foundering vessel. But as the lifeboat came almost within reach, the heaving line snapped—and the rescue boat drifted past the *Antinoe's* stern! A low moan of disappointment went up from both ships.

At eight o'clock that night Evans' blinker signaled, "Hurry! We're sinking!"

Immediately the *Roosevelt's* chief radio man phoned the bridge. Chief Officer Miller answered, then turned sharply to Captain Fried.

"This is still *my* party, Captain!" he said grimly. "Th' *Antinoe* is sinking—I'm lowering another boat at once!"

"Go to it, Bob—and good luck!" answered Fried. "I'll get the ship about and give you a lee to work in!"

Miller raced down to the boat deck—he knew there was little time to lose!

"I'm going to get those men off the *Antinoe!*" he shouted. "Who's going with me?"

"Count me in, sir!" yelled Fourth Officer Frank Upton, rushing up to the chief officer.

"I'm with you!" sang out Third Officer Thomas Sloan.

"I went in th' first boat, an' I'm goin' in this 'un!" shouted Seaman Alex Fugelsang.

"That goes f'r me, too!" roared Seaman Sam Fisher who had faced death when the first rescue boat was launched.

"I want t' go this time!" called out Deck Yeoman Wilson Beers.

"I went las' time, an' I ain't stayin' b'hind now!" cried out Deck Storekeeper Alfred Wall.

"*Ja*—me, too—las' two times I vas below—dis time I go!" boomed Otto Wilke, an oiler.

"I'm goin', too—we gotta save them guys this time!" yelled Engineer's Messman Deweese Caldwell.

Captain Fried veered the *Roosevelt* sharply across the *Antinoe's* trim clipper bow and brought her up off the disabled freighter's port beam, fifty yards away. The sea had moderated, though the *Roosevelt* still rolled and pitched as Fried ordered her hove to. Anxiously Chief Officer Miller stood by in the stern of the Lundin boat waiting for the instant to launch the rescue craft. Overhead the dark racing storm clouds thinned and a pale silver moon silhouetted the *Antinoe* wallowing helplessly below. Pigmy-like figures clustered near the sinking vessel's port rail.

"Lower away!" Miller boomed out the order. Blocks creaked and the fall lines whined through the sheaves as the lifeboat was lowered to the moderately rough water, while passengers and crewmen tensely lined the *Roosevelt's* starboard rails.

"Out oars!" ordered the chief officer, grabbing the tiller.

The moon was brighter now—and the powerful searchlight of the *Roosevelt* paved a broad path of illumination for Miller's rescue operation. The rolling, lifeless form of the *Antinoe* loomed ahead of them like a sinister monster as the rescue boat's crew stroked their way through the heaving swells.

"Best take us off from our stern!" shouted Captain Tose, clinging weakly to the aft rail. "We've secured a heavy line to a stern bitt—you'll find it dangling in the water off th' stern!"

"Aye," yelled back Miller, "we see it. Get some of your men ready t' come down th' line!"

Bobbing with the heavy swell, the rescue crew held the boat steady while the first of the *Antinoe* men slid down the rope, dropping exhausted to the bottom of the boat. Twelve times the operation was repeated—twelve men were safely in the lifeboat— men with faces black from oil and grime—men exhausted to the point of collapse! For them this ordeal was nearly over!

A pent-up roar burst from the throats of passengers and crew as the Lundin boat—up to its gun'ls in spray and spume—bobbed crazily toward the *Roosevelt* with its human cargo huddled in the bow and stern. Wearily the survivors pulled themselves hand over hand up the lines, ladders, and cargo nets slung over the *Roosevelt's* side. At the rail a half a hundred hands lifted them to the deck. A couple of dozen crewmen helped carry the *Antinoe* men to warm quarters below. Some of them limped badly, others had arms in crude slings—all of them were oil-soaked from head to foot and half-frozen from five days in bitter North Atlantic midwinter weather!

Simple stories of heroism were told. The fireman who stayed in the stokehold for two days with water up to his waist, trying to keep some sort of a fire going for steam—of Art Evans, their lone radio operator, who stood by in the radio shack keeping constant contact with the *Roosevelt* until even his emergency set failed and went off the air—then, after that, keeping the rescue ship informed by signal flags and blinker light.

" 'E's a grand guy, this Evans!" summed up one seaman. "Without him we'd have all bin lost!"

But there still remained thirteen aboard the sinking *Antinoe*, including her game little skipper, Captain Harry Tose. Black clouds began to blot out the pale moon, and the wind was rising. It was still a touch-and-go situation. The thirteen *Antinoe* men must be gotten off the foundering British freighter before an angry sea claimed its victim.

By 12:40 A.M., Thursday morning, January 28, the wind lessened and another boat was manned, lowered, and gotten away safely. But a huge wave suddenly reared up and nearly capsized the boat halfway to the *Antinoe*.

"Head into it, men—fast!" ordered the chief officer, shoving his weight against the tiller to steady the boat. "Now put y'r guts into it an' bend those oars!"

Once again they were under the line dangling

from the stern of the heavily listing *Antinoe*—once
again half-dead men slid down the line and dropped
to the bottom of the crazily bobbing boat.

"How many more?" yelled Fourth Officer Upton
through cupped hands as he stood in the bow of
the unsteady lifeboat. "Th' seas 'r' rising—there's
little time t' lose!"

A grimy seaman stuck his head over the edge
of the *Antinoe's* fantail.

" 'Ere's me gear—catch!" called down the sailor,
tossing along a bulky duffel bag.

"You go t' hell!" blasted Chief Officer Miller.
"I'll have no damn baggage!"

The sailor's duffel bag splashed into the water
alongside the boat—the sailor missed the gun'l as
he dropped from the swaying line and had to be
dragged aboard.

"Who's next?" shouted the fourth officer again.
"Hurry it!"

"Hit's th' Cap'n, sir," meekly answered the seaman just hauled aboard. "Cap'n Tose, sir—'e's th'
las' man!"

"Steady th' boat, men!" ordered Miller. Then he
hollered up to the *Antinoe's* skipper. "Easy does
it, Captain Tose—an' welcome aboard!"

Slowly—hand over hand—Tose came down the
swinging rope. He was so exhausted he nearly fell
as he dropped into the boat. Miller grabbed him
and sat him gently in the stern beside him.

"Thank you, Chief—an'—an' thank God f'r Captain Fried, an' th' *Roosevelt!*" His words were
barely audible to Miller, but their heartfelt meaning went deeper than the sea itself.

The official log of the Roosevelt closed the rescue operation with this entry:

1:35 A.M.—Thursday, January 28—All on board. Rescue work completed. Lifeboat badly smashed and stove in at forward end. Boat cut adrift and at 1:40 A.M. proceeded on. Partly cloudy and moonlight. High swells.

So ended the immortal saga of the "skipper who stayed"—Captain George Fried, master of the United States liner *President Roosevelt,* whose eighty-five consecutive hours on the bridge, that twenty-five men might be saved, mark him as a truly real man and master mariner!

Sources of Factual Material

Facts for this story were gathered from the marine news story "Scrapbook" of Mr. Raymond S. Camp in the Marine Historical Association's library at Mystic Seaport, Mystic, Connecticut, giving a complete account of Captain George Fried, master of the United States Line's *President Roosevelt,* and his rescue of the men of the British freighter *Antinoe* and their courageous skipper, Captain Harry Tose, in the North Atlantic, January 24 to 28, 1926, during one of the worst storm periods in fifty years. Mr. Camp's meticulous collection of clippings is a complete coverage of the rescue by the *New York Times,* the *New York Herald Tribune,* and the *New York Sun.*

II

"—REASON FOR ABANDONMENT, UNKNOWN!"

Gibralter, Dec. 13, 1872, 1:45 PM—The *Mary Celeste* (Aust. brigantine), from New York to Genoa, with alcohol, has been derelict at sea and brought here by three men of the *Dei Gratia* (British brigantine).

Gibraltar, Dec. 14, 1872—The *Mary Celeste* (British [?] brigantine) is in possession of the Admiralty Court.

THE FANTASTIC saga of the brigantine *Mary Celeste* began when these stunning words from *Lloyd's List* in London — together with a terse message from Horatio J. Sprague, United States Consul at Gibraltar — were telegraphed to Genoa, and to the Board of Underwriters at New York.

For some eighty-odd years, the *Mary Celeste* saga has mushroomed from fact to fantasy; from blood-and-thunder misdoings aboard, to dark deeds by her skipper and mate; from alleged barratry by her owners to defraud the insurance underwriters, to an accusation that the whole affair had been a stupendous "hoax"!

The mysterious *Mary Celeste* has fired the vivid imagination of many a writer and journalist—and the prolific Sir Arthur Conan Doyle got his real start in mystery story writing when he penned his own contribution to the *Cornhill Magazine,* in the

January, 1884, issue, under the assumed name of
"J. Habakuk Jephson"—trying to "unravel" one of
the greatest unsolved mysteries in the annals of
the sea!

Certainly the *Mary Celeste* herself could never
have raised a voice to help unravel the shroud of
mystery clinging to her down through the years.

Briefly, she had been built by Joshua Dewis
in 1861 at Spencers Island on Greville Bay, up in
the middle reaches of Nova Scotia. During the lusty
launching celebration on Saturday, May 18, 1861,
they christened her the *Amazon*—though she was
only 99.3 feet in length, from the fore part of her
stem to the aft side of her sternpost; her beam was
25.5 feet; her depth of hold, 11.7 feet, and her total
tonnage was 198.2 tons. Her hull was of mixed
woods — hardwood to the light-load line, spruce
above. Originally she was a single-decker, with
square stern and roundhouse forward and aft. Later
she was rebuilt into a double-decker. She was brigantine rigged—that is, her slightly raked "fore-'n'-
aft" masts were square-rigged forward and schooner-
rigged aft. And, instead of an upper and lower
tops'l, she carried a single large tops'l.

The *Amazon* started her career duly registered
under the British flag, with an A-2 classification—
but without British international signal letters.
Even at this early stage of her life at sea there was
a question of her proper registry. She was in the
lumber trade between Canada and England for a
period of six years, and, except for a collision in the
Dover Straits, her history during this time is somewhat obscured.

Still fogged in obscurity, the *Amazon's* destiny
finally comes to light in a letter from the Treasury
Department's Secretary, H. McCulloch, in Washington, to H. A. Smythe, Collector of Customs, in New
York, dated December 22, 1868. The letter, in substance, was an agreement to

... an application of Mr. Richard W. Haines, an American
citizen, for an American register for the foreign-built brig
Amazon, and accompanying papers showing that said brig
was wrecked in the waters of the United States; and duly
sold to the applicant for the sum of $1750; and has been
repaired at a cost of $8825.03,—exceeding three times the
amount of purchase price; all of which you certify to be
true, and recommend that said request be granted. I
transmit the papers herewith for file in your office and
authorize you to grant the American register for said
brig as requested, in any name the owner may desire.

Certificate of registry was issued to Richard W.
Haines, of New York, December 31, 1868, as sole
owner and captain of the "brig" *Mary Celeste* (the
name was apparently chosen by Captain Haines),
which had been the former "brig" *Amazon.* Immediately the certificate was surrendered, and another one issued to Richard W. Haines (with Haines
owning ⅞ of her) and Sylvester Goodwin owning
(⅛), Haines still captain. Nearly a year later—on
October 13, 1869—a third certificate was issued at
New York, listing as owners: James H. Winchester
(6/8), Sylvester Goodwin (⅛), and Daniel T.
Samson (⅛), with a W. S. Johnson as captain.
Still later, a fourth certificate indicated the owners
as James H. Winchester (4/8), Sylvester Goodwin

(⅛), Daniel T. Samson (⅛), and R. W. Fowler (2/8), captain.

Finally, on October 29, 1872, the *Mary Celeste's* fifth and last certificate was issued to its owners: James H. Winchester (12/24), Sylvester Goodwin (2/24), Daniel T. Sampson (2/24), and Benjamin S. Briggs (2/24). Benjamin Spooner Briggs succeeded R. W. Fowler as captain and part owner of the *Mary Celeste*.

Early in September of 1872, Winchester and Captain Briggs had surveyed the *Mary Celeste* at her Pier 44 berth in the East River. Certain major changes were planned that must be made before she took on her next cargo—and time was short. The *Celeste* went into screw dock for an extensive overhauling. A hurricane deck was built, and she became a twodecker—increasing her tonnage to 282.28 tons. She was lengthened to 103 feet, with a beam of 25.7 feet and a hold depth of 16.2 feet. Her bottom was newly coppered to the light-load line, and she was completely rerigged. Her hull, new deckhouses, and railings were painted. J. Lax Benedict, then deputy surveyor for the Port of New York, certified her changes. Captain Ben Briggs was concerned, too, about his cabin—after all, it must be made as comfortable as possible for his wife Sarah and their two-year-old baby daughter Sophia, who was accompanying them for the first time on a sea voyage. (The Briggses left their son Arthur, seven, at home with his grandmother, since he attended school.)

Five weeks later the *Mary Celeste* was ready for loading. By Saturday, November 2, 1872, she had a 1700-barrel cargo of alcohol stowed below decks —valued by its owners, Meissner, Ackerman & Company of 48 Beaver Street, at $37,000.

Captain Benjamin Spooner Briggs had an enviable reputation as a master mariner. He hailed from Marion, Massachusetts, and was descended from a long line of Yankee skippers who dated back to Plymouth Colony. Ben Briggs had already commanded the James H. Winchester & Company's brig *Sea Foam;* the three-masted schooner *Forest King;* the bark *Arthur* (on which he and his bride, the former Sarah E. Cobb, daughter of the Rev. Leander Cobb, of Marion, had taken their honeymoon voyage to European ports) —and, now, at thirty-seven, he owned an 8/24ths share in the *Mary Celeste.* Young Briggs had a bright future before him, and he echoed that thought the next day, Sunday, November 3, in a cheering letter to his mother:

We enjoy our melodeon, and have some good sings— shall want you to write us in about twenty days to Genoa, care of American Consul, and about twenty days after to Messina, care of American Consul, who will forward to us if we don't go there. Hoping to be with you again early in the spring.

The next evening, Monday, November 4, a couple of young sea captains met at the famed Astor House on Broadway for a simple "farewell supper," celebrating their departure on separate voyages to the Mediterranean. Old friends since their early years at sea, when they sailed before the mast together, they were—for the first time in their careers as shipmasters—sailing concurrent courses. One of these was Captain Ben Briggs, accompanied by his wife Sarah—the other was Captain David Reed Morehouse of Nova Scotia, master of the three-hundred-ton British brigantine *Dei Gratia,* now loading a cargo of petroleum for Gibraltar at a pier close by the *Mary Celeste.* Talk at the table had naturally centered around the coming voyages.

"So the *Mary Celeste* is loaded at last, Ben," Captain Morehouse said with a smile.

"Aye, Dave—and on time, too," beamed Ben Briggs. "Took some doing to get her so completely overhauled, what with a new coppering job, and all. But she's like a new ship, and I rather feel that Sarah, here, is pleased with her quarters aboard, too."

"You know I am, Ben," laughed Sarah Briggs lightly. "The *Celeste* is a beautiful little ship—not quite so roomy as the *Arthur,* but still a fine ship. And our baby daughter, Sophy, loves it, too. You see, Captain Morehouse, we've been living aboard since the twenty-sixth of October—got so it feels like 'home' already."

"What's this I hear about Mrs. Morehouse not being able to join you on this voyage, Dave?" questioned Captain Briggs.

"Unfortunately, it's true, Ben," nodded Morehouse. "Her mother is quite ill, up in Port Medway, so she thought it wiser to go to her—perhaps it's the best move."

"When do you expect to sail, by the way?" asked Briggs.

"Just as soon as we can get all the petroleum below decks on the *Dei Gratia,*" grinned Morehouse.

"Y' know, Ben, I think you've got a corner on all the *good* longshoremen along South Street—I'll be lucky if I can get cleared away in ten days."

As the farewell meal drew to a close, Sarah Briggs remained quietly in the background. While she knitted bootees for their two-year-old daughter, Mrs. Briggs would glance up occasionally to catch the drift of the conversation as Dave Morehouse and her husband talked cargoes, tradewinds, and old times. Suddenly Sarah Briggs thought of something that clouded her facial expression. She sat bolt upright and looked hesitantly over at Captain Morehouse—then she voiced a troubled thought she had in mind.

"Captain Morehouse, do you believe in ill-omens?" she questioned at length.

Ben Briggs shot an annoyed glance at his wife. "Sarah—remember? We weren't to speak of that, tonight!"

"Come, Ben," laughed Morehouse. "What's this all about?"

"Oh, nothing important, Dave," Briggs shrugged, still annoyed at his wife for bringing up such a subject at this time. "I foolishly mentioned to Sarah that the last cask of alcohol slipped out of the sling hoist last Saturday afternoon and smashed the ship's longboat to splinters—besides, we've a sixteen-foot yawl lashed to the main hatch top!"

"But Ben, dear," protested his wife, "that yawl is the merest cockleshell, compared to the smashed longboat!"

"You *are* going to replace it, aren't you, Ben?" questioned the master of the *Dei Gratia*. "After all, you must consider the safety of your wife and your little daughter—as well as the crew."

"The yawl will take care of our needs, Dave—besides there's no time—we're sailing on the morning tide," answered Ben Briggs testily. "Now that'll be enough of this silly talk of 'ill-omens'—the subject is closed!"

"Very well, Ben." Morehouse smiled weakly, shaking his head. "I suppose you know what you're doing—though I must confess it sounds a bit risky to me not to replace that boat."

To cover the "embarrassment" of the moment, Captain Morehouse was quick to raise his glass in a smoothly proposed "toast" to pleasant and profitable voyages for both vessels. Captain and Mrs. Briggs joined him heartily, and the incident was forgotten. Soon after, the three parted in good spirits, with cheerfully exchanged *bon voyages* for a successful passage across the Atlantic.

Sailing day for the *Mary Celeste* dawned next day, Tuesday, November 5. It dawned gray, cold, and unpromising. Captain Ben Briggs was early on the quarter-deck, gazing aloft, and gauging the sullen skies with a practiced weather eye. The wind was from the stern quarter, and he didn't like the looks of it—but he had a flood tide and meant to make the most of it.

Briggs ordered the lines off, and the *Mary Celeste* left her mooring at Pier 44 in the East River, sailing down bay under a light spread of canvas with ten people aboard—including his wife Sarah and their tiny daughter Sophy.

Captain Ben Briggs had shipped a crew of

competent seamen aboard the *Mary Celeste*. Albert Richardson, twenty-eight, of Stockton Springs, Maine, was his first mate; Andrew Gilling, twenty-five, also an able officer, was second mate; and Edward Herd, twenty-three, was cook and steward. The four fo'c'sle hands were equally able-bodied: Volkerk Lorensen, twenty-nine; Arian Martens, thirty-five; Boaz Lorensen, twenty-five, and Gottlieb Goodschaal, twenty-three. All these seamen knew their business of sailing a ship, and all were United States citizens of German birth.

As the *Mary Celeste* beat her way down toward Staten Island, Briggs became aware that the prevailing headwinds were much too strong for her, so he immediately ordered the vessel hove to in the lee of the island. On Thursday, November 7, the headwinds had dropped to a fresh breeze. Captain Briggs ordered up the anchor— and the pilotage record of the Board of Commissioners of Pilots of the State of New York, showed that Pilot Burnett had been assigned to guide the *Mary Celeste* down the Narrows into the lower bay.

During this time Sarah Briggs was below in the cabin, hastily penning a letter to the folks back in Marion. In it she wrote homily: "Tell Arthur [their school-age son] I make great dependence on the letter I shall get from him, and will try to remember anything that happens on the voyage which he would be pleased to hear—"Farewell." Pilot Burnett mailed that letter ashore in New York—little realizing that it contained the last words ever to come out of the *Mary Celeste!* Nor did Burnett feel at the time he took leave of the *Celeste's* company, waving to her as she stood to seaward, that he was destined to be the last person ever to lay eyes on those aboard!

Captain David Reed Morehouse, master of the three-hundred-ton bark *Dei Gratia,* cleared New York for Gibraltar on the fifteenth of November —just ten days after the *Mary Celeste* had sailed.

Out beyond the Narrows the *Dei Gratia* ran into unusually heavy weather, and for eight days she bucked and dogged her way through timber-twisting gales and tremendous seas. For hours at a time Captain Morehouse was on the quarter-deck, ordering reefed tops'ls, t'gallants, and stays'ls. The *Dei Gratia* plunged headlong into great mountains of water—she rolled on her beam's end, then shook the sea from her decks and plunged on again. Vaguely Dave Morehouse thought of his old friend, Captain Ben Briggs, and wondered how the *Mary Celeste* was faring in this onslaught of the elements. Why hadn't Ben taken time to replace that smashed long-boat? Were those seventeen hundred barrels of alcohol riding well in the hold—or were they chafing each other? God forbid! Morehouse's lips moved in a silent prayer as he thought of the sixteen-foot yawl for all hands!

The morning of December 4 had been violent. Squalls, strong nor'west winds with treacherous, tumbling seas. Around noon it cleared, though the sea was still running high. The wind came out of the north, and the *Dei Gratia* was on the port tack —her course, sou'east by east. John Wright, second mate, was on watch. Captain Morehouse stood grim-

ly by his side. Able seaman John Johnson was at
the wheel.

It was about 2:00 P.M., December 5, sea time
(afternoon, December 4—sea time being reckoned
from twelve noon of one day to twelve noon of
the next) with the *Dei Gratia* standing midway
between Cape Rosa, Portugal, and the southern-
most group of the Azores. Her position fixed at
38° 20′ North, and 17° 15′ West, as her helmsman,
Johnson, sighted a vessel off the port beam.

"Ship off t' win'ard, sir!" he shouted.

For a time Wright studied her. So did Captain
Morehouse. She was fully four miles distant, and
apparently a brigantine. Her course appeared to
be westerly, but presently Wright was aware that
she was hardly making a knot seaway. He further
observed through the glass that her sails were in
bad repair, and that she was yawing a bit—a clear
indication that she was without a helm.

"There's something wrong with that ship, Captain," commented Wright to Morehouse, handing
him the telescope. Morehouse nodded grimly, sensing something familiar about the cut of her sails.
Morehouse studied the vessel through the glass.

"She's a brigantine, right enough, John," observed Morehouse to his second mate. Then he
added to the helmsman, "Port your helm a point
or two, Johnson."

The *Dei Gratia* was then hauled to the wind,
and bore down toward the strange vessel at a faster
rate. Morehouse had misgivings as his own vessel
approached the stranger. At a distance of four hundred yards, Captain Morehouse hailed her. There

was no reply. The decks were deserted. Her hull had the appearance of being reasonably new, but her tattered sails told mutely that she had seen some rough going. Dave Morehouse's stomach felt like a ball of lead—he dared not voice the thought in his mind—not just yet, at any rate. Instead, he calmly turned to Wright. "Go fetch the first mate, John."

The second mate hurried below to get Oliver Deveau, who was off duty in his cabin. Meanwhile, Morehouse again studied the other vessel through his glass.

Fores'l and upper foretops'ls were gone—apparently blown from the yards in the same gale that the *Dei Gratia* had fought through. Her main stays'l lay in a heap on the for'ard house. The lower foretops'l had been set—though later it showed to be rent at the gaskets. The two heads'ls were set, while the jib, foretopmast stays'ls, and all other sails were reefed. Inasmuch as her heads'ls were sheeted fast on the port side—with the wind from the north, and her head bearing west—she was on the port tack. Captain Morehouse could see her steadily edging toward the *Dei Gratia,* though slowly. It was quite obvious to Morehouse that something was seriously wrong aboard her!

As the stranger angled to within a hundred yards of the *Dei Gratia,* Captain Morehouse could contain himself no longer. Impulsively he cupped his hands and roared, "Ahoy, *Mary Celeste!* F'r God's sake, Ben, answer me! It's your old friend—Dave Morehouse. What terrible thing has happened?"

But no answer came—only the wind tossing back his words.

Johnson looked strangely at his captain. Morehouse sagged visibly, and the lines in his weathered face seemed to deepen. Oliver Deveau, the first mate, and Second Mate John Wright came running to the quarter-deck—then stopped short.

"Holy Mother!" cried Deveau. "It's—it's the *Mary Celeste!*"

"Aye, Oliver," said Morehouse, recovering his poise. "You and John best lower a boat an' take Johnson, here, with you. But f'r God's sake be careful—you've a heavy sea, and I don't want to lose a couple of good mates and a seaman—there's something terribly wrong aboard th' *Celeste*—I—I want you to find out th' worst, and report to me!"

"Aye, sir," answered Deveau. "We'll find out!"

The *Dei Gratia's* boat was carefully lowered into the boiling seas and gotten away in good order—manned by the two mates and Seaman John Johnson. As the longboat neared the *Mary Celeste,* Deveau, standing in the bow, noted a puzzling oddity. A sliver of wood about six feet long, a half-inch wide, and probably three-quarters of an inch deep, had been stripped from both bows. There was no accountable explanation for this "damage"—either then or later. For the record, they were put down as "deep scratches."

"Pull around to the lee of her, Johnson," ordered First Mate Wright, "an' Deveau and I will board her an' see what's what!"

Once aboard, the two mates shouted loud halloos. Only hollow echoes came back on the wind. In

a matter of minutes Deveau and Wright were painfully aware of the situation aboard the *Celeste*.

"She seems completely abandoned, John." Deveau
shook his head.

"But why?" puzzled Wright. "What happened to
Captain Briggs and his family? Where's th' crew?"

"Those are tough questions to answer, right now,"
answered Deveau grimly. "But we'll damn soon
find out! Come on, John, we'll check topside, first!"

With the sharp eyes that long experience on
wind ships develops, Deveau and Wright set out
on an intensive tour of investigation. So thorough
was the *Mary Celeste* covered in the period of one
hour that, in a detailed survey made later by the
Queen's agent, little could be found to add—and
these findings, briefly given, were later subscribed
to, under oath, before the Vice-Admiralty Court
at Gibraltar.

The two mates went forward to the bow. Here
they found that the anchor and anchor chain were
in place. This precluded any question of the ship
parting her cable. Next, her masts and spars were
also in order, although some of the rigging was
broken, and a few pieces missing. The ratlines were
in bad shape, with no spares available. Sheets and
bracings were trailing over the side, and the standing rigging seemed to have had hard wear. The
Mary Celeste had three hatchways: fore, main, and
lazarette. The main hatch was battened down—fore
and lazarette hatch covers were off!

"There's something badly amiss here," commented Deveau, mystified at what he saw.

"Aye, there must be," nodded Wright. "Why

else would Cap'n Briggs cruise the North Atlantic in December with open hatches? Ain't it invitin' disaster?"

"There's more to it than that, John," answered Oliver Deveau in a quiet voice. "Captain Briggs was too good a seaman to leave hatches open at this time of year—and in this part of the Atlantic. It's our job to find out why he did!"

This was the first of several incongruities observed. However, the fact that the hatch covers had remained on deck at all, led the two mates to believe that the *Mary Celeste* had at no time been on her beam's end. Nor was there any likelihood that she had shipped heavy seas.

Further investigation by Deveau and Wright showed that five fresh-water casks stood intact in their chocks on deck. The door to the galley and companionway was ajar. The binnacle, torn from its lashings on the cabin roof, lay near the wheel —with the compass broken. The wheel and wheel gear showed no sign of damage.

The mates then inspected the hold, by way of the forward hatch. Below decks they found the cargo to consist of alcohol in wooden barrels—plainly marked on the head of each barrel—and, so far as the two mates from the *Dei Gratia* could determine, not one of them showed any indication of having been broken. (Two surveys, made later at Gibraltar, verified this.) They did find three and one-half feet of water in the hold. They also found two pumps, one of which was in good order. The valve of the other had been removed, ostensibly for the purpose of sounding through the opening in the well. A sounding weight, with line attached, lay near by.

"Likely as not, this leak was slow," remarked Deveau in passing, "or she'd have foundered long since."

"Aye," answered Wright. "That leak—and the open hatches. But I still can't understand what made 'em abandon ship!"

"Mebbe we will." Deveau nodded with a thoughtful scowl.

The two mates then made their way into the after hold. Here were the ship's stores—flour, meats, and potatoes—all in barrels. Supplies sufficient for an average complement for a six-month's voyage. *No liquors, beer, or wine were found there—or anywhere at any time.*

On the starboard side of the forward house was the galley. Here Deveau and Wright found a great deal of water. This was readily accounted for by the simple fact that a scuttle and sliding door, left open on the side, had allowed the sea to cascade through. The galley stove—also on the starboard side—was cold, and knocked slightly out of position. Pots, pans, and utensils, were clean and in their racks. There was no food in sight—either cooked, or being prepared. The galley had a single bunk which was in order and thoroughly dry.

Making their way through a sliding door in the forward house, the two mates entered the fo'c'sle. Here they found four bunks and three seamen's chests. There were the usual oilskins, sea boots, and various articles of sailors' clothing, either on the floor, or hanging from hooks. All were dry,

with no signs of mildew. Even a cigar case and a
pair of cuff links on one of the set chests were still
bright and untarnished. Several pipes lying about
on the other chests caught the attention of the two
mates and caused them to shake their heads.

"These sailors must have been in a helluva big
hurry—to leave their pipes behind," commented
Deveau.

"Aye," nodded Wright. " 'T ain't natural!"

The second mate's quarters were next, just abaft
the fo'c'sle, and on the port side. Nothing unusual
here, they found—a seaman's chest filled with dry,
serviceable clothing—a few personal papers, and an
old quadrant. That was all—Spartan simplicity and
no clues whatever.

Deveau and Wright made their way past the afterhouse, and found a spar lashed across the boat
davits at the stern—clearly indicating that no boat
had been launched. Closer examination definitely
proved that no boat had been carried there.

"By gad!" exclaimed Deveau as he surveyed the
empty davits. "This thing gets t' be more of a
mystery all the time; How th' devil did they get
away from this ship?"

"Remember those lashings we saw, back at the
main hatch?" Wright reminded him. "Probably had
another boat secured there."

"Mebbe you're right," conceded Deveau as both
men made their way back to the main hatch and
inspected it. "Aye—here are the marks on the tar-
paulin. But look—that boat was about two thirds
the size of the one that fitted th' davits aft—an' I'll
stake my last dollar that this boat on the main

hatch weren't more'n sixteen feet! Yet how in hell could Briggs, his wife an' kid—an' th' crew—take off from here in heavy seas without capsizing!"

"Could be they didn't get far!" hinted John Wright grimly as he followed Deveau to the afterhouse.

The afterhouse, built of light wood and sealed with pitch, was raised slightly above the deck— allowing space for five windows and a skylight. All of these windows were protected by heavy canvas nailed in place by wooden strips—all were undamaged except the skylight, which had a section of glass broken out.

Deveau and Wright stopped short at a door in the afterhouse—the door that led down the companionway steps to the main cabin below. The door was open, and swung crazily with the motion of the ship—creaking eerily.

"You feel th' same's I do—I mean about goin' down there an' finding that death's beaten us?" Deveau motioned toward the swinging door.

Wright grinned sheepishly, "Kinda spooky, ain't it?"

"Well, come on, then, John," said Deveau, gripping the second mate by the arm. "Let's get it over with!"

Once in the main cabin, Deveau and Wright found it damp, but there was no standing water. On one of the cabin's partitions was an ancient clock, broken and without hands. On a table, under the clock, lay the first mate's deck log—with the last known entries of the brigantine *Mary Celeste*.

"Y' know, John, th' old man's going t' take this

hard," said Deveau, checking the logbook. "Briggs was his best friend—told me once that they'd sailed afore th' mast together."

"Briggs cleared New York about ten days before us, didn't he?" questioned Wright.

"Aye, John," nodded Deveau. "Why?"

"Well, let's see when the last entry was made," suggested Wright. "That might tell us something, Oliver."

Together they traced the lines of fine Spencerian handwriting down to the bottom of the page: ". . . Eight AM, Monday, November twenty-fifth —on course E by SE—making eight knots, eastern side of Island of Santa Maria, the Azores—bearing SSW, about six miles distant——"

"Hmm, that's strange," puzzled Oliver Deveau. "There are no specific notations as to wind and weather in this last entry—that's the end!"

"Aye, an' pretty final, too!" added Wright grimly, as Deveau replaced the logbook on the table. "Let's keep on going—there must be a clue to this mystery somewhere!"

Next in the cabin was the dining table—cleared, with nothing on it except the "fiddle" (the "fiddle" being a metal projection to prevent dishes from sliding off in heavy weather). There were *absolutely no signs* of preparations for a meal nor was there a "half eaten meal" (contrary to a number of versions of the *Mary Celeste* story), and all plate ware was neatly stacked in an adjoining pantry. Deveau and Wright found that other pieces of furniture in the main cabin were in orderly arrangement. But the eyebrows of the *Dei Gratia's* mates raised slightly upon finding several old coats, and a pair of sea boots, in the main cabin—a place where they should not have been, under normal circumstances.

The chief mate's cabin—which opened off the main cabin—was checked next. This also was dry, clean, and in good order. Underneath the berth was the familiar chest, holding most of the mate's personal belongings, with nothing about it worthy of note. Near by was the ensign of the *Mary Celeste;* her own signal flag, and her international identification sign: "WT." A track chart of the North Atlantic was found, with the progress of the vessel plotted through the twenty-fourth of November.

The two men also found a cabin compass and another ancient quadrant. This was the second quadrant found—but Captain Briggs's sextant, chronometer, and *official log* of the *Mary Celeste* were never found. However, this was not surprising, since the skipper generally takes these instruments and records when he abandons ship! Also found were a kit of carpenter's tools; a new log reel; a pair of sea boots, greased and unused; a cargo receipt book, and a pair of sandglasses—all customary equipment to be found on almost any vessel afloat. A seemingly minor detail of a very small can of lubricating oil resting on its narrow bracket, satisfied the two mates, more than anything else that they had observed, that the *Mary Celeste* had experienced very little rough weather recently.

Captain Briggs's cabin—directly abaft the main cabin — was inspected next. Here, Deveau and Wright got a jolting eyeful! First of all, the berth bore the unmistakable imprint of a small child's body. Over in one corner of the cabin stood a high chair. Scattered about the cabin were toys, a pinafore, a couple of dolls, and "numerous articles of female wearing apparel." Here, for the first time during their investigation, the two men came face to face with mute evidence of a hasty flight!

"Good God!" exclaimed Oliver Deveau, closely examining the imprint on the bunk, then the clothes on the floor. "What've we got here! Look, John —the captain's kid was only a baby—a girl baby— hauled over the side by a panicky mother!"

"Aye, Oliver," added Wright caustically, "and one not knowin' what clothes t' take! Look at 'em —strewn all over th' place! An' look at th' woman's rubber overshoes there! See—she was puttin' 'em on—then suddenly she got out in a helluva hurry, an' left 'em! Wonder she thought t' take th' baby!"

"Perhaps you're right, John," Deveau agreed. "Now, let's look over the rest of the stuff here an' see if we can unravel this thing."

The men found two large boxes—both open, and full of men's clothing—in complete disorder. More evidence of haste! Also scattered about were many books and tracts, mostly of a religious nature. There was also a writing desk against one of the cabin partitions. On it were several mariner's charts, a valise—*and a sword in a scabbard!* Deveau drew it from its sheath, but neither he nor Wright could find anything of great note about it—except a few rusty spots. The first mate shrugged as he examined it, then replaced it in the scabbard and laid it back on the desk. Much has been said about the "blood on the sword found in the master's cabin of the

Mary Celeste." This so-called "blood"—analyzed later at Gibraltar—was definitely proven to be *rust.*

The two mates of the *Dei Gratia* further checked: a melodeon in good condition (this is the one sent from Marion, Massachusetts, as a gift of the family to Sarah Briggs) ; a small sewing machine; a medicine chest; and a sea bag filled with very wet woman's clothing—quite evident to be a washing ready to hang out. One of the compasses to the binnacle was found, with the card damaged by water. There was still no trace of the captain's logbook, sextant, or chronometer. Deveau also observed that none of the charts gave any indication of being hurriedly consulted.

Oliver Deveau and John Wright silently surveyed the perplexing scene in Captain Briggs's cabin, and shook their heads. What had actually happened? Why had nine adults suddenly taken off in a tiny cockleshell yawl without leaving a single clue? What "something" forced them to take this drastic and tragic action? Even after thorough inspection, the two *Dei Gratia* mates could find no answer.

Deveau turned sharply to the second mate.

"John!" he exploded. "I think I begin to see the picture aboard, here!"

The second mate shot a puzzled glance at Deveau. "What do you mean—'picture'?"

"Remember those open hatches, topside?" Deveau reminded the second mate.

"Aye," nodded Wright. "What about 'em?"

"I've felt, all along, that Briggs had a very definite reason for opening them," pointed out Deveau. "Now I think I understand why."

"Well, what's the answer?" questioned the second mate tartly.

"No answer, John—just a vague theory," countered Deveau. "Ever sniff an empty alcohol cask, John?"

"Aye, and it's likely to take my breath away, too," spoke out Wright with a sour look. Then he grinned. "Think I see what you're drivin' at, Oliver. But wait a minute—there was no such smell to the hold—remember?"

"Of course there wasn't," snapped the first mate. "That's just why Briggs left th' hatches open—to clear the hold of alcohol fumes!"

"Explosion could have blown 'em open, Oliver," added Wright.

"Perhaps," shrugged Deveau. "But I doubt it—we found no indication of an explosion in the hold."

"Seepage, mebbe?" suggested Wright.

"Not enough, perhaps, to cause outright leakage—things looked too tight and shipshape down there," answered Deveau. "But enough to cause dangerous fumes, an' give Briggs a very real fear of an explosion!"

Oliver Deveau and John Wright climbed to the deck, made their way thoughtfully to the lee rail, then slid down a halyard line to the waiting boat below.

"You fellows look like y' seen ghosts!" greeted Johnson sourly.

"Mebbe we did," replied Deveau dryly. "There certainly weren't any *real* people aboard!"

But both Deveau and Wright were thoroughly

satisfied that the *Mary Celeste* was seaworthy, and
that abandonment had likely been made in a moment of panic—partly prompted by the presence
of a woman and child aboard—and a highly dangerous cargo! At least this was the substance of the
observations made by the two mates of the *Dei
Gratia*. Very little truth has ever been added to
their findings—while much has been added which
is *untrue*.

Ten minutes later, Deveau, Wright, and Seaman
Johnson silently came aboard the *Dei Gratia*. Oliver
Deveau gave Captain Dave Morehouse a detailed
account of their findings aboard the *Mary Celeste*
—though, for the time being, he kept his *"theory"*
to himself.

Morehouse was visibly shocked by the tragic end
of his old friend, Ben Briggs, and his little family
—and the loss of the *Celeste's* crew. For several
tense moments all Morehouse could do was shake
his head sadly, and murmur to himself, "My God
—it happened—and with no boat at hand when he
needed one most—except that fool yawl. I warned
him to replace that smashed boat—I—I warned him!"

Dave Morehouse finally pulled himself together
and faced his two officers with a wan smile.

"Well, gentlemen," he said quietly, "what shall
be our next move?"

"Looking at it from a practical standpoint, Captain," ventured Oliver Deveau, "would you grant
me permission to sail the *Celeste* to Gibraltar?
There's the matter of salvage, you know."

After a consultation with all hands, Captain Morehouse gave Deveau his consent. He warned, how-

ever, that such an undertaking was not without risk as both vessels would be shorthanded in rough waters, and at a bad season of the year. But Morehouse knew Deveau to be an exceptionally good seaman, hailing from the seafaring town of Weymouth, Nova Scotia, and a man who had once commanded his own ship—in short, a man he knew he could put full confidence in.

Choosing able-bodied seamen Lund and Anderson to accompany him, Deveau gathered his sextant and almanac, borrowed a barometer, compass, and a hack watch, and tossed a few personal belongings into a sea bag. With their gear, and some food hastily prepared by the steward, the three men cast off for the abandoned *Mary Celeste*. It was then around 4:00 P.M., sea time, and the weather again looked threatening.

When Deveau and the two seamen boarded the brigantine, they realized they had their work cut out for them. First of all, there was the matter of three and a half feet of water in the hold. Seaman Lund was assigned to the one pump that worked, and in three hours he had the hold dry. On the way to Gibraltar she continued to leak, though twenty-five strokes of the pump, morning and night, were sufficient to keep her dry.

Meanwhile, Deveau and Anderson set about getting the gear in order. The main peak-halyards were broken, or missing, and had to be replaced. A spare trys'l was rigged as a fores'l; an upper foretops'l was made from spare pieces, and the mains'l was extended on the gaff. A compass was set up, the watches set, and by 8:00 P.M. the abandoned

Mary Celeste was making fair headway, although it was several days before the brigantine could be extended to any degree.

The *Dei Gratia's* first mate, and his two-man crew, were blessed with fine weather past Cape Spartel. But as they neared Gibraltar it worsened sharply, and they had extremely rough going from there on in. It became so severe that the *Mary Celeste* was forced to lay in at Ceuta on the Spanish Moroccan coast until the blow abated. Up until then they had spoken to the *Dei Gratia* several times a day, but off the Spanish mainland she disappeared. Deveau wasn't too worried, because he found his derelict brigantine faster and easier to handle than the *Dei Gratia*—the aura of mystery surrounding her didn't faze him in the least. To Gibraltar he was headed, and to Gibraltar he was determined to take her!

The derelict brigantine had brought death to ten people, and was destined for a strange future interwoven with fantastic legends. But to the mate from the Maritime Provinces she was simply a "prize," cast up on the floodtide of fortune. He accepted her for what she was—a "windfall"—an opportunity to get ahead. Out of the many people who had come in contact with her, Oliver Deveau, alone, found her to be a good omen.

On Friday, December 13, 1872, Deveau—unswerved by the ominous date—brought the *Mary Celeste* into the quiet waters of the Bay of Gibraltar and anchored her in the shadow of the great Rock. The *Dei Gratia* had already arrived twenty-four hours before. Word spread like wildfire that a strange, mysterious-looking derelict had been found at sea, with all hands lost. Soon, curious crowds swarmed the shore—and from that moment on, the legend of the *Mary Celeste* grew—swelling to a bizarre blend of fact, fable, and hearsay!

Frederick Solly Flood, Esquire—Her Majesty's Advocate-General, Proctor for the Queen in her office of Admiralty, and Attorney General for Gibraltar —immediately summoned Thomas J. Vecchio, Marshal of the Vice-Admiralty Court of Gibraltar, to his august chambers in the court and ordered him to slap a writ of libel on the derelict brigantine *Mary Celeste*. After the vessel was libelled, the claim for salvage was duly filed by Captain Morehouse in the Vice-Admiralty Court, as master of the salvaging ship *Dei Gratia*.

The *Mary Celeste* underwent a thorough examination on Friday, December 20, by two qualified experts appointed by the Court—Thomas J. Vecchio, Marshal of the Admiralty Court, and Mr. John Austin, Surveyor of Shipping for the Port of Gibraltar. They reported under oath that no sufficient reason for abandonment could be found. Still unsatisfied, there was another survey on December 23. This time by Flood, himself—together with Vecchio, Austin, and Ricardo Pertunato, an experienced diver who was employed to check the vessel's hull. Their combined report was the same: "——reason for abandonment, unknown."

Also, on orders from Flood, Dr. J. Patron, M.D., made laboratory tests on the sword found aboard the *Mary Celeste* for blood stains. In a report, dated January 30, 1873, Dr. Patron's tests showed conclusively that what were purported to be "blood stains" were in reality *rust*.

Accordingly, the proceedings for salvage were allowed to go forward, and after a lengthy assize—filled with much evidence (sic) and long reports—the august Advocate-General Flood gave his final adjudication: The master and crew of the brigantine *Dei Gratia* were awarded the sum of 1700 pounds sterling, or about 20 per cent of the total value of the vessel and cargo.

Here—officially, at least—the case of the derelict brigantine was closed. But her story will never die, and she holds her secret inviolate. She has gone to join the *Flying Dutchman*, the *Waratah*, and the lost fleet of La Perouse—all the dark ships of mystery, song, and story.

After the case had been settled at Gibraltar, the *Mary Celeste* was turned over to her principal owner, Captain James H. Winchester. With some difficulty a fresh crew was signed on, and she resumed her interrupted voyage to Genoa, March 10, 1875, under her new commander, Captain George Blatchford, of Wrentham, Massachusetts. She was then worked back to New York and put up for sale.

By now she was "jinxed"—a marked ship. No one wanted her—no seaman dared ship aboard her. She was finally "sold for a song" to a coterie engaged in questionable enterprises. In December, 1884, she left New York for Port-au-Prince, ostensibly with a "mixed" cargo of 4000 pounds of butter; 150 barrels of flour; 30 bales of dry goods; 975 barrels of pickled herring; 125 casks of ale; 54 cases of women's high-button shoes, and a large consignment of hardware. The cargo was insured by five different companies, and it proved to be the brigantine's last voyage.

She stranded on Rochelois Bank, in the Gulf of Gonave, January 3, 1885, almost within sight of her destination—and by "malice aforethought," her owners and captain were put to trial for barratry (the maritime offense for foundering a vessel to collect insurance). The outcome of this trial is unknown, but the end of the *Mary Celeste* is clearly recorded.

She left her whitened timbers on a coral reef—in the land of voodoo!

SOURCES OF FACTUAL MATERIAL

From Charles Edey Fay's *Mary Celeste: the Odyssey of an Abandoned Ship,* published by the Peabody Museum of Archeology and Ethnology, Harvard University, Cambridge, Mass. (1942), from George S. Bryan's *Mystery Ship, the Mary Celeste in Fancy and Fact* (Philadelphia: J. B. Lippincott Company, 1942), and from James Franklin Briggs' *In the Wake of the Mary Celeste* (New Bedford, 1944), have come the real facts of the celebrated mystery ship, *Mary Celeste.*

III

THE LONG, LONELY WATCH

As the 6,711-ton, 396-foot Isbrandtsen Line passenger-freighter, *Flying Enterprise,* cleared Hamburg for New York, December 21, 1951, carrying 2,600 tons of general cargo and ten passengers, she cautiously poked her nose out of the fogbound mouth of the Elbe River. Her master, thirty-seven-year-old Captain Hendrik Kurt Carlsen, had already radioed his family in Woodbridge, New Jersey, that he would soon join them—perhaps in time for the Christmas holiday. But that was before the thick "pea-souper" closed in on him in the English Channel. For nearly three days the *Flying Enterprise's* deep-throated siren blatted loudly from the Elbe to Land's End, while Skipper Carlsen—his eyes glued to the bridge's window for hours at a time—skillfully dodged shipping in the "gray-out" of the English Channel. The vision of "home for the holidays" went a-glimmering with every successive hour in that murky mass of formless fog.

Out past Bishop's Light and Lizard Head the *Flying Enterprise* shook the fog bank, and Captain Kurt Carlsen charted a speedier course north of the usual shipping lane to make up lost time.

On Christmas morning the glass dropped with ominous suddenness! By noon seas rolled heavily as a Force 7 gale lashed out of the northeast, and

snow swirled thickly around the ploughing, pitching *Flying Enterprise.* A weary night on the bridge,
in worsening weather, brought Kurt Carlsen to the
grim realization that this was no ordinary "winter
storm"—it was fast becoming a full-blown hurricane! More terrific, even, than the one off North
Europe back in 1926 that Carlsen had so often
heard old-timers tell about.

By daybreak, December 27, seventy-five-mile-an-
hour gusts—shot through with stinging sleet—buf-
feted the *Flying Enterprise,* churning up an angry,
mountainous sea that smashed at the starboard
quarter of Carlsen's ship with gigantic forty-foot
waves. Time and again she rolled on her beam's
end, and plunged her foredeck under tons of water
that raced along her weather deck, burying her lee
rail and finally sloshing out through her scuppers
as she shook herself free of each onslaught. She
was a solidly built ship—though Captain Carlsen
marveled to himself how she was ever able to take
such a pounding. In all his twenty-three years at
sea he had never known heavier seas—even during
his earlier training-in-sail days as a Danish naval
cadet.

Constantly maintaining a "full-speed" order to
the engine room, Carlsen managed to keep the
Flying Enterprise headed into the battering seas.
If he could continue this strategy he could edge
the cyclonic storm, then safely set a course westward toward Newfoundland, thence to New York.
True, it might be temporarily tough on his ten
passengers, but it held less danger than dawdling

along at half speed—besides it gave the ship better seaway to cope with the heavy weather.

But an angry and malicious sea is no respecter of ships, or men! Like a strong body puncher in the ring, the sea likes to weary its victims before thrusting home its "knock-out" punch. Carlsen and his *Flying Enterprise* were tenaciously battling such a sea—a sea that was just as tenacious and crafty as the skipper and his ship. The sea prodded and probed the *Flying Enterprise* with giant sledge-hammer blows of its massive waves—hunting for a vital spot on the ship's weather side . . . a loosened plate rivet, or a weakened plate! It raged in terrific fury, goaded on by a lashing Force 12 gale that roared with tremendous gusts—often laying the *Flying Enterprise* over on her lee rail.

Suddenly, one gigantic comber—towering above its fellows—crashed broadside against the freighter's starboard beam, abaft the bow. There was a sharp, cannon-like explosion—the sea had found its mark! A jagged one-quarter-inch crack opened across the steel deck at Number 3 hatch where, below, in Number 3 hold, 1200 tons of pig iron had broken loose and smashed against the port side of the ship when the forty-foot wave struck. The ragged crack extended nearly to the water line on the port quarter of the hull. The staggered ship heeled over and took a 45° to 50° list to port, never to come fully upright again. . . .

This was a grim danger signal! Carlsen immediately veered south in a skillful maneuver to put his wounded ship in the traffic lanes again, and to prepare for emergency conditions aboard the

Flying Enterprise. But there were to be many more batterings and side-slams against the crippled vessel.

At dawn, December 28, the entire ship's company aboard the *Flying Enterprise* were well aware that she had been dealt a cruelly mortal blow by the sea! She was taking water rapidly in Number 3 hold as she heeled over at a 60° angle. Down in the engine room, Chief Engineer George Brown and his assistants fought like demons to keep the list from developing further—and to keep the engines operating. They pumped out the water in Number 3 hold as it squirted in, under pressure, through the one-quarter-inch crack in the hull. But it fast became a losing battle when another cyclonic storm roared out of the northeast on the heels of the first. Terrific combers threatened to break the freighter in two—widening the jagged crack across Number 3 hold!

Captain Kurt Carlsen made rapid-fire decisions. He ordered the radio operator to flash out an S O S. Then he ordered all officers, the ship's forty crew members, and the ten passengers on deck with life jackets. Carlsen made it plain to them all that they were to abandon ship the instant rescue ships arrived alongside. Several junior officers begged Carlsen to let them stay aboard with him—his answer was an emphatic *"No!"*

Meanwhile, Chief Engineer Brown and the engine-room crew were frantically fighting to pump fuel from the listing side of the *Flying Enterprise* to the high side in a valiant attempt to bring the ship on an even keel. But the odds were sadly against them. One piece of equipment after another broke down, unable to stand the terrific strain brought on by the 60° list to port. Worst of all, the generator lasted about an hour. It pumped oil from its bearings faster than it could be put in. Oil was on the floor, on the steel steps, everywhere. Where it normally took ten seconds to cross the engine room, it now took five minutes. The ventilating fans went off when the power dynamo cut out, and the heat was terrific. By this time Chief Engineer Brown was quite certain that the wheel and rudder were "probably useless," and that the ship would be taking water faster than it could be pumped out. At this point Brown ordered all the engine-room crew on deck.

Ploughing t h r o u g h the rough seas were the freighters *Southland* and *Arion,* in response to the *Flying Enterprise's* sudden distress call. Within a few hours they were in sight of the stricken vessel. Following closely was the U.S. transport *General A. W. Greeley.* As the three ships converged on the heavily listing freighter they lowered boats that bobbed crazily toward the *Flying Enterprise.*

When Chief Engineer Brown went on deck, he saw a lifeboat some distance from the ship. Captain Carlsen was frantically waving it closer.

"In their judgment they think it's too risky to come in closer, Captain," pointed out the chief engineer to Carlsen. "Suppose I take one of the passengers and jump. . . ."

"That's risky, too!" answered Carlsen tightly. "You'd both be washed back against the ship. Wait a bit, I'll give the order to jump at the right time!"

Without exception everyone took the situation

calmly. No one jumped until Carlsen gave the order a few minutes later. Brown had already fastened a life jacket to a young girl and held onto her.

"Okay, Chief," nodded Carlsen. "God bless you, and go ahead!"

Carlsen tensely watched Brown and the girl clear the ship and hit the water. Five minutes later they were safely picked up by a boat from the *Southland*. Crewmen "paired off" with passengers and jumped safely. Less than an hour later all passengers and crew were aboard the rescue ships—only one casualty was recorded—an elderly Russian immigrant died later from exposure and cold. As he saw the last of his passengers picked up by the boats, Carlsen scrambled to the radio shack and contacted the rescue ships by radiotelephone and made an accounting of all persons on board.

With great difficulty Carlsen then made a thorough inspection of the *Flying Enterprise*, and calculated a fifty-fifty chance for salvage. He knew the list to port would increase with every hour, but he also knew that the forward and aft holds would give sufficient buoyancy to keep his ship afloat long enough to be towed back to the nearest port—if he could contact a powerful seagoing tug. This was the basis of Kurt Carlsen's decision—this was the calculated risk he intended to take, plus the dogged determination, courage, and sense of duty, to outwit an angry sea and save his ship!

Again scrambling along the starboard rail of the 70° careening deck, Carlsen managed to climb the superstructure to the crazily tilted radio shack. Contacting the three rescue ships, he advised them of his decision. As the crewless vessel wallowed in the rise and fall of the merciless swells, the skippers of the *General Greeley, Southland,* and *Arion* pleaded with Carlsen to abandon his ship. With a set jaw and a thin smile Kurt Carlsen told them in a quiet, tired voice, "Thanks—but I'm staying aboard until I'm towed or sunk!"

Then began the long, lonely watch of one man against the sea!

Cramped in an angle where the radio shack's port and starboard bulkheads (walls) became floor and ceiling, and the deck (floor) a bulkhead, Carlsen managed a four- to six-hour sleep of exhaustion that first night alone aboard the *Flying Enterprise.* Meanwhile, the seagoing tug *Turmoil* —one of Britain's fastest and largest—had been contacted. But Carlsen's ship would have to wait, because the *Turmoil* was tied up in other rescue jobs, he was told by radiophone. Probably would take several days, the operator continued. Then Carlsen turned in.

Morning found Carlsen hungry and stiff. In the only dry storeroom aboard his wallowing ship Carlsen found a whole pound cake, along with a quart of fresh water, some beer, and—most important— candles to provide him with light and heat.

After eating sparingly of the pound cake for his first breakfast, Carlsen boiled up a cupful of fresh water over the lighted candle and threw in some tea he had also found in the storeroom. Then he set up a "daily schedule" for himself. First, at 8:00 A.M. he established radiophone contact with the stand-by ships—advising them of the situation

aboard his own helpless vessel—and to learn of further developments about the tug *Turmoil*. Carlsen
then made another hazardous checkup of the *Flying
Enterprise*. What ordinarily would have taken a
short time, stretched into hours—clinging precariously to deck rails, climbing over slippery steel decks,
and crawling up companionway steps that swung
dizzily with every roll to port. Exhausted, Carlsen
threw himself on the improvised bunk made of a
mattress ingeniously wedged between the deck and
bulkhead of the radio shack and fell into a deep
sleep. Hours later he roused himself and signaled
the *General Greeley* over the radiophone that all
was as well as could be expected aboard the drifting, heavily listed vessel.

At 10:00 P.M., December 31—Kurt Carlsen's
fourth day alone on the 70° listing *Enterprise*—
the U.S. Navy transport *Golden Eagle* arrived on the
spot with orders to relieve the *General Greeley*,
which immediately headed for New York with
thirty-two survivors. As the *Golden Eagle* prepared
to stand by, Carlsen contacted her skipper, Captain
William E. Donahue, by radiophone and briefed
him on the situation to date. Carlsen's voice was
guttural and gave evidence of exhaustion. Charles
Gallison, the *Golden Eagle's* radio operator, made
an on-the-spot tape recording:

The wind was Force twelve [hurricane velocity] on December 27. The ship cracked right across the deckhouse
and down the side. When the wind veered, I came too
far north. I tried to steer south to get in the traffic lanes
where we had a chance of being picked up.

We were doing all right until dawn the following day

when another cyclonic storm came up with some terrific seas.

It was nothing but seas and water all over the place. One tremendous wave knocked her off course and it was then that the ship broke across the number three hatch.

The number three hold was full of water.

With the broken ship, I could not steer.

I must say everyone without exception took the situation very calmly.

They did nothing until I told them. No one jumped until I told them.

It was very touching to see the way the boys took it on the chin.

I saw one man crying, either through pain or fear, because he had fallen down and hurt his arm. There were no serious casualties.

Everything went fine and dandy. After nearly twenty-three years at sea, I guess we had it coming to us. We didn't want it to happen, we just couldn't help it.

You realize everything here is a problem, because I have to crawl around everywhere.

I'm putting the ship's papers in a watertight container within the orange lifeboat. See that they are dry and put in a safe place.

Carlsen sent the papers overboard the next morning, but they were lost in the still-mountainous seas. He tried to save the ship's log in the same manner, but the plan was called off because of the weather.

Meanwhile, on New Year's Day, word was gotten to Carlsen that the *Turmoil* had set out from Falmouth, bucking fifty-mile-an-hour winds with heavy hail showers and would not reach the *Enterprise* until late in the day, January 3.

Then suddenly Captain Carlsen was cut off from the outside world—sea water had seeped through into the battery room and the ship's regular radio set was out of operation! Smartly enough, Carlsen had anticipated just such a possibility, and had tinkered his "ham" short-wave set into service. Being an expert "ham" operator in his own right, he was still able to keep in communication with the *Golden Eagle* from his own cabin on the starboard quarter of the bridge deck. Water, by now, was getting dangerously close to the radio shack, due to the ship's heavy list to port.

It was now in the fifth day of Kurt Carlsen's long, lonely watch aboard the *Enterprise*. He was in good spirits, and he had maintained his "daily schedule," despite overwhelming odds. He still munched on the pound cake he'd found in dry stores, and added a bottle or two of beer to his slim diet. But he was beginning to get low on candles—his sole means of light and heat. He also found that he must revise his every-two-hour radio-phone signaling schedule — the only batteries he had in the "ham" set were getting weaker! He noticed, too, that the *Enterprise's* angle of list seemed greater—on his last tedious tour of the wallowing freighter he estimated a list of 80°!

At this point, Rear Admiral Walter Boone, United States Navy Eastern Atlantic commander, ordered the 2,300-ton destroyer *Weeks* to proceed through heavy seas from Bordeaux to relieve the Navy transport *Golden Eagle*. Captain Donahue of the *Eagle* communicated with Carlsen to that effect. Shortly before the *Eagle* departed, Carlsen said to the stand-by ship:

Everything is all right. There is nothing new, nothing exciting. I'm getting a little lonesome, but kind of getting used to it now.

I'm sorry that this has upset your schedule. You've lost a couple of days. We have a very valuable cargo of five tons of U.S. mail and 500 tons of coffee.

Under forced draft, the destroyer *Weeks* sped toward the vicinity of the floundering *Enterprise* —arriving to relieve the *Golden Eagle* about 3:00 A.M. January 2. Already new gales of another Atlantic storm lashed at the wallowing freighter—now about 350 miles off Falmouth, and drifting approximately 1.2 miles an hour toward the English coast.

The wild, stormy hours of January 3, 1952, were crucial ones for the *Enterprise* and her skipper, Kurt Carlsen. Hurricane-force winds still lashed at the half-capsized freighter as the premature darkness of a North Atlantic winter's night closed in on an angry sea. Carlsen trussed himself as best he could on the makeshift mattress bunk he had wedged in the angle between the deck and bulkhead of his cabin, vainly trying to snatch a cat nap on this seventh consecutive night of his long, lonely watch. But sleep was out of the question. Too many things were on Kurt Carlsen's mind—he was too nervous; too keyed up at the prospects of saving his ship. Some hours before, the operator aboard the *Weeks* had radiophoned him that the four-thousand horsepower British tug *Turmoil* had advised the destroyer she would reach the *Enterprise* within the next few hours. At two-hour intervals, Carlsen sparingly used the fast-ebbing power of his "ham" shortwave set to catch further news of the tug which was bucking her way through high seas toward the *Enterprise*—mindful that one lone man "stood watch" on her!

By the fluttering light of his last candle, Carlsen glanced quickly at his watch—the hours had ticked off faster than he realized. Even now the *Turmoil* might be churning the seas near by. He leaned closer to his set, fearful he might lose the weakening signal from the *Weeks*. Suddenly the destroyer's radio operator clipped out the words Carlsen had long waited for—the *Turmoil's* powerful searchlight beam was already darting over the dark seas, he was told, trying to pick up the floundering *Enterprise*.

Carlsen thanked the operator and snapped off his set to save the dying batteries. He scrambled cautiously out on the *Enterprise's* superstructure, feeling his way gingerly down the crazy angle of the companionway stairs, and crossing to the rail of the slanting starboard side. Carlsen knew his ship like a book, even in the dark of a storm-ridden night—but he edged along the rail, still cautious . . . one false step could mean instant death!

Still edging himself forward, Carlsen caught the broad path of the *Turmoil's* light, sweeping the twenty-five-foot swells on the lee quarter of the *Enterprise*. Now he saw the dark bulk of the British tug as she ploughed the seas between his ship and the *Weeks*. Tears of relief coursed down his cheeks and glistened as the glare of the searchlight caught him full in the face. Gad, she's close! thought Carlsen as he listened to the throb of her engines.

"Ahoy, Captain Carlsen!" roared the *Turmoil's*

skipper, Captain Dan Parker, through a megaphone. "Are you there, Captain?"

"Aye!" roared back Carlsen. "By th' starb'rd bow!"

"Stand by to catch a line!" boomed Parker.

Five times a heaving line whipped through the air—five times it fell short! Carlsen clung precariously to the bow rail with one hand and tried futilely to grab the thrown line with his free hand. Waves and spray lashed at him, nearly sucking him from the rail into the sea.

"Ahoy, *Turmoil!*" shouted Carlsen. "I'm going aft—try it there!"

"Okay, Carlsen!" yelled Parker. "Aft it is!"

Tortuously Carlsen crept to the heaving stern of the *Enterprise*. The *Turmoil's* searchlight beam flooded the rolling freighter in its brilliant white glare, pin-pointing Captain Carlsen's touchy progress along the outside of the dangerously slanting rail. He could hear the heavy throb of the tug's engines as her skipper maneuvered her closer to the bobbing stern of the *Enterprise*. Carlsen finally scrambled to the fantail—then clung to the taffrail of his half-submerged vessel, waving frantically at the *Turmoil*.

"Heave away!" ordered Carlsen.

"Heave away!" repeated Parker.

A "messenger line"—a slender line attached to a heavier line—shot across the boiling water between the *Turmoil* and the *Enterprise*. Carlsen grabbed at the line, but it slipped through his wet fingers. Twice the tug crew snagged a line to the aft rail— twice it parted before Carlsen could secure it to the stern bitt as both vessels rocked violently in the mountainous waves.

Suddenly, fog was closing in fast, swept along by forty-mile-an-hour winds. Captain Parker halted the chancy operation until the fog bank lifted. For a brief moment the *Turmoil's* port beam touched the stern of the *Enterprise,* and the British tug's First Mate, Kenneth Dancy, leapt aboard the disabled freighter—landing only a few feet from her skipper.

"Captain Carlsen, I presume. . . ." he said, grinning.

"Aye," answered Carlsen with a smile.

"Shake hands," said the *Turmoil's* first mate, still grinning. "Name's Dancy!"

"Welcome aboard, Dancy!" beamed Carlsen, pumping the first mate's hand. "Haven't much to offer you, but welcome just the same!"

"Thanks a lot, Captain," nodded Dancy. "My skipper, Captain Parker, wanted me to tell you he'll try to heave another line as soon as this fog clears —tonight if possible!"

"Good!" e x c l a i m e d Carlsen enthusiastically. "The sooner we can get a towline secured, the quicker we can start back to Falmouth!"

" 'Fraid it won't be as easy as that, Captain," said Dancy, smiling at Carlsen's enthusiasm. "If we can just get the heaving line secured tonight we'll be doing all right—first thing tomorrow morning we'll try to make fast the towline to the bow bitts, an' that'll be a touchy little operation in itself, as you'll see!"

"Then we'd better move up for'ard," suggested

Carlsen—adding with a grin, "be careful—because you'll find going for'ard on *this* ship is also a touchy operation!"

Together, Carlsen and Dancy clambered forward along the outside of the starboard rail, crawled down the slanting deck, then monkey climbed the tilting companion stairway to the bridge deck. Every few moments Carlsen stopped to let Dancy catch up with him.

"Gad, you're right, Captain!" grinned the *Turmoil's* first mate. "We've got the light from the tug on us—how th' devil did you make it in th' pitch dark?"

"After three years and forty-four crossings," laughed Carlsen, "you get t' know your ship from stem to stern—even in the dark!"

"But just one slip, ..." observed Dancy seriously.

"It's best not to think about it," commented Carlsen laconically. "Now, let's take a break, here, in the shelter of the bridge—perhaps a bit later the wind will blow away this fog bank, then we'll go up in the bows an' take that heaving line!"

For another half hour the two officers relaxed against a bulkhead outside Carlsen's quarters. While they talked and smoked, the *Turmoil* rocked in the rough seas near by, waiting for the weather to clear. As they talked they noticed the air clearing and the fog lifting. Carlsen glanced at his watch.

"Eight o'clock, Dancy," he remarked. "Th' fog's lifting, and we'd better be moving for'ard—and watch those crazy stairs as we go down to the deck!"

"Aye, sir," said Dancy with a nod.

Up forward, Carlsen and Dancy stationed themselves at the port and starboard bows. As the glare from the *Turmoil's* searchlight struck them Dancy signaled that they were ready for the heaving line, and the tug veered sharply across the bow of the *Enterprise*—then lay to, ready to heave the "messenger line." There were several misses and several parted lines. Several times, too, the *Turmoil* had to back off because of the heavy seas. Finally, at 9:30 P.M., in a moderated wind, Dancy and Carlsen caught one of the lines, made it fast to a bow bitt, and secured for the night. Tomorrow was another day—with a king-size question mark.

"Let's hit the sack, Dancy," announced Carlsen, "I'm dead tired, and I know you are. We'll both need plenty of shut-eye for tomorrow's business."

"Righto!" agreed the tug's first mate.

Carefully picking their way aft, the two officers again clambered up the companionway stairs to the bridge deck. With some difficulty Carlsen managed to open the door to his heavily listing cabin. Dancy followed him in and let the door slam, nearly falling flat on his face.

"I've a candle in my pocket," said Carlsen, "if I can find me a dry match."

A moment later a feeble yellow light revealed the topsy-turvy condition of Captain Carlsen's quarters. Dancy gave a low whistle while trying to balance himself.

"Gad, man, it's amazing!" exclaimed Dancy. "How ever you stuck aboard the *Flying Enterprise,* alone, for a week—like this—I can't make out—it's truly amazing!"

"You'd have probably done the same, Dancy—

given the same situation." Carlsen smiled. "Though it got pretty lonely toward the end, I'll admit. Now, then, how about a bite to eat—and a spot of beer?"

"Sounds capital!" grinned Dancy.

Kurt Carlsen broke off a portion of the remaining pound cake and opened a bottle of beer for his guest. Dancy lifted the bottle in a toast.

"To the success of our mission!" he said gayly.

"Aye, to the success of our mission," smiled Carlsen wearily.

Dancy nibbled at the cake, sipped his beer, and marveled at Carlsen's ingenuity—the mattress wedged securely in the angle of the cabin's deck and bulkhead; Carlsen's "ham" short-wave set, and the many other things that had made life at least bearable aboard the heavily canted *Enterprise* during Carlsen's long, lonely watch.

Meanwhile, Captain Carlsen pulled a mattress from the upper bunk and wedged it between the deck and bulkhead, just ahead of his.

"When you're finished, Dancy, you'd better hit the sack," he said with a smile. "I'm going to contact the *Weeks* before I turn in."

Carlsen flicked on the switch and called the *Weeks*. A moment later he heard the destroyer's operator telling him that the *Weeks* was running low on provisions and fuel, and that the Navy had ordered the destroyer *Willard Keith* to relieve her. The *Keith* would be alongside the *Enterprise* by dawn to take over stand-by duty, the operator continued. Then, before he signed off, he wished Captain Carlsen and the *Turmoil* the best of luck!

Carlsen and Dancy were up with the gray dawn next morning—January 4. The wind was down, but there was still a rugged kick to a sea that refused to give up the *Enterprise*. There was a rising barometer, a gentle west-northwest breeze—and a feeble sun tried to break through the low-hanging overcast. But trials and tribulations were destined for Kurt Carlsen, Dancy, and the British tug *Turmoil* that day!

Trouble started almost immediately—heartbreaking trouble that sorely tries the souls of men. It started when crewmen of the *Turmoil* attached a heavier line to the "messenger line" and signaled for Carlsen and Dancy to haul the line aboard the *Enterprise*. As they hauled the heavy line through the rough water between the rocking ships, the "messenger line" snapped—and all the tedious and dangerous work of Carlsen and Dancy in securing the line the night before suddenly went by the board!

"Stand by to receive another heaving line!" sang out Captain Parker from the deck of the *Turmoil*.

"Heave away!" roared back Carlsen, bracing himself in the bows of the *Enterprise*.

Half the morning was spent before the *Turmoil* managed to get a line aboard the rolling derelict freighter. Gingerly the tug's crew attached the heavier line and dropped it gently over the side of the pitching *Turmoil*. Carlsen and Dancy hauled in the "messenger line," hand over hand—foot by foot it came over the bow, with Dancy gently snubbing the slack around the bow bitt. The end of the heavier line was just out of the water—nearly within reach of the two weary officers—then disappointment struck again! A sudden twenty-foot swell rose out of the sea and side-slammed the *Enterprise,* throwing Carlsen and Dancy off balance! The heaving line frayed itself out on the sharp steel of the foredeck, and the heavier line fell into the sea with a disheartening splash—a whole morning's work gone for naught!

"Avast heaving!" roared Carlsen. "We're taking a break to get reorganized!"

"Okay," sang out Captain Parker from the starboard quarter of the *Turmoil.* "We'll try it again, later!"

Meanwhile, Commander Leslie J. O'Brien, Jr., of the stand-by destroyer *Willard Keith,* had watched the morning's unsuccessful attempt to get a towline aboard the *Enterprise*—and had also observed a "break" in the operations. He now ordered the *Keith* to come alongside the wallowing freighter.

"These men must be damn'd low of provisions," he observed to one of his lieutenants. "See to it that a line is shot across and have the galley send some hot chow over there!"

"Aye, sir!" the lieutenant said with a grin.

For the first time in over a week Kurt Carlsen had a "hot meal"—he and Dancy ate "royally" on a steak dinner with all the "fixin's," boosting their morale and giving them the added strength they must have for the grueling task of securing a towline on the bow bitt aboard the rolling *Enterprise.*

In the first few hours of the afternoon failure still dogged Carlsen and Dancy in their herculean attempts to get a towline aboard. Undaunted, Captain Dan Parker, of the *Turmoil* yelled encouragement to the pair on the *Enterprise,* saying he'd "try an' try again" until a towline was secured! Darkness ended a day of defeat, with Carlsen and Dancy leg and arm weary.

"You two get a night's rest," yelled Parker. "Meantime, I'll think of a way to get that towline aboard first thing in the morning!"

"Good night!" chorused Carlsen and Dancy. "We hope you're right!"

The fifth day of January, 1952, dawned gray and drizzly, with a still-heaving sea. Thin banks of fog dimmed the outlines of the *Turmoil* and the *Keith.* With the compliments of Commander O'Brien, Carlsen and Dancy scrambled topside with full bellies, ready to tackle the towline ordeal again up in the bows. Captain Parker wasted no time. He veered the *Turmoil* sharply in close to the bows of the *Enterprise* and heaved a line! Carlsen caught it cleanly. Dancy put all his weight into it, and slowly they dragged aboard a heavier line—then, finally, the towline itself—a five-inch steel cable— securing it around the bow bitt at 9:37 A.M., after an hour of feverish work!

"Towline fixed!" they chorused jubilantly.

Slowly the giant four-thousand-horsepower British tug *Turmoil* moved through the moderately rough seas. There must be no sudden pull—no drawing taut the towline—it must stay at least forty feet under the water. This was one race that must be run slowly to win! Some one thousand yards astern was the powerful 440-ton French tug *Abeille 25* —under contract with the *Turmoil* to stand by in case of trouble—having arrived from Brest during the night.

Then began the long, long trip—on what might well be the last leg of Kurt Carlsen's great epic of the sea—to Falmouth, England, 320 miles and four days away!

But the sea is a stubborn, capricious thing—it rarely relents, even to a man of Kurt Carlsen's stature! And the North Atlantic in January is as dangerous as the Indian Ocean in typhoon season —its whims are just as uncalculated as they are terrible! Warnings came of southwesterly gales not far to the north as the little convoy slowly made its way toward Falmouth on January 6. First came the powerful British tug *Turmoil,* then, some 750 yards behind her, the lop-sided *Enterprise* with Carlsen and Dancy still aboard, and hovering close to her was the stand-by destroyer *Willard Keith* and the French tug *Abeille 25* a thousand yards astern the *Enterprise.*

"Weather overcast with intermittent fog banks," radioed Commander Leslie J. O'Brien, Jr., of the *Keith.* "Sea moderate. Visibility eight miles to one mile in fog. Barometer 30.52, steady. Wind 10 knots. Course 074 true. Captain Carlsen in fine spirits."

The sea craftily bides its time. It is now January 7. Carlsen and the *Enterprise* are within 110 miles of Falmouth—and safety! Carlsen's vessel rides easily in tow and there seems less of a list to port. All appears well aboard the *Enterprise.* Carlsen and Dancy are far more concerned by what the *Keith's* radio operator told them this morning—the uncom-

fortable prospects of facing the company of report-
ers and the battery of newsreel cameramen who
would swarm dockside at Falmouth. At this moment
it was a more terrifying thought to them than the
ordeal aboard the *Enterprise*—and they frankly agree
that it scares them!

"Wind slight. Swells from west ten feet high,"
radioes the *Keith's* operator later. "Reduced speed
to 3 knots this morning. *Enterprise* listing 50°,
rolling to 65°, immersing port wing of bridge occasionally, due to swells."

The sea stirs itself into heavier swells. The wind
begins to pick up. The fury of another North
Atlantic cyclonic storm unleashes itself, threatening the helpless, wallowing *Enterprise* with near-
gale blasts. But the five-inch steel cable towline
holds, and the *Turmoil* edges slowly toward Falmouth a hundred miles to the northeast.

But by 1:30 A.M., January 9, the full fury of
the new storm hurls itself upon the hapless freighter. The five-inch steel towline snaps like a piece
of string, and the merciless sea pounces on the floundering derelict, side-slamming her with twenty-
five-foot combers that crash broadside against her
weather beam. The staunch four-thousand-horsepower tug *Turmoil* rocks and rolls in the mountainous seas, helpless to get a new line aboard the
careening *Enterprise*—now only a scant thirty miles
off Lizard Head, southeastern tip of England, twenty
miles south of Falmouth.

Grimly Carlsen and Dancy fight their way to the
pitching bows of their stricken vessel. Time after
time Carlsen and Dancy struggled to get another

tow rig aboard—time after time it's touch and go as the mounting seas smash over the *Enterprise,* rolling her to 80°. Up in the bows the two officers cling to the railing as they go about the dangerous task of reclaiming the towline shackle for still another try.

Rain squalls hiss blindingly across the deck, driven by hurricane-force winds. It's shortly before 3:00 A.M. as the foredeck dips deep into the on-rushing combers, spewing the angry sea over the fo'c'slehead.

Carlsen is outside the rail of the port bow, dangerously closer to the raging waters than Dancy. Half-submerged, Kurt Carlsen gamely clutches the rail until the *Turmoil's* first mate clambers down the slanting fo'c'slehead and drags him back aboard. Dancy drags Carlsen up to the starboard bow and comparative safety. For several minutes Carlsen clings to the rail, breathing heavily from complete exhaustion.

"That was a close brush, Captain!" yells Dancy above the wind. "It's too bloody dangerous to attempt another tow tonight!"

"Aye, I'm afraid so," agrees Carlsen weakly. "I'm too beat!"

But stubborn men of the sea like Carlsen and Dancy never quit! After a brief cat nap, the two officers again tackled the tortuous towline job at daybreak. For the next tedious thirteen hours they gamely fought a losing battle with a treacherous sea that gave them no quarter—and for thirteen hours Captain Dan Parker tried to maneuver the rolling *Turmoil* into positions of vantage for the two struggling men in the bows of the wallowing *Enterprise*. But the sea had too much strength and power. Hour by hour the doomed freighter settled deeper—now she was nearly on her side at an almost 90° angle! How much more could she take before she capsized? How long could the intrepid Kurt Carlsen and the game Ken Dancy stay aboard her? Hour after hour they faced frustration—still they fought the angry sea against overwhelming odds! Still before them danced that one glimmering hope—the next heaving line would hold—and they'd rig another towline around the bow bitts! Even as dusk closed in, veteran tugmen at the scene gave them a fifty-fifty chance that they could snag a tow and reach Falmouth next day!

All that night the sea surged and raged around the hopeless hulk that was once the *Flying Enterprise* — the pride, the very life of Captain Kurt Carlsen!

As the dawn of January 10 grayed the stormy skies, Commander Leslie J. O'Brien, Jr., of the guardian stand-by destroyer *Willard Keith* stood on his bridge and scanned the half-sunken hulk with his binoculars. Earlier, a weak signal from Carlsen's "ham" set had been intercepted by the *Keith's* radio operator. The almost inaudible voice of Captain Carlsen came across the rough waters that separated the rocking destroyer and the sinking *Enterprise*—a reluctant concession that an angry sea was smashing all hopes of securing another towline aboard her . . . then followed a faintly audible apology that he, Carlsen, must sign off to conserve the fast-waning power of his set for "emergency" signals only.

The *Keith's* operator radioed a waiting world:

"Unable to pass tow this weather which believe typical of this area, therefore outlook not favorable immediate future."

All morning, strange gurglings below warned Carlsen and Dancy that the 1,200 tons of pig iron had suddenly shifted further to the port side, widening the crack in the hull and admitting a greater inrush of water. This could be the "beginning of the end," they knew! Perched precariously on the starboard side of the foundering *Enterprise,* Carlsen clung grimly to his "ham" short-wave set and dutifully kept the *Keith* and *Turmoil* informed of the worsening conditions aboard his sinking ship. Dancy, grim-faced, balanced himself beside Carlsen.

Shortly before 3:00 P.M., Carlsen held his last "three way" conversation. He was talking with Commander O'Brien of the *Keith* and Captain Dan Parker of the tug *Turmoil.*

"We'll plan to get off by way of the funnel when the time comes," he was saying to Captain Parker.

"How long are you going to wait?" asked Commander O'Brien anxiously. "From here it looks bad. . . ."

Suddenly the doors of the wheelhouse exploded from the pressure of the inrushing water. Fifteen seconds later Carlsen and Dancy were well aware that the *Enterprise* was sinking fast—that further delay could mean disaster and death if the badly battered hulk took a sudden dive. Scrambling over the superstructure—now on its side—the two officers made it to the ship's funnel, jutting out over the rough water. For a brief second Carlsen took a backward glance at his fast-dying ship—it was then that he fully realized he'd lost his grimly fought battle to a power and strength beyond his control . . . the cruelly merciless sea!

"Jump for it, Captain—th' funnel's takin' water!" Dancy's voice was urgent.

"We'll jump together, mate!" snapped Carlsen, grabbing Dancy's hand.

At 3:26 P.M. the *Keith's* operator said, "Carlsen and Dancy have jumped from the funnel!"

At 3:32 P.M. the *Turmoil's* operator flashed the word, "We've got 'em both!"

On the rolling deck of the *Turmoil* Captain Kurt Carlsen, wrapped in blankets, glued tearful eyes on his beloved *Flying Enterprise* as she lay flat on her side. Dancy stood beside him, an arm around his shoulder. At 3:39 P.M. the *Enterprise* slowly went down by the stern. By four o'clock her starboard bow just showed above a triumphant sea. Ten minutes later Kurt Carlsen saw the last of his ship as the sea did the only decent thing during the whole ordeal—it shrouded its victim in a pure white funeral spray . . . and Kurt Carlsen's "long, lonely watch" came to a sad end at the mouth of the English Channel, a scant forty miles short of Falmouth!

Sources of Factual Material

The complete factual account of Captain Hendrik Kurt Carlsen and the *Flying Enterprise* comes from another fine marine scrapbook compiled by Mr. Alfred Irwin Abt, in his "Ships—1952, Vol. 1," also in the Mystic Seaport library. Mr. Abt's carefully selected clippings from the *New York Times*, the *New York Herald Tribune*, the *New York Daily Mirror*, and the January 14, 1952, issue of *Life* thoroughly cover "The Carlsen Saga" from December 27 to December 31, 1951, and from January 1 through January 10, 1952—the day when Captain Kurt Carlsen, and Mate Dancy of the tug *Turmoil*, were taken aboard the British tug from the funnel of the fast-sinking *Flying Enterprise*.

IV

AN AFFAIR OF DISCIPLINE

THERE WAS BUSTLE and scurry aboard the glistening new brig-o'-war *Somers* as she rode gently at her pierhead in the Brooklyn Navy Yard on that bright September morning of 1842. Midshipmen and apprentices swarmed her trim deck. The *Somers* was the first training vessel of the United States Navy and marked the full realization of a long-felt need. More, too, she symbolized a personal triumph for Commodore Matthew Perry, who had sponsored her against strong opposition.

For all her rakish beauty, the *Somers* was not a large vessel. She boasted a deck length of 103 feet, a 25-foot beam, and an 11-foot depth of hold. Her single-spar deck was cut up into cramped quarters. Head room below was less than five feet. With her complement of 120 men, she was badly overcrowded. Seven midshipmen were bunked in the steerage within a space of eight feet by fourteen feet. Many of the apprentices found they were forced to sleep on deck and most of them, having neither bunks, lockers, nor a seat at mess, had to fend for themselves. It was to be a Spartan life at sea—hard and tough—a rugged training to make rugged and competent officers out of raw, green youngsters. It was the Navy's way to make 'em learn fast.

In command was one of the most talented officers in the Navy—Alexander Mackenzie, who had been hand-picked by Commodore Perry to inspire the future officers with the highest traditions of the service.

The *Somers'* orders were to sail for Africa with dispatches for the *Vandalla* stationed there. She then was to return via the West Indies, completing a three months' training cruise of some seven thousand miles.

As the last naval cadet was mustered aboard, a carriage clattered noisily down the cobbled lane leading to the *Somers'* pierhead. A tall, arrogant youth in midshipman blues threw open the door and jumped out when the cabbie reined up the horse within yards of the *Somers*.

"Here, fellow," he laughed, tossing the cabbie a silver dollar, "my name's Spencer and I may not be welcome aboard that scow. Wait a bit for me!"

Commander Mackenzie spotted him from the *Somers'* quarter-deck and muttered silently to himself, "God Almighty — they've sent me Philip Spencer!"

How this wild, unbridled son of the Secretary of War came to be included in the group of selectees has never been explained. Following two trials by a naval court for gross insubordination and attempts to incite mutiny aboard two vessels of the United States Navy, young Spencer had been dismissed "for the good of the service." Unfortunately, through political pressure, he had been reinstated and returned to active duty. His unsavory reputation as a troublemaker was known far and wide throughout Navy circles, and Commander Mackenzie winced inwardly as young Spencer arrogantly swung aboard the *Somers,* minus his gear.

"Mr. Spencer," Mackenzie greeted him, "I suggest that in the best interests of this training cruise you seek an immediate transfer!"

"Aye, sir," answered the Secretary's son with a surly glance at the *Somers'* commander, then strode back down the gangplank toward the waiting carriage.

"To Commodore Perry's quarters," he ordered the cabbie as he leaped in and slammed the door, "and look lively!"

The cabbie wheeled the horse about sharply and the carriage clattered back up the land. Moments later, young Spencer faced Commodore Perry across his desk. The Commodore tapped his finger tips against the mahogany top as he studied the "blacklisted" midshipman and listened to his plea for a transfer. For several seconds there was silence, the veteran Navy man still tapping the desk in deep thought. Slowly he shook his head.

"No, Mr. Spencer," Commodore Perry said at length, "I'm afraid I cannot grant your request for a transfer at this time—this cruise is exactly what you need to learn the Navy's first law—discipline! Report at once for duty aboard the *Somers!*"

"Very good, sir," answered young Spencer, though his face fell when he heard the Commodore's decision. He saluted halfheartedly and returned to duty on the *Somers,* much to Mackenzie's displeasure as well as his own. So it was that when the brig cleared next morning, September 13, outbound for Fayal in the Azores, the mischief-making Spencer was aboard.

He lost no time in capitalizing on his reputation as a "hard case." The *Somers* was scarcely out of sight of land before he started sowing the seeds of discontent among his shipmates and, due to the insufferable conditions brought about by overcrowding, Spencer found fallow ground for his mischievous activities.

"You fools!" he sneered. "You blasted young idiots—leaving comfortable homes to cast your lot with this stinking hulk! A set of officers who sit smugly in their quarters, aft—a doddering old man for your commander—and you sweat and strain your bellies out—for what?"

Day after day Spencer continued to castigate his shipmates with stinging invectives. He boasted of his own superiority and enlarged upon their conditions to such a point that many of them came to fear and hate him. Soon he began to work on the *Somers'* crew, forward. He stole tobacco and distributed it among apprentices and crew, contrary to regulations. He inveigled the wardroom steward into stealing brandy for him. He got drunk and announced boastfully to the foremast hands that he had served on the *Adams* and the *Potomac,* that he was a sailor of the seven seas and looked upon his fellow cadets as being childish.

Outward bound, the discipline aboard the *Somers* appeared to be good. Spencer, by apparently following orders, got but scant notice from his superiors. But in secret he defied every regulation and grew more brazenly mutinous with each passing day.

The *Somers* touched a Fayal, paused briefly, then laid a course for Funchal, where she arrived October 5. Then, against strong headwinds, she beat her way to Santa Cruz in the Canaries. Here, inquiry was made as to the whereabouts of the *Vandalla*. This vessel being unreported, the *Somers* pushed on to the Cape Verde Islands and signaled Porto Traya on October 21. Still no word of the *Vandalla*. Commander Mackenzie then laid a course for the mainland.

On November 10 the *Somers* made a landfall, rounded Cape Mesurado, entered the mouth of St. Paul's River, and brought up in Monrovia. Here Captain Mackenzie learned that the *Vandalla* had cleared for the United States.

Meanwhile, young Spencer kept tongue-lashing his mates into sullen fury against their superiors. Then Commander Mackenzie made a decision that was as unfortunate at it was expedient. In fear that overcrowded conditions might speedily turn the *Somers* into a floating morgue, Mackenzie suddenly decided to quit the blazing equatorial heat of African waters and ordered shore leave cut to one day.

A few days later the *Somers* weighed anchor and set a course for the West Indies. There was much grumbling below decks and tempers were short. Spencer took full advantage of this ugly undercurrent among apprentice seamen and midshipmen alike. Again he lashed into them unmercifully.

"What are you—a bunch of suckling infants?"

sneered the troublemaking midshipman. "One-day 'liberty' and back you trot to teacher, like a lot of schoolboys! One day 'liberty'—and back you go to sea—with a hell of a wide water between you and your next landfall! The Old Man has you wrapped around his little finger like a wisp of hemp—you've got all the squashy innards of a jellyfish! Navy men, you call yourselves — bah! You haven't the guts to complain out loud—much less fight for your rights!"

Under the sting of his constant needling, discipline aboard the *Somers* worsened rapidly and Spencer's seeds of discord soon began to bear fruit. In this foment of discontent and tension, the brig beat westward through light airs and intense heat. Only the breezes from the northeast trades made life aboard endurable. Nevertheless, the *Somers* made daily runs of two hundred miles under a merciless tropic sun. Murmurings grew louder and finally reached the quarter-deck.

Commander Mackenzie then resorted to the "lash" in approved Navy tradition. As required by regulations in the punishment of youthful offenders, the "cat" was applied with only four of its nine tails, but it drew blood freely just the same. These systematic lashings spread hysteria and a wave of nameless terror among the already distraught cadets. Orders from the officers had often to be repeated before they were carried out with great indifference. Again the dreaded "cat" would strike into raw flesh! The *Somers* became a floating hell.

By clever contrivance, Midshipman Spencer escaped the lash. He was servile to the point of abjection under the eyes of Commander Mackenzie, while below deck he preached open mutiny. He visioned himself as a future pirate chief and he laid plans to take the *Somers,* as he had unsuccessfully schemed to take the *Adams* and the *Potomac.*

On a sultry, dark evening following one of Commander Mackenzie's worst "cat sessions" with recalcitrant apprentices, Spencer succeeded in recruiting a pair of "hard cases" to help him further his fantastic plans.

One of these recruits was the bo's'n's mate, a giant of a man who answered to the name of Cromwell. He was an ex-slaver and a savage at heart. The other man was Seaman Small—a short, wiry man who made up in guile what he lacked in size.

Talking low in the black recesses of the fo'c'sle, these three formed a nucleus for the half-hatched conspiracy.

"Had my eye on you for some time, Spencer," stated Cromwell without mirth. "You're smart, Spencer—think I'll go along with you—know a trick or two myself. How about you, Small—kicking in with Spencer?"

"Maybe I will," the taciturn Small answered, eyeing Spencer warily. "What's in it for us, Spencer?"

"Enough to make it worth your while, I'll wager!" snapped the truculent midshipman. "If we play our cards right this vessel is as good as ours—if we play our cards right!"

"Then what?" questioned Small with a thin smile.

"Not so fast, Small," answered Spencer sharply. "I'm making the plans."

To his newly recruited lieutenants who had

soaked up much of the world's evil while knocking about the ports of the seven seas, Spencer briefly laid bare a cold-blooded plot—cold-blooded even
by the standards of Cromwell and Small. He had,
he said, won over Neville, an ordinary seaman—a
man handy with dirk or pistol. A steward named
Wales had thrown in with him—a good man to
have in charge of mess and supplies. Altogether,
he figured, some twenty men had allied themselves
with his "cause."

Then Spencer outlined the procedure of his
daring plan: Each of the conspirators was assigned
a definite post—being committed in writing by
Spencer on a paper which he concealed in his
neckerchief. As Spencer was assigned to the midnight to 4:00 A.M. watch under Rogers, the officer
of the deck, the attack would be made by Spencer.
A "fight" would be staged by the plotters well forward of the mainmast. Spencer was then to part
the "offenders" and escort them aft for disciplinary
action. Once they were well aft and clear of the
gangway, Rogers was to be killed and thrown overside; the hatches would be instantly battened down
and the keys to the arms chest secured. With the
mutineers armed, Spencer would go below and kill
Commander Mackenzie, after which all would in-
vade the wardroom and steerage—systematically putting to death all officers, warrant officers, and midshipmen. Then they would return to the deck, slew
the guns around, muster the remainder of the crew,
and throw overboard those who would be of no use
in their plans.

The brig would be stripped down; spare spars,

yards, gigs, and all impediment would be destroyed, and a course laid for the Spanish Main. All prizes would be sunk and all prisoners murdered. Thus their grim secret would remain hidden.

"Gad, Spencer," grinned Cromwell malevolently, "you ain't forgot nothing!"

Even Small agreed grudgingly.

The trio parted for the present.

Midshipman Spencer, while on duty at the jib downhaul, one day found it to be jammed. In a raucous voice, plainly audible to the whole crew, he roundly cursed the jib, its lacing, and the man who invented it—knowing full well that the lacing was Commander Mackenzie's own idea.

The revolt thus came out into the open. Commander Mackenzie sensed that it was widespread. Not knowing whom he could trust, he realized that any impulsive action on his part might precipitate the very thing he wanted to avoid. Delay was in his favor. Sparring for time, he altered the course for New York and drove the brig to the utmost.

As the days passed and the appointed night for the staged "fight" drew closer, Spencer, Cromwell, and Small actually thought that their secret "masterplan" was still *secret*. But as Machiavelli long ago expounded, no secret is truly secret if shared by more than one. It is also quite possible that there were as many flaws in Spencer's plot as there were parties in the plan.

Wales, the steward, was no sailor and certainly was not a pirate. The more he pondered the terrible gravity of the thing, the more panic-stricken he became. He made an unsuccessful attempt to warn the crew, but only succeeded in arousing the suspicions of the plotters who then began shadowing him closely. Shortly afterwards, however, in going about his routine duties, Wales seized upon an opportunity and unburdened himself to Purser Heiskell. The amazed Heiskell assured Wales that an immediate report would be made to Commander Mackenzie.

But even as Wales and Heiskell talked, Wales was painfully aware that he had been detected by Cromwell, Small, and Wilson, who had begun an advance to encircle him. Tossing all caution to the winds, Wales turned quickly and ran up to Lieutenant Gansevoort, the officer of the deck, and blurted out the plot.

Meanwhile, Commander Mackenzie weighed the situation. The enormity of the thing was staggering; such a bold mutiny plot had no precedent in the annals of the United States Navy. But now he had strong, concrete evidence that Midshipman Spencer was *actually* plotting to take over the *Somers;* that Spencer had sought to obtain, through the surgeon, sailing directions for the Isle of Pines, that he, Spencer, had made specific inquiries of Midshipman Rogers of the chronometer rate and had been seen examining charts of the West Indies.

Even though the mutineers had made no overt move, Commander Mackenzie decided to act and to act at once to avert disaster. The crew was piped to quarters and Mackenzie called a meeting of the officers. Among them was Spencer himself. Mackenzie's sharp eyes seemed to drill into Spencer's evil mind.

"I understand, Mr. Spencer," opened Mackenzie sarcastically, "that you aspire to command the *Somers!*"

"Oh, no, sir," answered Spencer, a wan smile playing for an instant on his face.

"Did you not tell Mr. Wales, sir," continued Commander Mackenzie, boring in deeper, "that you had a project to kill the commander, all the officers, and a considerable portion of the crew of this vessel, then convert her into a pirate?"

For a second Spencer's face blanched and he wiped cold beads of perspiration from his brow.

"I—I may have told him so, sir, but only as a joke."

"You admit that you told him so?"

"Aye, sir—but as a joke!"

"This, sir, is joking on a forbidden subject," roared Mackenzie. "This joke may cost you your life!"

Spencer was searched, but no papers were found. The midshipman was committed to double irons and shackled to the port arms chest on the quarter-deck, out of reach of the crew. Lieutenant Gansevoort was assigned to guard the prisoner and to see that he did not escape or make contact with his fellow conspirators.

The next day was Sunday, the twenty-seventh of November, dawning fair after a night of mounting tension. The brig ran free under a following wind and at quarters a rigid inspection of the crew was made. Church was rigged and divine service was held.

In the afternoon the wind fell off and the skys'ls

and royal stu'n'ls were bent. Apprentice Gagely, aloft on the main royal yard had a closer brush with death when Small and another seaman drew in on the sheet with such force that the main t'gallant mast sheered off at the cap. As young Gagely fell, he managed to grasp part of the rigging as the mast crashed to the deck. The better part of the afternoon was consumed in clearing away the wreckage.

Yet, in the confusion brought on by the dismasting, Mackenzie had time to note that most of the mutineers had assembled at the maintop.

The men were piped to evening mess. After supper they returned to work. The main t'gallant mast was fitted, skys'l and yards crossed, the canvas bent. Again Mackenzie noted that the plotters mustered at the maintop.

Night closed down. The officers stood a sharp watch—tense and ready. Then Mackenzie acted fast. Cromwell was seen descending the main weather shrouds. At a sign from the commander the officers closed in and Cromwell was placed under arrest— taken to the quarter-deck and shackled to the starboard arms chest in double irons. Questioned briefly, he sat in sullen silence. Moments later, Small was seized and clapped in irons. He, too, kept a surly silence when questioned.

Affairs worsened. Instead of bringing order, the arrests marked the passing of any pretense of discipline. Musters went unanswered; orders were flagrantly ignored.

Fist fights and petty thievery broke out up forward. Again and again the "cat" bit deep into

human flesh and blood flowed—to great agony but
to little avail.

In this deplorable state of chaos the brig lumbered
on until Wednesday. On that day, at 9:00 A.M.,
Greene, MacKinley, Wilson, and another seaman
were put under arrest.

This now brought the number of prisoners to
seven, nearly filling the quarter-deck. Commander
Mackenzie then drew up a letter which was immediately posted in the wardroom:

U.S. BRIG SOMERS
November 30, 1842

GENTLEMEN:

The time has arrived when I am desirous of availing
myself of your counsel in the responsible position in which
as commander of this vessel, I find myself placed. You are
aware of the circumstances which have resulted in the
confinement of Midshipman Spencer, Boatswain's Mate
Samuel Cromwell and Seaman E. Small, as prisoners, and
I purposely abstain from entering into any details of them,
necessarily ignorant of the exact extent of disaffection
among a crew which has so long and so systematically and
assiduously been tampered with by *an officer*. I have determined to address myself to you and ask your united
counsel as to the best course to be now pursued, and I
call upon you to take into deliberate and dispassionate consideration the present condition of the vessel, and the contingencies of every nature that the future may embrace
throughout the remainder of the cruise and to enlighten
me with your opinion as to the best course to be pursued.

I am, very respectfully, gentlemen, your most obedient

ALEX SLIDELL MACKENZIE, *Commander*

As a result of the letter, a court of inquiry was
held by the officers of the *Somers,* exclusive of Com-

mander Mackenzie and three midshipmen who held the deck, with witnesses examined under oath.

On Thursday the findings were delivered to Commander Mackenzie in writing by Lieutenant Gansevoort. Their recommendations were that Cromwell, Small, and Spencer should be executed without delay for the safety of the vessel and the good of the service. The judgment confirmed Mackenzie in his own views.

The petty officers were armed with pistol and cutlass and the main yard was rigged for a hanging. Midshipman Spencer was notified that he had just ten minutes more to live.

Now in the shadow of the noose, disgraced, and soon to die, Midshipman Philip Spencer, U.S.N., conversed with his commander.

In hushed whispers Spencer admitted his guilt to Mackenzie. He felt that the world was against him. He expressed concern that his execution might damage his father's career. His only request was that he be shot instead of hanged. He admitted he had plotted to take the *Adams* and the *Potomac,* adding that he was possessed with a mania for revolt.

The ten minutes grew to an hour as the commander took notes which later were admitted for evidence.

Then the execution began. The prisoners had said their farewells. All were blindfolded. Spencer and Cromwell were placed slighty abaft the gangway and opposite each other. Small was led a few steps forward on the hammocks. The nooses were about their necks. The lines led over the main yardarm to the deck below where they were tailed by three groups of men under the command of an armed petty officer.

Spencer had received permission to give the command to swing away.

For a moment an awesome stillness settled over the deck.

"I am ready, Mr. Spencer," said Small in a steady voice.

Spencer's eyes welled over with tears, his voice shook and he was unable to give the word. Through Browning he asked that Commander Mackenzie give the signal of execution.

"Stand by!" ordered Mackenzie. "Fire!"

"Whip!" echoed Lieutenant Gansevoort.

Along the deck there was a scuffle of running feet and three bodies leaped into the air. A gun boomed out, the American colors were run up. The whips were made fast and the crew listened to a solemn address by their commander. Then three rousing cheers were given by all the ship's company for their flag and country as the three bodies swayed in the air overhead. The mutiny was ended.

On December 15—three months, almost, to the day since she had sailed—the *Somers* reached New York and tied up to her pierhead at the Brooklyn Navy Yard. Four of the mutineers were still in irons. Commander Mackenzie was duly tried by a naval court on four charges growing out of the mutiny. The charges: murder, oppression, illegal punishment, and conduct unbecoming an officer.

The trial marked an epoch in naval history, created a political uproar, and won international attention. Commander Mackenzie ably defended his

position. After a trial lasting forty days, Mackenzie
was acquitted. President Taylor confirmed the verdict.

Thus, the only organized mutiny in the history
of our navy was effectively squelched by the vigorous action of the fearless commander of a tiny
brig-o'-war.

Sources of Factual Material

The facts of the first—and only—attempt at mutiny
in the United States Navy are ably covered by Rear
Admiral Livingston Hunt (SC), U.S.N. (Ret.) in
Naval Institute Proceedings, LI (November, 1925)
2063-2100, and by George R. Clark, in his *Short
History of the United States Navy* (Philadelphia:
J. B. Lippincott, 1927), pp. 214-18. In 1844, James
Fenimore Cooper, noted historical novel writer and
historian of the United States Navy—an ex-navy
man himself—chose to make a hotly controversial
issue of the attempted mutiny aboard the *Somers* and
its subsequent quelling by Commander Alexander
Slidell Mackenzie and his officers. In his long account, "The Cruise of the *Somers,*" Cooper soundly
lambastes the court-martial as "a brazen piece of
whitewashing." In so doing he set up two schools
of thought on the matter: (1) Commander Mackenzie was not justified in hanging Midshipman
Philip Spencer, Samuel Cromwell, and Elisha Small;
or, (2) Commander Mackenzie was fully within his
authority as commander to quell the incipient mutiny aboard a vessel of the United States Navy as
quickly and as effectively as possible. Even today

these two schools of thought exist. The present writer leaves the reader to draw his own conclusions —but it must be borne in mind that Midshipman Spencer had been a "trouble-maker" twice before, aboard two other United States naval vessels; had been "let out" of the Navy "for the good of the service"; but, because of "high political connections," had been "reinstated" with the rank of midshipman. The outcome of the attempted mutiny aboard the *Somers* was instrumental in establishing the United States Naval Academy at Annapolis a few years later.

V

DEATH WATCH ON THE R.M.S.
TITANIC

LIKE A PHANTOM SHIP on a smooth ebony sea, the sharp towering bows of the great new 882-foot, 45,000-ton White Star luxury liner *Titanic* clove the black expanses of the North Atlantic at a twenty-one-knot clip as she sped westward toward New York on her maiden voyage. Among her three hundred and twenty-five first-cabin passengers were many world notables—even a few of her two hundred and eighty-five second-cabin passengers were internationally prominent, and those happy seven hundred and ten passengers of her third cabin dreamed of peace and freedom in a new world. All felt secure in the knowledge that the *Titanic* was the last word in modern ship construction and —*unsinkable!* Far below in her cargo hold were 1,400 tons of machinery, merchandise, and valuables worth $420,000. Commanding her palatial magnificence, and her crew of eight hundred and ninety-nine, was Captain Edward J. Smith, seasoned veteran of forty-three years at sea. She had cleared Queenstown, Ireland, at 2.00 P.M., Thursday, April 11, 1912—and now it was Sunday night, April 14 —with the Irish coast some 1,500 watery miles behind her!

By nine o'clock that night Chief Operator George

Phillips knew he had had a hectic day in the *Titanic's* wireless shack. All sorts of crazy messages were being flashed out on the air by the ship's passengers, intrigued by Marconi's miracle invention. They must see how it worked—this new style "ship-to-shore" communication without wires—and so they slapped a wire basket full of many messages on Phillips' desk. For hours he had "pounded brass," and he was dead tired—yet the pile of "Marconigrams" seemed to be endless. Five dollars per week and board was little enough to pay a hardworking operator, thought Phillips wearily.

At his left elbow on the desk lay the *Titanic's* "wireless log-book." Interspersed among its entries of messages received were warnings of icebergs—all dated Sunday, April 14. From the *Baltic,* at 3:00 P.M.: "Greek steamship *Athinai* reports passing icebergs and large quantity of field ice today in latitude 41.51 north, longitude 49.52 west." From the *Californian,* at 6:30 P.M.: "Latitude 42.3 north, longitude 49.52 west. Three large bergs five miles to southward of us." Later, from the *Amerika:* "*Amerika* passed two large icebergs in 41.27 north, 50.8 west, on 14th of April."

Harold S. Bride, relief operator aboard the *Titanic,* then posted the ice warnings under a glass frame in the chartroom, directly above the navigating officer's table. Captain Smith and First Officer William M. Murdoch studied them, checking the chart to estimate in what latitude and longitude the *Titanic* would be in reference to the icebergs at a given time. Even as the two officers studied the warnings, the mighty *Titanic* continued to plough ahead through the glasslike sea at twenty-one to twenty-three knots—approximately twenty-six to twenty-eight miles per hour, land speed.

At nine o'clock Captain Smith went up on the bridge where Second Officer Charles H. Lightoller was on duty.

"We're favored with a fine, clear night, Mr. Lightoller," said the *Titanic's* master, smiling.

"Aye, sir," answered the second officer.

"But have you seen the ice warnings in the chartroom yet?" asked the captain. "Seems there *are* a few icebergs around."

"Afraid I've been on duty since they were posted," said Lightoller. "What latitude and longitude do the warnings give?"

"Well, the last message came from the *Amerika*," answered Captain Smith. "They gave forty-one point three north, and fifty point eight west, two large icebergs."

"What position is that in reference to ours?" asked Lightoller.

"Mr. Murdoch and I estimated that we would be in the vicinity of ice about eleven o'clock tonight," answered the captain quietly.

"Which means we'd best reduce speed, sir," suggested the second officer.

"If it is in a slight degree hazy we shall have to go very slowly," agreed Smith. "But in any event keep the lookouts on their toes—I've a dinner engagement now, so carry on until Murdoch relieves you."

"Aye, sir," smiled Lightoller. "I will—and have a good time, sir."

As Captain Smith left the bridge, Lightoller immediately phoned the lookout up in the crow's-nest on the foremast.

"Fleet?"

"Aye, sir."

"Lightoller speaking. The skipper says to keep a sharp lookout for ice!"

"Aye, sir!"

Still the majestic *Titanic* sped westward through the frosty, starlit night, averaging twenty-one knots!

Down in the luxurious first-class smoking room on Deck B a group of prominent men were discussing the comparative speeds and luxury of competing transatlantic liners. Among them were Major Archie Butt, military aide to President Taft; Clarence Moore of Washington, D.C.; Frank D. Millet, the world-famous artist; Colonel Archibald Gracie, of New York; Mr. John B. Thayer, second vice-president of the Pennsylvania Railroad; and Mr. George D. Widener, a son of the Philadelphia streetcar magnate, Mr. P.A.B. Widener. Mr. Charles M. Hays, president of the Canadian Grand Trunk Railway, who was returning home after an extensive study abroad of hotel equipment for the new extension to his own great railroad system, was addressing his distinguished fellow passengers.

"The White Star, the Cunard, and the Hamburg-American lines," said he, unaware that he was voicing a grim prophecy, "are now devoting their attention to a struggle for supremacy in obtaining the most luxurious appointments for their ships, but the time will soon come when the greatest and most appalling of all disasters will be the result."

Up on the bridge, Second Officer Lightoller had opened the window on the starboard corner of the bridge for a quick breath of fresh air. It was nearly ten o'clock—the hour when First Officer Murdoch would relieve him on the bridge. Behind him the helmsman stood silently at the wheel—he would be relieved at the same time by Quartermaster Robert Hitchins. The night air was cold and clear—so clear that the stars seemed low enough in the heavens to touch. There was no moon. The sea was black and smooth. Automatically Lightoller scanned the horizon with his binoculars for possible stray icebergs. Not a sign of ice! A shiver shook Lightoller and he closed the bridge window—but, as he still peered out, Captain Smith's words drifted through his mind, "If it is in a slight degree hazy we shall have to go very slowly." But it wasn't hazy, and the *Titanic* sliced effortlessly through the cold sea at unreduced speed!

At 10:40 P.M., another grim ice warning from the *Californian* crackled in over the *Titanic's* antenna: "We are stopped and surrounded by ice!"

Phillips quickly scribbled the message down on a bit of paper and handed it to Bride.

"Get this to the bridge in a hurry!"

First Officer Murdoch studied the paper Bride handed him and shook his head. "Captain Smith's orders are not to reduce speed unless it hazes in —and it's as clear as bell outside."

Bride shrugged and left the bridge. Then Murdoch turned to Hitchins.

"Better keep a watchout for small floes of ice."

"Aye, sir."

At a little past 11:30 P.M. Seaman Louis Klein had just completed two hours of his six-hour patrol on the promenade deck, starboard side, when a passenger at the rail called to him.

"Look, quick!" he said tensely. "See the hill over there!"

Klein rushed over and followed the passenger's arm as he pointed a little to starboard of the *Titanic's* bow.

"That's an iceberg!" whispered Klein hoarsely. Klein rushed forward to notify the bridge.

"What's wrong?" yelled Third Officer Herbert J. Pitman, on his way to the bridge.

"Big iceberg off the starb'd bow, sir!" answered Klein over his shoulder as he raced for the foremast and the lookout's crow's-nest.

"Iceberg!" shouted Klein as he swung up the ratlines. No answer from Fleet or Lee.

Scrambling into the crow's-nest, Klein vigorously rang the alarm bell three times to warn the bridge! Then he roused the benumbed, dozing lookouts. Klein then slid down the ratlines to the promenade deck. Fleet, instantly awakened by the alarm, grabbed the phone and called the bridge.

"Iceberg ahead!" he roared into the phone.

"Thank you," came the calm reply from the bridge.

But it was already too late! With the *Titanic* rushing through the water at a twenty-one-knot clip, the officers on the bridge saw the great iceberg loom up just ahead of her bows!

"Hard a-starboard! Hard a-starboard!" yelled

Murdoch to Hitchins at the wheel. He called the engine room, "Reverse engines—iceberg!"

But a sixth-of-a-mile-long ship can't be maneuvered as quickly as a tiny cabin cruiser. Slowly the great *Titanic* veered to port—but it was too late! There was a slight grating sound that lasted only a second or two. Up in the crow's-nest Fleet and Lee breathed a sigh of relief as the great ship grazed the towering berg.

"That was a damn'd narrow shave!" whispered Fleet.

"Too damn'd close if you ask me!" answered Lee tensely.

Seconds later the majestic *Titanic* listed five degrees to starboard, settling slightly by the head. The engines stopped. Captain Smith rushed out of the chartroom to the bridge.

"What's happened?"

"We've struck ice!"

"Close the watertight emergency doors immediately, Mr. Murdoch!"

"They're already closed, sir!"

"Call a carpenter—tell him to sound ship!"

"Aye, sir!"

Quartermaster Hitchins stood at attention at the wheel, awaiting further orders. Third Officer Pitman, Mr. Boxhall, fourth officer, Mr. Lowe, fifth officer, and Mr. Moody, sixth officer, all stood by for orders. Captain Smith quickly stepped across the bridge to the wheelhouse and studied the clinometer—it showed a distinct seven-to-eight-degree list to starboard.

"Mr. Pitman, phone the wireless shack and tell

Mr. Phillips to send out a call for help as far as he can—I fear we will need it."

"Aye, sir."

A moment later Pitman had Operator Phillips on the phone.

"Mr. Moody, break out the distress rockets—we shall need them, too."

"Aye, sir!"

"Mr. Boxhall, go down and check the lower decks for possible damage."

"Aye, sir!"

Second Officer Lightoller hurried onto the bridge, still adjusting his jacket—having been off duty in his quarters since being relieved by Murdoch at ten o'clock. Captain Smith and First Officer Murdoch greeted him grimly and quickly briefed him on the situation. Smith paced the bridge a few steps in thought, then faced his officers.

"Gentlemen, prepare to take your boat stations," said Captain Smith quietly. "I want no panic among the passengers—that is one reason I am not sounding the ship's siren for a general alarm. Uncover all lifeboats and get them ready for lowering away. See to it that every passenger is served with a life jacket, though I firmly believe that the ship is capable of staying afloat—her sixteen airtight compartments will take care of that. These orders I have given you are precautionary—and I repeat, I want no panic aboard."

Up in the *Titanic's* wireless shack neither Chief Operator George Phillips nor his relief operator, Harold Bride, felt the shock when the ship struck.

In fact, Bride was asleep on his bunk, just off the wireless room, when Phillips called him.

"Harold, wake up—the ship's stopped!"

"Wha-what's the matter?" asked Bride sleepily.

"Don't know yet," answered Phillips. "Take over while I scout around outside."

A few moments later Phillips was back with a puzzled look on his face.

"Everything's queer as hell out there. You can't see anything, but you get the feeling that all's not as it should be, aboard."

"See any ice?"

"No, it's too dark—suppose you find out what's wrong while I take over here."

After a more thorough investigation Bride returned to the wireless shack and found Phillips sitting tensely at the key, pounding out C Q D's in rapid-fire order.

"Captain says we've struck ice!" said Phillips out of the side of his mouth. "Got to get help, fast!"

"Yeah, I know," answered Bride tightly. "She's got a list to starboard, too!"

For a solid twenty minutes Phillips pounded brass. Intermittently he listened for an answer from other ships—then he continued wearily to flash out the C Q D's, irritably pushing aside the wire basket full of unsent "Marconigrams." Suddenly an answer crackled in. Bride stood tensely by his side.

"It's the *Frankfort*—Hamburg-American Line!" said Phillips, still listening intently. Then Phillips exploded. "Well, Goddam him! 'What's the matter, old man?' he says calmly! I'll fix him!"

"You're a fool! Keep out!" angrily pounded out Phillips on the key.

Moments later H. T. Cottam, wireless operator aboard the *Carpathia,* answered, giving her position. At that moment Captain Smith came into the wireless shack and handed Phillips a piece of paper.

"Here's our position—41.46 north, 50.14 west."

He was advised that the *Carpathia* had just answered the *Titanic's* distress call and had given Phillips their position, telling him that the *Carpathia* was turning about and heading for the *Titanic!* Captain Smith quickly calculated the time the *Carpathia* would arrive, then hurried back to the bridge.

Fourth Officer Boxhall reported to the bridge at about the same moment that Captain Smith returned.

"What damage did you find, Mr. Boxhall?"

"Steerage and all decks in the vicinity of where the iceberg struck are intact—there's no trace of damage, sir."

"What about sounding ship?"

"The carpenter reports she is taking water, sir —and the mail room is flooded. The clerks are moving the mail sacks now—the sacks are floating on the water."

"Then time is of the essence," announced Captain Smith in his quiet voice. "Go to your boat stations and prepare for immediate lowering. Mr. Moody, inform the stewards to arouse all sleeping passengers, and instruct *all* passengers in the use of their life jackets. And remember, gentlemen—women and children go first!"

There was nothing in the manner of the *Titanic's* brush with the submerged section of an iceberg to arouse any undue anxiety among her first-cabin passengers.

Colonel Archibald Gracie had his stateroom on Deck C—Number 51—starboard side. A sudden shock and scraping noise, forward, aroused him from sleep. Hastily he glanced out into the corridor, but found no commotion. Returning to his room he could hear a loud roar of escaping steam—and the ship was suddenly motionless. He dressed hurriedly and left his cabin to investigate. He went up on the Boat Deck. There he found a young man, and together they made their way about the deck to discover what had hit them. But from vantage points, where the view wasn't obstructed by the lifeboats, nothing could be seen either near the ship or on the horizon. They made a complete tour of the deck, but aside from seeing a middle-aged couple from the second cabin strolling arm-in-arm, they found nothing out of order. The steam exhausts in the stacks now set up an unearthly din.

Gracie continued alone down to the glass-enclosed Deck A, port side, and looked over the rail to see whether the ship remained on an even keel. Nothing seemed to be wrong. Entering the companionway, Gracie passed Mr. J. Bruce Ismay, managing director of the White Star Line, accompanied by a member of the crew, hurrying up the stairway. Colonel Gracie noticed that Ismay was hatless and preoccupied, so he didn't speak to him. But a sixth sense told him that the White Star official's face was paler than usual, though he was bravely trying not to show his feelings in fear that he might alarm passengers he might meet.

At the foot of the stairway Gracie met a number of men passengers investigating the situation as he was. Among them was his friend, J. Clinch Smith.

"What seems to be the trouble, Clinch?"

"I think we've sideswiped an iceberg, Colonel."

"Bad?"

"No one up to now seems rightly to know—but at least here's a sample."

Smith unclenched his hand and showed Gracie a flat chunk of ice and smiled.

"Want to take it home for a souvenir?"

No, there was no panic among the first- and the second-cabin passengers—not even among the women. Many of them had already retired for the night. All stories up to this point were the same— a slight shock, and a distinct grating sound. Those in the first-cabin smoking room on Deck B hardly looked up from their cards. A few more venture- some went out on deck to learn what had happened to make the engines stop. Whatever it was, this giant of the seas could *never sink*—sixteen airtight compartments would keep her afloat, no matter what struck her!

But the postal clerks in the mail room, below, knew differently—men like John S. Marsh, William L. Gwynn, Oscar S. Woody, Iago Smith, and E. D. Williams! They were feverishly moving the bulky mailbags to the deck above—working in freezing sea water that was already rising around their knees! Many of the *Titanic's* stewards knew, too—but they kept smiles on their faces, ready to assist their passengers when this night should suddenly become a nightmare!

As the ship's officers were about to leave the bridge for their boat stations, Mr. Thomas Andrews, Jr., designer of the *Titanic* and representative of her builders, Harland & Wolff, burst in on them —hatless and wild-eyed!

"For God's sake, Captain Smith, order the lifeboats manned!" he screamed. "This ship is doomed —she's taking water faster than her pumps can handle it—and twenty-three of her twenty-nine boilers have a full head of steam! Engineer Bell is down there now doing his best to have steam blown off the boilers, but there's still grave danger of a monstrous explosion!"

"Thank you, Mr. Andrews," answered Captain Smith with grim restraint. Then he calmly turned to his officers, "Gentlemen, you have had your instructions—carry on."

But panic had already broken out down in the "black hole" of the *Titanic's* huge boiler rooms. The "grating sound" heard topside had been a giant finger of ice from the submerged section of an iceberg ripping through the ship's "single skin" plates, just abaft the starboard bow, and tearing a three-hundred-foot gash along her bottom. The sea had flooded Lower Deck G—was dangerously deep in Number 6 and Number 5 boiler rooms, and steadily rising in Number 4. A hundred and fifty stokers, trimmers, and firemen were trapped when the watertight emergency doors automatically clanged shut. Others struggled, fought, and clawed their way up the greasy steel ladders that led to the upper decks

—many fell to their deaths, or were drowned. Later, one little Cockney stoker put it graphically when he was asked how he escaped:

"Hit's this way, sir, in them there big ships, that us blokes below 'aven't much o' chance when 'ell breaks loose—that we 'aven't! The bunkers are so placed that when we has to break out our diamonds we 'ave to go a good bit along the channels, and that's w'ere I was w'en she struck the chunk o' ice!

"First thing that I knowed I feels her bumpin', then she kinds o' quivered an steadied 'er bloomin' self, and then I 'ears the sound o' water rushin' somewhere. Then she shakes all over, same as a 'ound w'en he leaves the water, and then she settles back easylike.

"'Blow me,' says I to meself, 'the blessed old 'ooker 'as done somethink to 'erself.' I 'ops it for out and as I goes I 'ears the poundin' an' swashin' below. All o' us were on the same lay an' there was as pretty a bit o' monkey climbin' as you could wish to see!

"As I was sayin', I 'opped it and took to me nails —upward bound. I 'eard the poor beggars droppin' off below me, and they swore 'orrible, but I kept on climbin' 'till I reaches the top gratin' o' the engine room and pokes me 'ead out.

"The stars were shinin' an' ice was ev'rywheres. One o' the hofficers comes runnin' by. 'Wot's wrong, sir?' I arsks. 'Nothink!' 'e says, an' keeps on runnin'! The yells an' fights was somethink fearful below, so I peeks down through th' gratin'! Lor lumme, sir, but they was fightin' fearful!

"I see one chap 'it another wi' a spanner (wrench) an' 'e split 'is 'ead open—that 'e did! Th' poor chap cannoned from 'eads an' shoulders all th' way down, an' th' last I see o' 'im 'e was movin' fingers pitiful like an' th' rest was tramplin' over 'em. Aye, hit's true that men be animiles sometimes, an' on board that there ship that night we wasn't standin' on no ceremony!

"Some got up whole men—most o' 'em 'ad an ear gone, or a bit of nose missin' an' th' likes o' that, an' wot good was it t' get on deck at all?

"There wasn't no room for th' likes o' us in th' boats, so most o' us knowed, 'cause there was women an' kiddies t' go an' there wasn't room for us all, so we took it as best we could an' tried t' think of th' good things that we 'ad done in th' world that might promise us 'alf a chance in th' next.

"Hit ayen't near so easy as you might think t' wait calmlike for th' bloomin' old tub t' tyke 'er last wallow. 'Specially w'en you knows you must wallow along o' 'er. An' th' sea looked so cold!

"Hi've sweated me 'eart out in th' tramp ships o' th' world. Hi've seen it 135° in th' stokehole o' a stinkin' South American tub, but as I looked out on th' ice I felt th' chill o' death that so far's I could see was bound my way, I wished that I was back on any old craft at all.

"No, there wasn't no excitement 'special. Wot's th' use o' it, anyway? 'If we've got t' go'—as I said t' th' rest o' 'em—'let's go as Britishers!' Hi don't mean t' brag, sir, nor say anything that anybody might think themselves hoffended at, but I do mean one thing, and that is that th' Britisher knows jolly well how to die!

"Th' bloomin' boats cleared away, an' there was more'n one lump in th' throats o' us all as we watched 'em slide off int' th' dark with them as we considered was worth more than our lives. Some son o' a sea cook began t' blubber an' whine, but we soon quieted 'im, never fear!

"Then came th' 'ell o' it, as we felt th' sea grippin', reachin' hits finger for us. Nearer an' nearer the blessed swash o' th' water came until we all f'rgot an' went mad, sir.

"Mad is the only word that can tell you wot 'appened then. For a man can keep cool just so long, an' beyond that there styge 'e's 'elpless!

"Seems t' me that I can still 'ear the roar o' steam, th' 'orrible screams for 'elp, an' above all these 'ere desperate noises, the faint notes o' th' band that were playin' as we went down.

"Saved? 'Ow was I? Arsk me somethink else, sir. All I know was bein' picked up by a bloomin' boat that 'ad thirty wimmin' an' 'ere I am."

Throughout the ship, officers and stewards quietly warned, "All passengers on deck with life jackets!"

Lawrence Beesley, an English passenger—who, like Colonel Gracie, had felt the ship stop—had dressed and was investigating the reason. He crossed to the port door of the vestibule leading out onto the Boat Deck and noticed one of the officers uncovering the aftmost lifeboat on the port side—Number 16. Curiously enough, Beesley noted, no one paid any particular attention to him.

Below, on Deck A and Deck B, stewards were calmly fitting passengers into life jackets. Other stewards were rousing passengers who had already retired—many of these refused to be disturbed, so secure were they in believing "nothing could sink the *Titanic*." These were to die in their staterooms!

Out on Deck A, on the port side, aft, were Colonel Gracie; Mr. and Mrs. Isador Straus; Colonel and Mrs. John Jacob Astor; Gracie's friend, J. Clinch Smith; Hugh Woolner, son of the English sculptor; and a young lieutenant in the Swedish army, H. Bjornstrom, who knew Mrs. Gracie's relatives in Sweden. Also in the group were Mrs. E. D. Appleton; Mrs. R. C. Cornell, wife of the well-known New York justice; Mrs. J. Murray Brown, wife of the Boston publisher; and their friend Miss Edith Evans. All were curiously watching the preparations for lowering boats when one of the ship's officers came by.

"Our wireless operator, Mr. Phillips, has contacted several ships," he announced with a smile, "and at least one of them is bound to be along soon to rescue us. The boats are being readied to ferry passengers to the rescue ship."

As the officer left, Colonel Gracie spied a bright light off the port beam.

"Look — see that light off there!" He pointed across the water reassuringly. "That's our rescue ship!"

"Whereabouts, Colonel Gracie?" asked Colonel Astor.

Just then a lifeboat was lowered with it's gun'l level with the Boat Deck above, shutting out their view. Gracie and Colonel Astor had to lean over the rail to see.

"Right over there, Colonel," pointed out Gracie with difficulty. "Why—why the light is growing dimmer—it's disappearing. . . ."

A strange hush fell over the group. The "light" disappearing over the horizon was later proven to be the *Californian!*

Suddenly rockets flared from the *Titanic's* bridge, zooming into the crisp night air and hiding the stars as they burst with resounding explosions to spread a cold, eerie glare over the heavily listing liner. Sharp orders were barked out by the officers stationed at their sixteen boat positions on the Boat Deck—eight on the port side and eight on the starboard side of the sinking ship. Other officers were feverishly tearing away the tarpaulins from the four Engelhardt "collapsible" boats atop the officers' cabins. Twenty lifeboats . . . and a ship's company of 2,223!

"Women and children first—all men stand clear!"

Small groups of passengers with their life jackets secured, stood by, listening with amusement to the grim-faced officers as they repeated the call, "Women and children first!" What manner of monstrous joke was this? Didn't those officers know that the *Titanic* was the world's largest *unsinkable* ship? Why in the world should one be so foolhardy as to spend a few freezing hours in open boats while waiting for a rescue ship to come to their aid? Lifeboats, indeed, was the general thought among these first-cabin passengers. We'll walk the spacious decks to keep warm while we wait—or, better still, we'll go below to warm saloons, smoking rooms, or even our comfortable cabins!

So the call for "Women and children first!" went practically unheeded. At Number 5 boat, Third Officer Herbert J. Pitman was trying his level best to persuade passengers to get aboard. Fifth Officer Harold Lowe was feverishly getting the davit falls straightened away in preparation for lowering Number 5 when J. Bruce Ismay came running up to him.

"Lower away, lower away, lower away, lower away!" he screamed frantically in Lowe's ear.

"Get th' hell out of here, and I shall be able to do something!" blasted Lowe angrily.

"I am afraid, my dear man, you don't know who you're talking to!" flared Ismay.

"I don't give a good Goddam who I'm talkin' to—now stand back outa th' way!" ordered Pitman. "I'm officer in charge here, an' I'm givin' th' orders —y' understand!"

Ismay quieted down, but hung around to help load Number 5 boat, which by now had thirty-five of the more venturesome souls aboard—including four men. Pitman had called for more women, but found there were none in sight. The thirty-foot lifeboat was registered to carry sixty-five persons, though the risky task of loading from the deck made it unwise to put aboard more than thirty-five or forty for fear of "buckling" the boat. Finally Number 5 was the first boat to be safely lowered and gotten away.

Down in Deck G, all hell was breaking loose! Steerage passengers, in complete panic, were screaming and cursing in half a dozen tongues—clawing fingers and flailing fists gouged or belted country-men and stranger alike as more lifeboats were lowered past the third-cabin deck without stopping. . . .

"We're being deserted!" they screamed in desperation to ship's petty officers and stewards. "We're being deserted!"

More steerage passengers piled down into their deck, shouting and crying and dragging after them bundles of their sole possessions from the Old World. Men, women and children! They had been topside and had heard the dismal warning, "Iceberg ahead!" before the *Titanic* had struck. Now they were like so many frightened sheep, milling aimlessly, round and round. . . .

"Quiet, you people!" ordered a young petty officer. "We have sideswiped ice, but there is no danger—and you're not being deserted! Besides, this ship cannot sink!"

Calmed by the officer's words, the third-cabin passengers stood by—quiet but bewildered—wondering what would happen next. Then, suddenly, up from the *Titanic's* stokeholes came the "black gang"! Armed with stoking bars, shovels, ashpan hoes and levelers, they converged on the steerage people—knocking many down and trampling on others as they tried to beat their way to the loading ports. Seamen and stewards battled them in warlike, hand-to-hand combat and slowly pressed back their savage attack—forcing many of them back down into the stokehole and death!

When the first lifeboat stopped at the steerage deck the human "rat-race" began all over again. Panicky men forced themselves to the front, with no thought but for themselves and their precious bundles—most of them were "single men." Women and children went down before their maniacal surge. Again seamen, stewards, and petty officers converged on this new onslaught. Pistol shots rang out. Several slumped where they had stood, dead—the rest, cowed, moved back. But before the sailors could act, that first boat to stop at Deck G was soon half full of men—threatening to "buckle" it with their weight. Seamen manhandled them unmercifully and dragged them bodily from the boat, letting women with children take their places. Many of the steerage women had great bundles on their heads or in their arms, and they fought like demons when they were told they'd have to leave them behind to save room in the lifeboat.

Every boat that came down after the first two— and was not already full—stopped at Deck G to take on a few more passengers. But those who left in the last boat declared afterward that there were still hundreds crowding the loading port, shrieking, screaming, and praying—many of them completely mad with fright as the ship continued to list heavily to starboard.

Eighty-five stubborn engineers under Chief Engineer John Bell—nearly one hundred feet below the Boat Deck—fought to keep the ship's electro-power turbine engines turning, without any thought of their own lives. Electric power still lighted the great *Titanic* until her final plunge—and the eighty-five engineers went with her!

The desperate situation hadn't reached the panic

stage among first-cabin passengers, even an hour after the *Titanic* struck ice.

"Don't worry, the *Titanic* will not sink, and we will all be saved," Colonel John Jacob Astor assured every frightened woman he helped into the lifeboats. They were the same words he whispered to his bride of a few months as he kissed her good-by and set her in Number 4 boat—planning to follow her in another boat. Those were also the plans of George D. Widener, Henry B. Harris, and Charles M. Hays as they bid their own wives farewell and helped them over the gun'ls of the lifeboats—but their plans never matured. . . .

Meanwhile, up in the wireless shack Chief Operator George Phillips stuck by his key, pounding brass—telling Operator H. T. Cottam of the *Carpathia* of the desperate situation aboard the slowly sinking *Titanic*. Bride acted as messenger between the bridge and Phillips.

"They're putting off the women and children, George," relayed Bride on one of his trips to the bridge. "And it looks like th' ship's settling deeper by th' head!"

At that moment Captain Smith himself stuck his head quickly in the door of the wireless shack.

"Our engine rooms are taking water, Phillips," he said calmly, "and I'm afraid the dynamos won't last much longer."

"I know—th' power's getting weaker, Captain," nodded Phillips. But Captain Smith had already gone. Phillips pounded out the grim words to the *Carpathia*: "Engine Room is Filling Up To Boilers!"

"I'd better get our life jackets!" called Bride from the tiny bunk room off the wireless shack.

"Yeah," grinned Phillips, "this tub'll sink fast when she does go!"

Bride got out their overcoats, heavy boots, and the two life jackets. While Phillips picked up the *Olympic* and told them the *Titanic* was sinking fast by the head, Bride slipped an overcoat on him and fastened on his life jacket for him.

"That water's goin' t' be damn'd cold, George," pointed out Bride as he tightened the last strap on Phillips' life jacket.

"Yeah, I know," answered the *Titanic's* operator with a wry grin. "Better see what's going on out on deck—we can't last much longer up here—power's getting weaker by th' minute, soon those dynamos 'll quit altogether!"

Bride found most of the lifeboats gone. Men were milling around the remaining boats. Some were fighting to get aboard, others stood silently by. He recognized Colonel Astor who was still helping the last of the women into lifeboats in this section of the sinking ship. Major Archie Butt stood by him and leveled a pistol at the men threatening to "rush" the boats—warning them that he would shoot the first one who tried! Bride felt the dangerous slant of the deck as the *Titanic* buried her bows deeper in the sea. Cries and shrieks shrilled in his ears from all sides as panicky passengers suddenly realized the end was near. He heard Colonel Archibald Gracie earnestly entreating the Isador Strauses to get into one of the remaining lifeboats.

"No," said Mr. Straus firmly, "I do not wish any

distinction in my favor which is not granted to others."

"I will not be separated from my husband," said Mrs. Straus with deep determination. "As we have lived, so will we die—together."

Down in his cabin, a half an hour before, Benjamin Guggenheim had given this message to his room steward, Johnson.

"I think there is grave doubt that the men will get off," he said in a matter-of-fact tone to Johnson. "I am willing to remain and play the man's game, if there are not enough boats for more than the women and children. I won't die here like a beast. I'll meet my end as a man."

Guggenheim paused thoughtfully for a moment, then he continued.

"Tell my wife, Johnson, if it should happen that my secretary and I both go down and you are saved —tell her I played the game straight out to the end. No woman shall be left aboard this ship because Ben Guggenheim was a coward."

He paused a moment as if he were dictating a letter. Then he spoke softly again.

"Tell her that my last thoughts will be of her and of our girls, but that my duty now is to these unfortunate women and children on this ship. Tell her I will meet whatever fate is in store for me, knowing she will approve of what I do."

Only a few lifeboats were left, now. Panic-stricken passengers screamed louder for help—and clambered harder for places in the remaining boats. The band blared away with ragtime tunes on the slanting aft deck. Bride rushed back to the wireless shack to find Phillips up to his knees in water, still pounding at the brass key—still advising the *Carpathia!*

Suddenly Captain Smith shouted from the bridge to the two Marconi men in the wireless shack, "Abandon your cabin! It's every man for himself, now!"

"You heard th' skipper—let's get th' hell outa here!" yelled Bride grimly. "There's not much time—she's going fast!"

"Wait a minute, Harold!" whispered Phillips hoarsely. "What time is it?"

"Nearly two o'clock!" shot back Bride, glancing at his watch.

"Maybe they'll get this, an' maybe they won't!" shrugged Phillips. "Power's almost gone!"

Leaning heavily against the careening table, Phillips pounded out his last message to the *Carpathia!*

"TITANIC SINKING FAST! HURRY!"

As the two wireless men sloshed their way from the water-filled shack, the vague strains of "Autumn" came back to them from the band gamely playing on the tilting deck above them. Phillips ran aft and that was the last Bride ever saw of him.

Bride made his way to the Boat Deck, climbing with difficulty up the steep angle of the slanting deck. He found that Number 4 lifeboat had been lowered—the *last* of the sixteen lifeboats to leave the ship. Even then the electric deck lights were still burning—he glanced at his watch—1:55 A.M.! He saw Colonel Astor, Benjamin Guggenheim, and Major Butt calmly clinging to the port rail, smoking.

Men were struggling against time with the last of the Engelhardt "collapsible" boats—the Engelhardt Boat "B"—near one of the ship's funnels. Twelve men were trying to "boost" it down to the Boat Deck from atop the officers' cabin. Among them was Second Officer Lightoller. Bride rushed over to lend a hand as a large wave came awash of the deck and carried the heavy boat off. Bride had a hand on the oarlock. The next thing he knew he was in the boat—but the boat was upside down and *he was under it!* Fully realizing that he was wet through—and under water—he knew he had to fight for his life, yet he also knew he must not breathe or he'd be done for. Somehow he managed to fight free and felt a life-giving blast of fresh air!

Struggling men were in the water all around Bride—hundreds of them. All were depending on the buoyancy of their life jackets to keep their heads above the freezing water. But nowhere could he find George Phillips. Vaguely he could still hear the band playing "Autumn" aboard the fast-sinking *Titanic*. Smoke and sparks were rushing out of the last funnel. Gradually the ship turned up slowly on her nose—like a duck diving for a fish. Bride had only one thought in mind—to get away from her suction before she went down, and he began to swim madly from her. He was about 150 feet from her when the *Titanic*—her after-quarter sticking straight up into the black night—began to settle slowly. He heard piercing cries for help—agonized screams of panic—all blended in one horrible roar as boilers, machinery, crockery and furniture smashed down through the length of her!

Bride had a sickening feeling in the pit of his stomach as the last of the waves washed over her great rudder and gigantic propellers — then the *Titanic* was gone!

Reaction set in on Bride. The freezing water was taking its toll. He was shivering and numb with cold, but he knew he must keep up some sort of exercise to save himself from freezing to death. Suddenly there was a boat near him and he gamely made a supreme effort to swim toward it. But it was hard, hard work. A hand darted out at him just as he was sinking, and he was hauled aboard. It was the same Engelhardt Boat "B"—still bottom up—that he had so short a time before got out from under with his life!

Bride found just room enough to roll on the edge of the boat, near the stern. He lay there, numb, and physically exhausted. Nothing seemed to matter to him, now, nor did he care what happened. Vaguely he wondered if Phillips had been picked up. A drowsy mental haze further numbed his senses. Somebody sat on his half-frozen legs and wrenched them badly, but somehow he had neither the heart nor the strength to ask the other survivor to move. Terrible sights and sounds were all around him. Bobbing heads showed ghostly white against the black sea. Men screaming for help— swimming, then sinking with a deathly gurgle. It all seemed like some fantastic nightmare from another world. A very tangible vapor of smoke and steam overhung the hellish scene, giving the supernatural effect of a Dante's Inferno.

"Is Phillips aboard?" Bride heard himself say.

"You mean the wireless operator?" came a familiar voice from the bow of the bottom-up boat.

"That you, Mr. Lightoller?" Again Bride spoke as in a dream.

"Aye," answered the *Titanic's* second officer, "but Phillips isn't with us."

"We—we left the wireless shack t'gether," continued Bride with hesitancy. " 'Fraid we lost each other when she sank!"

"Well, we got a couple of passenger survivors, and a score of crewmen—mostly firemen and a couple of cooks," called back Lightoller. "But no Phillips. Who are you?"

"Bride — relief operator." The Marconi man's answer electrified the other survivors.

"Bride! Thank God!" yelled back Lightoller. "Tell me, Bride—what ships did Phillips raise?"

"The *Baltic, Olympic,* and the *Carpathia,*" Bride spoke the magic words, and for the first time the thirty survivors clinging to the bottom of the up-turned Engelhardt Boat "B" took on new hope of rescue. "Th' *Carpathia's* on her way, Mr. Lightoller—Phillips kept in constant contact with her operator until the wireless shack flooded, an' Captain Smith ordered us out! By the way, what became of the captain?"

"I kin answer that," said Harry Senior, one of the *Titanic's* firemen. "Th' cap'n reached this boat. We pulled 'im on, but 'e slipped off, an' we ayen't seen 'im since—poor fellow!"

"I c'n vouch for that," corroborated J. Maynard, entree cook. " 'E slipped off when a funnel crashed into th' sea near us—couldn't 'old on. 'E's drown'd by now, God rest 'is soul!"

By now the survivors on the bottom-up Engel-hardt were standing nearly knee-deep in water—some facing the stern, some facing the bow. Bride, still pinned to the bottom of the boat, breathed when he could—often the waves went over his head. A man near him rolled off into the water with a soft splash—dead from fright and cold! Colonel Archibald Gracie, and young J. B. ("Jack") Thayer, Jr.—the only two passengers aboard the Engelhardt —had miraculously escaped the final plunge of the *Titanic* and stood back to back. It was a ticklish situation. The slightest mismove of any one of the survivors could easily capsize the fragile craft. But Lightoller's knowledge of how to handle small boats kept the boat "balanced"—and Bride's announce-ment that the *Carpathia* "was on her way" gave the survivors strength and purpose to battle for their lives!

"Don't th' rest o' you think we oughta pray?" asked a burly fireman near Bride.

"Aye, that I do," spoke up John Collins, another cook.

"Then let every man call out his religion," sug-gested the fireman.

"Catholic . . . Episcopalian . . . Methodist . . . Presbyterian . . . Baptist!" sang out the men.

"Let us all repeat the Lord's Prayer," said the fireman solemnly.

Then a chorus of thirty voices boomed out across the black waters—and the bright stars in the dark heavens above seemed closer to the sea. . . .

Finally dawn dimly grayed the sky. Far over the horizon to the east, Second Officer Charles H. Lightoller spied the masthead light—then the running lights—then the blaze of cabin and porthole lights!

"It's the *Carpathia*, boys!" he cried, half sobbing.

A low murmur of cheers swept over the sea from men, women, and children in the other lifeboats. Seven hundred and ten had seen the rescue ship . . . but Colonel John Jacob Astor was not among them . . . nor was Major Archie Butt . . . nor was Benjamin Guggenheim . . . nor were the Isador Strauses, nor the nearly sixteen hundred other passengers, officers, and crew of the great White Star liner, H.M.S. *Titanic,* which had sacrificed herself on a pinnacle of ice—for a *speed record!*

Sources of Factual Material

Again the writer called on Raymond S. Camp's invaluable marine scrapbook to glean the facts in the *Titanic* disaster from the great newspapers of the time, particularly the *New York Times* and the *New York Herald.* These papers covered the sinking with their usual fine accuracy—including the New York and Washington Senate Inquiry testimony. There is the little-known fact that Seaman Louis Klein was the *first* crew member of the *Titanic* to realize the closeness of an iceberg to the giant White Star luxury liner. Klein was on watch patrolling the *Titanic's* promenade deck, starboard side, when a passenger called him and pointed out what he (the passenger) thought was a "hill." Seaman Klein then rushed up to the crow's-nest, only to find that the lookouts were dozing. He quickly sounded the alarm bell, rousing them, and it was then that one of the lookouts phoned the bridge. This was a story from the *New York Herald* with a Cleveland date line on the Sunday before the Washington Senate hearing was to convene. In the course of the testimony, Seaman Louis Klein was called to the stand, but his testimony so embarrassed White Star officials that he was "spirited away" and gave no further "damaging" testimony.

Since finishing this chapter on the *Titanic*, the writer has talked with an ex-seaman who once shipped with a sailor who had been aboard the *Titanic* that fateful night. It was common knowledge among the *Titanic's* crew, he said, that there were nearly five hundred steel workers aboard, still completing steel work on the lower hull, and that work on the airtight safety compartments had not been completed at the time the *Titanic* struck the berg. It was his belief, he said further, that the final toll of 1,600 who went down with the *Titanic* didn't include the steel workers!

For further facts on the *Titanic* the writer consulted Colonel Archibald Gracie's *The Truth About the Titanic* (Mitchell Kennerly, New York, 1913) ; Lawrence Beesley's *The Loss of the SS Titanic* (William Heinemann, Ltd., London, 1912) ; and J. Bernard Walker's *An Unsinkable Titanic* (Dodd, Mead & Company, New York, 1912) .

VI

LAST LOG OF THE *VERONICA*

SOME SHIPS, like some men, have histories that were destined to be tranquilly lived and were, so to speak, written in the far-flung waters they sailed. Quietly they took their appointed places in the affairs of the world and fulfilled their missions without fuss or fanfare, to the end of their days. Others, like the bark *Veronica* are marked for disaster; and in their crimson wake follow greed, lust for undeserved power, and—always—misfortune!

The shipping firm of William Thompson & Company of St. John, New Brunswick, had had its share of misfortune. Doing business out of that thriving port in the latter years of the nineteenth century, the Thompson outfit lost ship after ship. Some foundered, one capsized, another caught fire at sea. Still others went "missing," never to be heard from again.

Nor was the firm of Thompson & Company at fault. Their vessels were staunchly built and the ships' officers were chosen with great care. Their fleet was frequently overhauled and cargoes were meticulously stowed. Yet they lost vessels with a consistency that defied all explanation.

Then, not content with heaping woe upon woe, the fates, with rare satanic malevolence, chose the 1,093-ton bark *Veronica* as a stage for the climax

of the Thompson firm's long string of calamities
—a mutiny, the brutality of which has scarcely a
parallel in all the annals of the sea!

Trouble smouldered ominously in the fo'c'sle of
the ill-fated bark shortly after she cleared Ship
Island off Biloxi, Mississippi, on the dawn tide,
October 15, 1902, carrying a pine lumber cargo
to a Montevideo, Uruguay, firm on the east coast
of South America.

An ugly flare-up over a girl back in Biloxi sparked
a fight between two crew members during morning
mess. Hot words flew back and forth across the
table. Moses Thomas, young mulatto cook and steward of the *Veronica,* tried his best to quiet them.

"C'm on, Gus," cajoled Thomas, "le's break it
up—an' you, too, Paddy! Don' wanna see you boys
in irons f'r fightin'—so break it up!"

"*Ja!*" jeered the sullen twenty-eight-year-old German seaman, Gustav Rau. "Show me the man on
this vessel who can put *me* in irons!"

"Sure an' oi'd give me right arm t' try!" roared
back Patrick Doran, rising quickly from the table.
"Y' wu-r-thless spalpeen!"

"Let's see ya try it!" raged Rau, hurling his
bowl of steaming porridge at Paddy Doran.

This was too much for Doran to take. The rugged Irishman from Prince Edward Island grabbed
Rau by the front of his heavy jersey and with sheer
brute strength dragged the German sailor across
the table. Otto Monsson and Ludwig Flohr, members of the crew, rushed in to help Rau. But
Paddy Doran scared them off with dire threats of
the same kind of medicine. They wisely retreated.

In the melee, Willem Smith, a young Hollander; Alec Bravo, a Hindoo; and Julius Parsons, a fellow Canadian—all able-bodied seamen of the *Veronica* —scattered to the dim corners of the fo'c'sle. Johanssen, another member of the crew, was aft doing his trick at the wheel. Rau, still groggy from Paddy Doran's fist, reeled past him up the companionway.

Quickly revived by the tangy sea air as he stumbled out on deck, Gustav Rau turned sharply and swung heavily at the surprised Doran who had followed closely behind him up the companionway stairs. Momentarily stunned by blows from Rau's flailing fists, the big Irishman stood his ground and threw up both arms to guard his head.

"Still like t' try an' put Gussie in irons, Doran!" leered the surly German, boring into Paddy.

"Sure an' thot oi would!" roared Doran, ripping into Rau and forcing him to give ground foot by foot along the deck toward the skipper's cabin.

Aft, in the captain's quarters, Alexander Shaw, elderly master of the *Veronica,* and his hardy Nova Scotian first mate, McLeod, were studying the chart when they heard thumps and shuffling feet on the deck above them.

"What in tarnation is that racket!" exclaimed McLeod, rushing to a window in the raised deck of the afterhouse.

"Second mate's probably got the boys holystoning the deck, Mac," answered the mild-mannered Shaw with a kindly smile. "Come, now, stop fretting about it."

McLeod shrugged and the two officers returned

to scanning the chart before them as the *Veronica's*
master laid out the course. "Now, as I see it, we'll
follow the eighty-eighth latitude south through the
Gulf of Mexico to the twenty-fourth longitude,
then we'll set a course east on the twenty-fourth
through the Florida Strait, then. . . ."

With a sudden crash and a sharp tinkle of glass
on the cabin deck, Gus Rau's foot came through
the same window McLeod had just vacated. Captain Shaw glanced up from the chart and surveyed
the broken window light with Rau's foot still pro-
jected through it. The old skipper scratched his
head in amazement that such a thing should happen on any vessel of his. Cheers and catcalls broke
loose from the crew on deck. McLeod bounded
up the afterhouse companionway and out on deck.

"What's the meaning o' this?" demanded the first
mate as he saw Paddy Doran, his huge fists still
clenched, standing over the prostrate form of the
bloody-faced German. The rest of the crew broke
the circle they had formed around the two fighters
and moved back a step.

"It's Gus Rau, sir," spoke up Moses Thomas, the
cook, "it was him who started it—I tried to stop
'em both, sir!"

"All right, Rau, get up!" barked McLeod. "The
rest of you break out the buckets an' holystones
an' get t' work on these decks!"

The first mate swung around to the Irishman.
"You, Doran—what have you to say for yourself?
Come on, speak up!"

"Aye, sor!" answered Paddy humbly. "What

would *you* do if a pig loike Rau slung a bowl o' hot porridge at ya?"

"The same thing you did!" retorted McLeod. "Now, get for'ard with the rest of 'em!"

As Paddy Doran ambled forward rubbing his knuckles, McLeod prodded Gustav Rau with his foot. Rau stirred uneasily and stared up sullenly at the mate through bloodshot eyes.

"Get up!" bellowed McLeod. "Take y'r blasted foot out o' that window an' get up!"

"Someday," hissed Rau venomously, raising himself painfully to his hands and knees, "I'll kill that Doran!"

"Right now y'll go for'ard an' get busy with a holystone!" ordered the first mate. "Another brawl like this, Rau, an' y'll both be in irons—y' understand? Now, get!"

The surly young German seaman rose slowly to his feet and slunk forward, sullenly muttering dark threats and ignoring the mate's promise of irons. McLeod watched him a moment, shook his head, and returned to the afterhouse.

As he made his way unsteadily along the lee rail, Rau caught sight of Patrick Doran, alone, in the waist of the vessel. The rugged Irishman was down on one knee tying a shoelace, his back to the scheming German. The others had gone forward to the storeroom to carry out the mate's order.

Johanssen, the helmsman, who, from his vantage point on the raised poop deck had witnessed the fight between Doran and Rau, now saw Paddy Doran stooped over and also caught a fleeting glance of Gus Rau stealthily crossing the deck to the mainmast, intent on drawing a belaying pin from the pinrail there.

"Look out, Paddy!" the Swede shouted warning. "Rau's right b'hind ya!"

With a swift upward motion of his huge right fist, Doran swung around and caught the German in the midriff. The surprise blow sent the mendacious sailor sprawling and the belaying pin clattered to the deck. In a flash the Irishman was on Rau for the second time, punishing him unmercifully.

By now some of the crew were out on deck, loaded down with buckets and holystones. Julius Parsons, the Canadian, caught sight of the two men thrashing around.

"They're at it again!" he yelled, edging toward the fighters. "Doran'll kill him this time!"

The others stopped short and watched grimly, but they held their distance, mindful of the mate's dour warning. Rau struggled free momentarily and made a grab for the loose belaying pin. Doran beat him to it, kicking the pin into the scuppers. Then he caught the German off balance with a crashing right to the jaw. Gustav Rau buckled heavily to the deck just as McLeod rushed angrily toward them from the afterhouse.

"What did I tell you two about fighting, Doran!" he bellowed. "Did you think I didn't mean it?"

"Sure and oi'll have no dur-rty spalpeen tryin' t' bash in me head with a b'layin' pin!" exploded the angry Irishman.

Rau lay still on the deck, blood oozing from his battered nose and mouth. McLeod looked down at

him, dubiously, then at the circle of seamen. The
first mate singled out Parsons who stood nearest.

"You, Parsons!" commanded the mate. "Fetch
a bucket of water from overside—and look lively!"

As Julius Parsons drew the full bucket up over
the rail, McLeod snatched it from him and doused
the length of the German with cold sea water. Doran
stood back, glowering first at the mate, then down
at Rau who stirred uneasily.

"All right, you men—he's still alive. Toss him
in his bunk!" barked the first mate angrily. "Then
get on with the business of holystoning this deck!"

"No irons f'r him, sor?" questioned the big Irishman, narrowly, as several seamen picked up the
limp German.

"No, you've given him punishment enough,
Doran!" was McLeod's short answer. It was an
error of judgment that was to change the destiny
of every last man aboard the *Veronica!*

Under clear skies and a fair wind the *Veronica*
knifed through the indigo-blue waters of the Gulf,
following the course set by Captain Shaw. Sunny
days and starry nights lent a false security to all
aboard the bark, officers and crew alike. Nearly
forgotten was the bloody scuffle between Rau and
Doran—forgotten by all but Gustav Rau!

Inwardly infuriated and morosely nursing a loss
of face among his fellow crewmen, the big German
kept to himself for hours at a time. Physically recovered, but more surly than ever, Rau set about
planning with calculating coldness the murder of
one Patrick Doran! Cunningly he spread his in-
sidious venom in the fo'c'sle. For the most part it

fell on deaf ears, but there were those who listened hungrily—Willem Smith, Otto Monsson, and Ludwig Flohr!

Despite the fact that their food and treatment had so far been good; that Doran himself had offended no one and was recognized by all as being the ablest seaman among them—still Gustav Rau successfully inflamed these three into actually believing the stalwart Irishman should be killed!

The bark had cleared the West Indies and was in the region of the doldrums when matters came to a head!

One night, as the *Veronica* was making bare headway in light airs under a star-studded sky, Rau caught sight of Patrick Doran standing lookout on the fo'c'sle head. A malevolent grin twisted his face as the German nudged Flohr, who stood close to him in the shadows.

"Look, Ludwig!" whispered Rau thickly as he pressed a sailor's knife into young Flohr's hand. "Here's the chance we been waitin' for—now we strike!"

It *was* a most favorable moment from Rau's standpoint. Doran's dimly silhouetted figure paced slowly from port to starboard and back—lost, no doubt, in his own thoughts. No one was near and Doran's position was obscured from view by the fores'l sheet.

Young Flohr blanched at the thought of actual murder! Down in the fo'c'sle, talk of killing Doran was—well, just talk. But now the hour to strike had come! Flohr was at first appalled at Rau's fiendish order, then openly alarmed that the actual

deed was delegated to him by the very man who
bore the grudge!

"I couldn't even kill a chicken, Gus," pleaded
the young German. "How could you expect me
to kill a man!"

"*Ja!*" snarled Rau, angrily snatching the knife
from Flohr. "You're th' chicken!"

Young Flohr fled aft in terror as Willem Smith
silently crossed the deck to Rau's side.

"Somethin' go wrong, Gus?" he asked in a harsh
whisper.

"*Ja!*" hissed the mad Rau, "Flohr's scared—we'll
do the job ourselves!"

"Better mebbe t' use b'layin' pins," rasped Smith,
"less likely t' leave blood!"

Rau agreed in guttural assent. Arming themselves with iron belaying pins the two crept up on
the fo'c'sle head toward Doran, who was at his post
gazing out on a placid sea. But Doran, warned by
a seaman's sixth sense, whirled around and caught
sight of the German's bulky form in the shadows.

"Lookin' f'r more trouble, Rau?" challenged the
big Irishman.

"Why, Paddy," mocked Rau with a humorless
guttural laugh in an effort to draw Doran off guard,
"why in hell would I do that!"

"An' you, Smith!" roared Doran, catching a fleeting glimpse of Smith's shadowy figure. "Sure an'
what's y'r little game—you two?"

"Nothin', Paddy, nothin'," murmured Smith in-
nocently. "Nice night—so we're out f'r some air."

"Where's Flohr an' Monsson?" persisted the Irishman suspiciously.

Smith closed in on Doran. "Flohr's aft, too, I guess."

"Oi'm not so sure o' that," said Doran stooping to peer under the fores'l.

"Quick!" whispered Rau to Smith the instant the Irishman's eyes were off them.

The two renegade seamen rushed Doran with a series of crashing blows with the belaying pins. Staggered but game, the dazed Irishman fought back at them until he was dropped to the deck with a smashing blow on the head. In the melee, Smith was accidentally dropped by a wild swing from Rau.

The noise of violence brought the first mate forward on the run.

"What th' hell's the row!" bellowed McLeod. "Who's on watch up there?"

. "Paddy was here just a moment ago," answered Rau from somewhere in the darkness. Smith was standing up rubbing his head. "He was fightin' with someone!"

Screened in the black shadows of the fores'l, Rau and Smith waited for McLeod as they gripped their weapons tighter.

"You two'll be in irons f'r this night's business!" barked the first mate as he gained the ladder to the fo'c'sle head.

"*Ja, ja*—we know!" rasped the mad German now poised in the darkness of the *Veronica's* bows with Smith beside him. "Always threats—well, come an' get me, McLeod!"

As McLeod reached the fores'l, Rau and Smith jumped him. With swift shattering blows they crushed his skull like an eggshell. The mate crumpled to the deck in a bloody heap.

Monsson, hearing the commotion, deserted the wheel and rushed forward with young Flohr to join the blood-maddened mutineers. Rau ransacked McLeod's pockets, securing his revolver and extra cartridges.

"Monsson—Flohr!" bellowed Rau with a guttural curse. "Over the side with the mate!"

There was a faint splash off the port bow as McLeod's body sank into the murkiness of a dark sea. Flushed by the undeserved success of the mate's murder in cold blood, Rau suddenly flashed the gun at Monsson, Smith, and Flohr.

"From now on y'r takin' orders from me—y' understand!" The German's voice was hard, with the sting of a lash in it. His eyes were slits as he leveled McLeod's revolver at them, waist-high. "One false move from you boys and you'll get a lead slug in th' belly—understand that, too! Now, get Doran into that paint locker—on th' double!"

The three mutineers meekly dragged the unconscious Irishman to the paint locker and dumped him in.

Without a helm the bark fell off the wind and began to yaw. This, together with the wild confusion forward, brought the *Veronica's* elderly master on deck. Amazed at finding no one at the wheel, Captain Shaw bent over the binnacle to check the course just as Gustav Rau and his three renegades ran aft. As the dim figures raced toward him, Shaw straightened and peered into the dark.

"McLeod! What's the meaning of this?" he demanded, mistaking the shadowy Rau for the first mate. "Where's the man at the wheel?"

Rau quickly melted into the darkness and hurled his belaying pin at the old shipmaster who stood in the dim light of the binnacle. As the captain doubled over in pain and staggered forward, the blood-crazed Rau whipped out McLeod's pistol and opened fire on him at close range!

Severely wounded and greatly shocked by the sudden viciousness of the attack, Captain Shaw barely managed to escape Rau's fury in the comparative safety of his cabin a few feet away. The captain collapsed in a chair beside the chart table, breathing heavily. With one hand he clutched at his stomach, while the other hung limply at his side. Blood from a shattered shoulder slowly trickled down his arm and hand, dripping to the floor from his fingertips in thick, claret-hued dots.

The second mate was off duty and asleep in his cabin. Aroused by the shots, he reeled sleepily out on deck, unarmed. Surprised by the sudden appearance of the second mate, Rau turned his fire on him.

"Swine!" snarled the infuriated German, emptying the gun at the officer, "we don't want prisoners!"

The second mate, badly wounded, stumbled blindly into the chart room where Captain Shaw sat in agony.

"They're after us!" gasped the mate as he forced his back against the closed door.

"I—I know!" the old shipmaster whispered hoarsely and shook his head weakly. "That I should live to see mutiny on *my* vessel!"

Painfully the two officers managed to barricade the door against the renegades.

Out on deck, Rau and his henchmen went into a hasty huddle, unaware of the officers' serious condition.

"Lis'n, Gus," argued Willem Smith, "they got rifles an' ammunition in there! We got one revolver—they could pick us off like flies if we tried to attack 'em!"

"*Ja! ja!* I know that, ya fool!" grunted the German impatiently. "But we've got aces in our sleeves! We'll hole 'em up with boards! If we can't get in, then th' fools can't get out—see! Quick, now—look lively!"

Boards and doors were torn away and nailed over ports, the skylight, and the entrance to the captain's cabin. Shaw and his second mate were "holed up." Lying flat on the deck of the chart room to avoid possible cross fire from the mutineers, the two badly wounded men managed rough bandages to stop the flow of their waning life's blood. Shaw had gotten it through the neck, the shoulder, and lower legs, as well as the clout in the stomach from Rau's belaying pin. The mate was worse off. He'd been hit in the stomach, with great loss of blood.

Up forward, Julius Parsons, the Canadian; Alec Bravo, the Hindoo; and the Swede, Johanssen, stood before the glowering Rau. They were dim figures in the eerie light of a hurricane lamp held high by Gustav Rau, and their shadows threw grotesque silhouettes against the fo'c'sle bulkhead.

"Well, boys, this is th' showdown!" Rau smiled

grimly, but his humorless voice was flint. His smile
faded as he took a step toward them, covering them
with McLeod's reloaded revolver. Bravo and Johanssen cowered, but Parsons held his ground. Ludwig Flohr, Otto Monsson, and Willem Smith hung
back in the shadows of the mains'l behind Rau
and watched. For a moment there was silence as
Rau looked around him.

"Where's th' cook — Thomas?" he questioned
sharply. *"Ja*—th' cook—where is he?"

"Moses Thomas is a sick man," volunteered Parsons, levelly. "He's barricaded in the galley. I have
no doubt but what he's terror-stricken because of
your crazy antics!"

"So!" blustered the furious Rau. "We'll see about
that—now!"

With cruel vindictiveness the mutineers, led by
Rau, advanced across the deck to the galley. The
German pounded heavily on the door with the butt
of McLeod's pistol. There was momentary silence
as Rau waited for Thomas to open up.

"Come out!" ordered Rau, leveling the revolver
waist-high toward the galley door.

"Never!" came Thomas's scared voice from within
the galley. Rau emptied the gun with splintering
reverberations through the panels. The cook called
for quarter and came out on deck, hands high
over his head. The spiteful German reloaded and
stalked toward Moses Thomas with the evil intent
of murdering him on the spot.

"Hold it!" yelled Smith, grabbing Rau's arm
from behind. "Use y'r head, Gus. Who's t' dish
up th' grub if y' kill Mose, here?"

Reluctantly Rau relaxed his gun hand. It was unassailable logic. No cook—no grub! It was as simple as that.

"Go get some coffee!" ordered Rau with an angry grunt. "Make it fast—and hot!"

"Yassir!" answered the grateful Thomas with a wide grin at Smith; then he disappeared through the galley door.

Gustav Rau turned sharply and faced Bravo and Johanssen, who still stood near the fo'c'sle head. He took a step or two forward, the hurricane lamp held above his head and shining into the bewildered men's eyes.

"Well, how do we stand?" he asked ominously. "Are we all still good friends—or would ya like a taste of lead?"

"We'll kick in with ya, Gus," replied the two sailors, nodding.

"And you, Parsons?" snarled the German sarcastically. "What's *your* pleasure?"

"I refuse to be a party to mutiny!" declared the Canadian quietly. "And I daresay I'll someday see you all hanged for pirates!"

Parsons then brushed brusquely past the dumbfounded Rau. He entered the fo'c'sle, slamming the door and battening it after him. At that moment Moses Thomas came on deck with a pot of steaming coffee and a half-dozen mugs. After the coffee was done with, Gustav Rau beckoned to Willem Smith.

"Smit'," whispered Rau, "we'll lock the cook in th' sail room 'til mornin'—then we'll let him out, understand? F'r mess he's out—other times he's locked up—see? Watch Bravo an' Johanssen—I don't trust 'em!"

"Aye, Gus," grinned Smith, glad to be in the German's good graces.

Without helm or lookout the *Veronica* drifted fitfully—but the mutineers seemed to care little about the vessel's welfare. They had other matters to tend to. Smith locked up Moses Thomas in the sail room of the forward deckhouse. Rau, on a hunch, stalked to the paint locker where Doran was slowly bleeding to death. The vengeful German with an evil grin was intent on finishing off the hated Doran, if he was still alive.

"Water!" moaned Doran weakly as he heard footsteps on the deck near by. "F'r God's sake, gimme water!"

"*Ja*—water!" answered the vicious Rau, "I'll give you a drink of water, Doran—a damned good drink!"

Motioning to Flohr and Monsson, Gustav Rau ordered the dying Doran hoisted to the rail. With a vicious kick, Rau booted the helpless sailor into the sea.

"Have a good drink, Paddy," he sneered. "It'll be y'r last!"

With the killing lust roused to fever pitch the quartet of madmen, led by the crazy German, rushed aft to finish their nefarious job on the gravely wounded Captain Shaw and his second mate. In a harangue of profane oaths, Rau, standing near the skylight, demanded that the captain come on deck at once.

"He is too ill to move," the second mate answered weakly. "He is dying!"

"That's too bad, mate," jeered Rau. "Guess the boys'll have t' move him! Pine lumber in the hold burns fast—*ja!*"

"My God!" screamed the second mate, "you wouldn't. . . ."

"Monsson—Flohr!" bellowed the German, "rip off them boards from the skylight! Bravo an' Johanssen—get lamp oil from th' storeroom, fo'ard —then stand by!"

As Flohr and Monsson ripped off the skylight boards, Rau kicked in the glass and stood by with McLeod's loaded gun leveled at the two officers below.

"Got any bargains t'night?" snarled Rau. "I'm here t' do a little tradin'—if ya got what I want, Cap'n!"

At this the elderly shipmaster, gathering his remaining strength, rose painfully to bargain with the mutineers. Anything met, he reasoned, could scarcely be worse than the possible doom awaiting him and the second mate. Shaw stumbled to the smashed skylight and faced the leering Rau.

"Give us some water," pleaded the old captain, "and I'll give you my gold watch!"

"What th' hell would I do with a gold watch?" spat Rau contemptuously. Then turning to Monsson, "Fetch th' Cap'n a bucket of fresh water."

A bucket of water was drawn from a cask and lowered down the skylight—just out of reach of the two officers.

"Now, we'll bargain, Herr Captain!" laughed Rau sarcastically. "First, we'll want th' sextant to shoot th' beautiful sun and th' pretty stars with—then we'll want the chart to tell us where t' go—and last, the parallel rulers t' make lines on the charts. Then y'll get y'r water—*ja!*"

"Rau, you're a damn'd contemptible rascal!" exclaimed Shaw angrily. "But we've no choice—we're dying men!"

After this one-sided exchange was completed, Monsson and Flohr secured the skylight at Rau's command. For three days and nights the mutinous crew navigated the *Veronica* on the general course set by Captain Shaw. During this time the two suffering officers received no attention either from crew members or from their German ringleader.

Then one day, Rau, with overwhelming cruelty, decided to finish off the two officers without further delay. With fiendish cunning he devised a diabolic "shooting game" that only he and his henchmen could win.

Grinning sardonically, Rau supplied Smith, Flohr, and Monsson with rifles and ammunition he chanced to find in a little-known arms chest hidden in the closet of the ship's store. Stationing himself and his mutineers at strategic points on the poop deck, abaft the now barricaded entrance to the captain's quarters, Rau laid bare his sadistic plan.

"Lis'n, boys—I've a surprise for you," he began in sharp, guttural tones. "We're going to play a little shootin' game! When I give th' command for th' mate t' come out of the cabin, you, Smit', will shoot if he runs away! You, Johanssen, will take the wheel an' wait f'r orders from me—understand? Monsson, you, Bravo, and Flohr, stand by f'r orders. Got it? Now, we're ready for our little game t' start!"

Rau's armed renegades stirred uneasily with their new-found weapons. This "game" was not entirely to their liking, but they had little choice in the matter. They'd thrown in with Rau, and Rau had them covered with McLeod's gun. He knew that none of them had guts enough to take a pot shot at an armed man when a miss meant suicide! Calmly bracing himself against the starboard rail, Rau grinned at his crew's nervous tension. That's what he wanted—when he gave a sudden command, they'd all be trigger happy!

"Come out, mate!" he barked.

The second mate, wan and white-faced from loss of blood, stepped falteringly through the cabin door. He blinked, shading his red-rimmed eyes, being momentarily blinded by the stinging rays of a tropic sun. The mate found himself circled by hostile crewmen, armed and waiting. With ebbing strength he staggered along the starboard deck of the vessel.

"You, Smit' fire!" ordered Rau.

Smith fired at the fleeing officer, striking him in the shoulder. Desperate, now, the mate chose another way out! With a grave last effort he climbed the rail and plunged headlong into the sea, swimming away from the *Veronica* as fast as his waning strength would allow.

"Johanssen!" Rau bellowed at the helmsman. "Turn th' vessel about—quick!"

The bark answered the wheel sharply and quickly overhauled the struggling swimmer. Like a man possessed, Rau ruthlessly emptied his gun into the body of the second mate until it slowly sank from sight.

Captain Shaw was next! Ordered out of his cabin, the old shipmaster stubbornly refused!

"You, Bravo!" rasped the infuriated German. "Take th' axe—get him out!"

Bravo grabbed a fire axe from its cleats on the cabin bulkhead and hacked savagely at the barricaded door. A few moments later Captain Shaw staggered weakly from the passageway. Flohr, who was nearest the aged officer, was ordered by the merciless Rau to shoot the commander! But, coming face to face with the pitiable sight of the bleeding and broken old man, he lost his nerve. Flohr instinctively backed away as if he had seen a ghost in broad daylight!

"Kill him!" screamed the mad Rau, jabbing his own empty gun into young Flohr's ribs. "Kill him —or I'll put a bullet through ya!"

Flohr, thoroughly cowed and confused by Rau's threats, fired three times at Captain Shaw who stood only a few feet away. Whether by accident or design, young Flohr missed his target!

"*Dumkopf!*" raged Rau, tossing his empty pistol to the deck and seizing Flohr's rifle. "Outta th' way—I'll finish th' job m'self!"

Bellowing blasphemies at the blundering Flohr, Rau pushed past him to within a pace of Shaw, who stood by with his hands over his eyes. The German jammed the rifle butt to his shoulder and jerked the trigger irritably and an instant later the veteran shipmaster sagged to the blood-splattered deck! At his order a couple of Rau's renegades unceremoniously dumped the old man's body over the rail.

"Now, I'm y'r commander!" grinned Rau in his evil hour of triumph. "Smit'—you're second in command! Johanssen, you stay at the wheel—Monsson, Flohr, and Bravo, you go aloft and trim canvas. We'll stay on th' course set by the late Captain Shaw!"

The *Veronica* slowly worked her way southward as if in trepidation of the vile secret she carried— or the fate that awaited her!

As watch followed watch and day followed day, the awful impact of their atrocious acts began to dawn upon the mutineers. They held council in the captain's cabin and made a grave decision. The *Veronica* must be destroyed—the only mute witness to their crimes must go!

With this objective in mind, the longboat was made ready for a voyage to the Brazilian coast not too far distant. Indeed, it was close—too close for the peace of mind of the mutineers! The name on the longboat was laboriously erased. Stores and fresh water were put aboard, seams were carefully caulked, and all preparations made to scuttle and abandon the *Veronica* on the high seas!

The vicious Rau now concocted a truly amazing tale in a grim effort to account for the loss of their vessel with all her officers. The story was mulled over, trimmed, and finally memorized by all but Bravo and Johanssen! These two couldn't repeat it correctly no matter how much it was rehearsed. Something had to be done. So Rau decided that

these two dull wits would have to die. The fewer
the witnesses the better the chance to escape the
gallows!

"Johanssen!" barked Rau, setting into motion another one of his diabolically cunning plans. "Stow
th' flyin' jib!"

The sail hung limp under the boom. As Johanssen went along the boom out over the water
to obey the order, Rau and Smith opened fire on
him! Riddled by bullets, the big Swede's lifeless
body splashed into the sea. For a brief moment
a scarlet tinge marked the spot of his going.

Bravo was then ordered by Rau to haul up the
slack in the foresheet which was trailing in the
water. Realizing only too well the full implication
of the order, the Hindoo, nevertheless, carried it
out. His reward was a lead slug in the base of
the skull and a grave in the sea!

"Let *me* kill Thomas!" piped up young Flohr,
trying to impress Rau with his false courage. "He
knows too much, anyway!"

"Nobody's killing the cook!" barked Smith, rap-
ping Flohr sharply across the mouth with the back
of his hand.

For the second time Smith had saved the life
of Moses Thomas—and the noose drew closer!

Julius Parson, who had refused to join the mutineers in their nefarious plans, had ensconced himself in the fo'c'sle these many days. From the first
he had scorned every overture and had often repeated that he'd one day see them all hanged. But
thirst is a terrible betrayer!

In the dead of a dark night Parsons sought to

escape from his self-imposed prison through a tiny skylight—he must have water! He became hopelessly stuck, halfway out. In his desperate exertions to free himself he made a commotion that attracted the attention of Monsson, aft at the wheel.

Locking the wheel, Monsson stole silently along the port rail to investigate. As he crept toward the fo'c'sle he snatched up an iron belaying pin and listened to Parson's struggles, punctuated by frequent groans. A fiendish grin twisted over Monsson's face. He climbed stealthily up the ladder to the fo'c'sle head, concealed by the fores'l sheet, but he carelessly stubbed a toe on a hawser ring in the deck that gave out a metalic "clink."

"Water!" moaned Parsons. "Gimme water!"

"Only got *hard* water," sneered Monsson. Then he bounded across the deck and in cold blood bludgeoned the Canadian's brains out with the belaying pin. Left hanging, half in and half out of the skylight, Parsons remained, to the end, a ghastly relic of a terrible, nightmarish voyage—wrought of violent deeds!

With the shore of Brazil a blue-gray blur on the horizon dead ahead, all witnesses murdered, the longboat stocked and ready for a quick getaway, and their story well rehearsed, the mutineers fired the *Veronica!* Flames—fed by kerosene-soaked mattresses, broken-up boards, chairs and tables—shot skyward. In minutes the vessel was a roaring pyre. All hands were in the longboat that swung out from the stern davits.

"Lower away!" ordered Rau, grinning satanically. "Abandon ship!"

As they swung free of the *Veronica's* stern, the mutineers stood by in the longboat until the stately old bark burned to the water's edge. Then Rau took a bearing, ordered the jury sail set, and the longboat, with Monsson at the tiller, bore away SSE for the hazy coast of Brazil.

The *Veronica* had been destroyed and abandoned on December 21. On Christmas Day the longboat made a landfall. Before closing in to the shore, the wily Rau took stock and commanded that most of the gear and provisions be jettisoned to give the deceptive appearance of having abandoned ship in great haste. Carefully they rehearsed their story for the last time, then went ashore.

The mutineers found themselves on Canniera Island, port of call for a Liverpool steamship line. Barely had they set foot on the beach when a steamer drew in toward the green harbor of the island.

From a vantage point deep in a clump of mangroves, Rau studied her through the glasses as she dropped anchor. He made out the *Brunswick* on her rusty port bow. As she took on cargo from a dingy little lighter, Rau suddenly decided they would board her, tell their sad plight of fire at sea, then secure passage to Europe, or to the British Isles if possible, using a trumped-up argument that he "wanted to find out if Captain Shaw's boat had been picked up."

"Ahoy, *Brunswick!*" bellowed the G e r m a n through cupped hands as the boatload of mutineers neared the port bow. "Where's your home port?"

"Liverpool!" answered the bow watch, leaning

over the rail to size up the down-at-the-heels crew in the longboat. "Who are you?"

"Shipwrecked seamen!" returned the wily Rau. "Sole survivors of fire at sea! Could we speak with the captain?"

The request was granted, a rope ladder was thrown over the side, and the mutineers climbed aboard. Once on deck, Rau, cocky and verbose, did the talking for the rest. He poured out such a tale of woe that Captain George Browne, master of the *Brunswick*, was just a little skeptical of the whole deal from the start.

However, the captain heard Rau out. The crew *did* look woebegone, the nearest consul was miles away, and there were no witnesses against them— so, with whatever misgivings Browne might have kept to himself, he accepted the erstwhile mutineers as shipwrecked mariners. They were given food, clothing, and quarters.

On the passage eastward the men of the *Veronica* were berthed forward with the crew of the *Brunswick*. But Rau, in another one of his strange mental quirks, demanded a berth, aft, that befitted his rank and dignity—claiming now to be an officer. He kicked up such a row that he got the undeserved berth.

The more Captain Browne studied Rau the more firmly convinced he became that the man was, at least, worth watching.

It was in the middle night watch of the tenth day out, as the *Brunswick* approached the Canaries, that Captain Browne was suddenly aroused by furtive poundings on his cabin door! Opening the door, he was amazed to see the *Veronica's* mulatto cook, Moses Thomas! Thomas was crouching low so as not to be seen by the watch and was obviously in a state bordering hysteria. Trembling and crying, he asked to be allowed to come in—that his life was in grave danger! Still puzzled, but realizing Thomas's terror was real, Browne admitted him and inquired what was wrong.

Moses Thomas poured out the whole tragic story!

"The *Veronica* was captured an' burned by those fellas you've picked up!" he sobbed loudly. "They murdered the cap'n an' officers! They killed five of my shipmates, an' now they're tryin' t' kill me!"

The little mulatto cook choked back the tears and continued.

"Las' night," he stumbled on, haltingly, "Gustav Rau tried t' murder me in my quarters! But he was stopped by some of the *Brunswick's* crew!"

Moses Thomas glanced wildly around the cabin —then dropped to his knees before the master of the *Brunswick*.

"I—I got to tell everythin', Cap'n!" he moaned. "If Rau *does* get me, well—leastways th' truth'll be known! *I* wasn't with 'em, an' they know it! They *got* t' kill me so's nobody'll ever know!"

Thomas broke down and sobbed in terrified anguish. Captain Browne closed the ports and drew the blinds. He, too, was shocked, but not altogether surprised. The captain got out the ship's official log, swore Thomas on the Bible, and took down the narrative almost word for word.

When he was finished, Browne put his hands on the mulatto's shoulders.

"Son," he said in a fatherly tone, "you've done a great service tonight—you've shown a courage few men would dare to, under the circumstances. Continue to bear up as if nothing had happened; I'll see to it that you get proper protection."

Relieved of his terrible mental burden, Moses Thomas left the captain's cabin by way of another door, a much quieter man in mind and spirit.

Fully aware, now, of the desperate characters he had aboard, Captain Browne knew he was in a bad spot. To attempt clamping them into irons might endanger the lives of his passengers—among whom were a number of women and children. He held no doubts as to the very real threat that the mutineers were heavily armed with hidden weapons —or that, facing the gallows, they would hesitate to use them! Hadn't they, all too successfully, seized one vessel? What was to prevent them from taking another—especially since there was a strong German element among the *Brunswick's* crew—fellows, who, very likely, would "throw in" with the "castaways" if it came to a showdown! Browne, carefully weighing the situation, chose to take the advice he'd given young Thomas—act as if nothing had happened and play for time!

To forestall suspicion, Captain Browne arranged a "benefit" in the main saloon of the *Brunswick,* next night, which succeeded in raising a sizable sum for the "survivors." The following day Rau made another crude attempt to murder Moses Thomas! Again, Thomas escaped!

The *Brunswick's* master ordered an immediate search of Rau's quarters. Two hidden pistols and a quantity of ammunition were seized. Rau sulked and said nothing. He schemed in sullen silence. Moses Thomas must die!

At Madeira, Browne set in motion machinery that ultimately trapped Rau and his mutineers. He sent a cable to England reporting the loss of the *Veronica* and that he had five of the survivors aboard. That and nothing more. But at Lisbon, Captain Browne laid the whole sordid story before the British consul, who in turn advised him to proceed to England as if all were well. For if arrested in Portugal, the consul explained, the prisoners would have to be extradited, resulting in a loss of valuable time through red tape.

The mutineers suspected nothing as the *Brunswick* steamed leisurely toward England. But wires to British authorities went out immediately from the Lisbon consul.

When the Brunswick docked at Liverpool, the "survivors," led by the unsuspecting Rau, began putting questions to the very officers sent to pick them up—asking bluntly whether "Captain Shaw's boat had been picked up at sea." The British officers snapped handcuffs on the whole lot and whisked them away to the Dale Street Gaol!

A short time later Moses Thomas made his appearance before an English magistrate. He was duly sworn and thoroughly examined. His statement coincided in every particular with those previously made to Captain Browne in his cabin on that fateful night aboard the *Brunswick*. The Crown's case was further strengthened when Flohr made a complete confession. Then Smith, the noose already tightening around his neck, accused Thomas as being the ringleader. Flohr's story refuted Smith at every point—and the Crown used his evidence to protect its case.

The surly Rau, together with Otto Monsson and Willem Smith, were indicted for the murder of Alexander Shaw, master of the bark *Veronica!* Added to this was that clincher and horror of maritime law—*piracy!*

The wheels of English justice turn slowly and there were many cases to be tried before the mutineers' trial came up. For five torturing months Rau, Monsson, and Smith had timeless days to think over their vile crimes.

At long last, the trial was held before Justice Lawson at the Liverpool Assize, St. George's Hall, May 12-15, 1903. On the stand Rau vehemently declared Thomas and Flohr hatched the mutiny and did the killing. The jury was out a scant twelve minutes. Their verdict: Monsson—a lad of eighteen at the time of the indictment, a fairly good record and no previous arrests—was recommended to mercy. He, alone, escaped the gallows. Rau and Smith were sentenced to death by hanging!

Thus, the last log of the *Veronica was writ in blood* and *signed* by the King's Hangman when Rau and Smith dangled from the gallows in the yard of Walton Gaol!

Sources of Factual Material

The facts of this story came from the minutes of the trial held before Justice Lawson at Liverpool Assize, St. George's Hall, May 12 to 15, 1903.

VII

THE "WORKAWAY" GUY AND THE SEA TRAMP

THE BEATEN-UP little tramp freighter S.S. *Tashmoo* poked her 324 feet of rusty hull out through the Golden Gate, wallowing her pudgy 3,249 tons in the long rolling swells of the Pacific. Like a fat old lady she settled herself solidly in the gray-green water far below her legitimate load line. As each roller smashed against her bows the salty spume cascaded over her fo'c'slehead and drenched her deckload of lumber from stem to stern.

Captain Olav Brieland, the *Tashmoo's* skipper, stood grim-faced on her paint-chipped bridge, legs apart and fists jammed into the pockets of the pea jacket he wore against the marrow-chilling 'Frisco fog on that morning of April 24, 1928. His thoughts were not happy ones.

"Why in hell don't they get smart an' quit loading this damn'd tub t' th' gun'ls," he grumbled to his first mate who stood shivering beside him.

"Same reason they didn't sign on a radio operator," retorted the first mate sourly. "An' th' same bloody reason they never fixed that burnt-out transmitter so's it could use an operator—'cause they scrimp on every bloody cent they shell out for repairs...."

The thought the mate voiced was a gross understatement and he knew it. He knew that the *Tash-moo* was overloaded, undermanned, and utterly unseaworthy. So did Captain Brieland. Both wondered how any port in the civilized world could ever have the nerve to clear her for her unsavory conditions. She began her voyage at Seattle, her home port, and now she was bound south from 'Frisco for the Panama Canal, and, if she held together, they figured she'd maybe make her port of destination, Norfolk, Virginia.

The tramp *Tashmoo* carried a "mixed cargo." From fruit, to copper, to oriental rugs—topped off by a full deckload of lumber. She bulged at her hatches, listed nastily to starb'rd because of poor stowing, and laid dangerously low in the water. Brieland knew it would take a lot of luck to get her $500,000 cargo to the East Coast.

Captain Brieland was also painfully aware that the owners of the *Tashmoo* had greedily seized upon the loose wording of the Maritime Act of 1912 which was applicable to ships at sea having a complement of fifty persons or more. The *Tashmoo's* crew of twenty-eight and passenger list of eleven totaled only thirty-nine—all of whom, by an unhappy dispensation of Congress, were left quite free to drown, burn, starve, or perish in any manner that pleased the fates. These unsavory visions occupied the worried thoughts of the *Tashmoo's* skipper and his first mate as they glared grimly through the spray-streaked windshield of the shoddy little freighter's bridge.

The *Tashmoo* dawdled down the California coast in a smooth sea, still listing to starb'rd. Some days

later she put into San Pedro to take on oil and
five of her crew "jumped ship." It took a lot of
tall talk by Captain Brieland to sign on replacements.

Among those who had shipped aboard the *Tashmoo* at 'Frisco was one Arthur Finch, an unem-
ployed electrician. Two considerations had prompted Finch's action—first of all, he was broke, and,
second, he had the prospects of a good job on the
East Coast, if he could get there. Finch had applied
as a deck hand, but was told there were no openings topside. So he was signed on as a "workaway"
and was given the job of "assistant steward" for
the six-thousand-mile voyage at a stipulated monthly
wage of *thirty cents!* The amount was as *irregular*
as it was *miserly*—one dollar being the recognized
minimum consideration of *all* contracts. But, then,
there were many *irregular* things about the *Tashmoo,* as Arthur Finch was fast finding out.

Several days out of San Pedro, as the *Tashmoo*
lurched southward down the coast of Mexico with
an increasing list to starb'rd, there was still another
note of distress.

One squally dawn the chief engineer climbed
down into the bowels of the beleaguered sea tramp
and faced an almost insurmountable problem. He
found her boilers wheezing from an aggravated case
of leaky tubes. Nor was that all. The port feed
pump had finally broken from the constant wrack-
ing of crashing seas between San Pedro and the
ship's present position off the Mexican coast, and
the starb'rd pump was bucking like a crazy porpoise
from the extra load thrown on it. As a consequence

the injectors stuck and the gaskets were sprung. All this, without a single replacement part aboard for anything! Even the very supports of the *Tashmoo's* boilers were threatening to break away and the Chief was fit to be tied.

"Listen!" he roared over the phone to the bridge, recounting conditions in the engine room. "We're in a helluva mess down here! Th' boilers 'r bein' pumped drinkin' water and the port injector's fouled up. Th' starb'd injector's sprung a gasket an' if we get any heavier seas we're done for!"

"Do th' best y' can," bellowed back Brieland, mopping his brow.

"With whot!" yelled the Chief caustically.

When the *Tashmoo* reached the waters of the Gulf of Tehuantepec and headed into a stinging gale that registered eight on the Beaufort scale, things really got out of control. Even the most un-initiated among the eleven passengers sensed that something of great magnitude was wrong.

The *Tashmoo* was making a bad time of it. Her quartermaster soon discovered that she wasn't re-sponding to her helm properly. She would not "head to," but, instead, developed a nasty little trick of broaching dangerously—a side-slipping action which very nearly caused her to founder then and there! Wallowing broadside, she'd ship tons of tumbling water through her already strained plates, down her skylights and past her warped hatch covers. That's when her list to starb'rd hovered dangerously to a thirty-degree angle, making it virtually impossible to pass along her decks without clinging to a rail.

The gale shrieked and whined through her whipping guy lines and roared past her stubby masts, rising to near hurricane force. The hapless *Tashmoo* reeled, pitched, and staggered in and out of green mountains of water like a mortally wounded sea creature. The deckload of lumber broke loose, shifting and crashing into the superstructure with a booming force that threatened to wrench it from its foundation and carry it overside into the boiling sea.

Below decks, lubricating oil drums smashed against each other like sailors in a drunken brawl. Drum heads sprung open and oil, mixed with water, sloshed around the legs of terrified firemen and lapped ominously against the hot plates of the firebox. In some unaccountable manner the ship's fresh water supply line got fouled up and drinking water was fed through the injectors and into the boilers. But the damage was already done before it was discovered and the ship's company was put on rations. Water in the engine room rose and dynamos grounded. The main boilers went cold as the power auxiliaries konked out, one by one, and the burners quit.

With engines dead, the *Tashmoo,* now completely at the mercy of the sea, began to drift westward out of the steamer lanes and into the trackless wastes of the Pacific. A hastily constructed sea anchor tore away from its moorings and distress pennants were quickly whipped to shreds before they were halfway up the halyards.

Day followed day and no ships were sighted. In the intense heat of a tropic sun food stores began to spoil. Water was on shorter rations. Distress became acute. Deep lines etched the faces of the *Tashmoo's* skipper and his first mate. A dim ray of hope raised spirits of crew and passengers when the chief engineer managed to tease life into one of the power auxiliaries and again got the engines going and headed for the Mexican coast. But this respite was short-lived. After a few hours the power went out, the engine stopped, and few held hope of ever seeing land again. Over and over, prayers were said and hymns sung, led by Arthur Finch, the assistant steward, in the sea tramp's main saloon. Grimly he tried to keep up what little morale was left among the passengers.

About one o'clock Sunday afternoon, May 6, Captain Olav Brieland, haggard and unshaven, turned over in his mind the tragic problem of survival which now beset them all. There seemed to be no answer to it. Up on the bridge Brieland's eyes, in a worried, abstract way, followed Finch as he crossed the deck. Suddenly those eyes lighted up.

"Finch!" he shouted. "Come up here a moment!"

"Aye, sir," answered the puzzled Finch as he climbed the ladder to the bridge.

"I'm not going to mince words, Finch," said the played-out skipper. "We're facing death, Finch, imminent death—unless something is done an' done damn'd quick!"

"I know, Captain," answered Finch wearily, "things look pretty black—passengers are pretty well done in, too, and we've some injuries among the crew."

"Now, then, Finch," continued Brieland grimly,

"there's just one possible hope—and that's to get a message out over the burnt-out transmitter!"

The skipper watched Finch's reaction to his suggestion of getting an S O S on the air.

"How?" asked Finch at length. "How do you propose to get the thing into operation?"

"You know something about radio, don't you?" questioned Brieland, half hopefully, half accusingly. "Foley, the third mate, says you do!"

"Don't know a thing about it," shrugged Finch. "I've done plenty of electrical work, but not radio."

"But give it a try, Finch," persisted the captain. "I'm only askin' you to give it a try!"

"Hell, Captain, I've never seen a transmitter in my life," countered Finch. "Why don't you get your engineers in on the job?"

"I did, last trip," groaned the *Tashmoo's* skipper. "They damn'd near burned out the radio shack!"

"If that happened before, sir," answered Finch, shaking his head, "then it would be my luck to set the ship afire. No, thanks!"

"Listen, Finch, you know electricity," he pleaded, "they didn't. I'll take th' chance of fire! Only do something—anything you like—get it running—I'll —I'll relieve you from all your other duties!"

Arthur Finch pondered the skipper's impossible request for a moment, then shook his head.

"My God, man!" exploded Brieland in desperation. "It's—it's a matter of life an' death for all of us—I'm only askin' you to *try!*"

"Very well, sir," nodded Finch finally, fully realizing the tough spot Brieland was in. "I'll give it a try—but I warn you, Captain, don't expect a miracle!"

"Good boy!" grinned Brieland, slapping Finch on the shoulder.

The *Tashmoo* was taking on heavy seas and rolling sluggishly as Finch struggled aft from the bridge to the radio shack. He found it a veritable jungle of broken and burned-out wires—a maze of mysterious gadgets and gismos. Switches, cracked by the heat of the previous fire, fell from the blackened walls when he touched them. To the ever-present threat of death by drowning was added the strong likelihood of electrocution, but Finch pitched in. One of the passengers grabbed the door jamb of the radio shack and looked in.

"Watch yourself, Finch," he warned. "I got a helluva jolt trying to fix that thing!"

"You tried to fix it!" exclaimed Finch. "When?"

"Yesterday," answered the passenger leaning against the radio shack door. "That's when I damn'd near got electrocuted!"

"Come in and help me, then!" called out Finch urgently. "This can mean *all* our lives!"

"I'm not coming in," answered the passenger vehemently, "but I'll help identify some of those hanging wires over there.

With the *Tashmoo* rolling and pitching under them, Finch and the passenger went to work. But neither of them could hit the combination for a correct hookup of the loose wires. Finch rustled around the drawers of the operator's desk but couldn't locate either a blueprint or instruction book. He ran his fingers through his tousled hair nervously and shook his head in bewilderment. Then he dashed past the surprised passenger onto the tilting deck.

"Hold the fort, friend!" he flung over his shoulder, "I'm goin' below. The chief engineer must have the blueprint of these gadgets somewhere!"

But the chief didn't. By the time Finch raced back along the careening deck to the radio shack he was soaked to the skin from the heavy spray. Once in the shack, Finch made him a test lamp of an ordinary socket and a couple of lengths of wire. Then it struck him that there was no power—the engines were dead! And there was no electricity to test with! In the semidarkness Finch looked around.

"Behind you," called out the passenger, "there's a bank of storage batteries on that rack on the wall! I gotta leave you for now—I got a sick wife down in my cabin."

Bracing himself against the operator's table to withstand the sharp pitch and roll of the helpless ship, Finch pondered the ways of the *Tashmoo's* radio set. He had an idea that alternating current was used for wireless work but he wasn't too sure. Then he realized that with the bank of storage batteries he could run the D.C. motor which, in turn, would drive the A.C. generator—*if he could get the motor going*. The transformer was hooked up under the table. Frantically he kept testing with the lamp, crossing the 110-volt terminals. He got a light. This encouraged him to go on. But when he threw the switches, nothing happened. He knew he had to be careful. This was the point where the passenger had gotten a severe electric jolt! He very gingerly threw the switch again. Thirty-nine lives depended on him to get an S O S out to the world! Again, nothing happened.

By now several passengers and crewmen had gathered around the radio shack door and were needling him with an endless chain of questions.

"Kin ya git it goin', Finch?" a rawboned deck hand asked.

"Could I send a message to my wife, Mr. Finch?" questioned a middle-aged passenger.

Finch would pause to wipe the sweat from his forehead and explain that there wasn't even the remotest chance that the set would ever work again. Not ever! That sent them away for a while. Then, free at last, Finch tried to start the D.C. motor, failed, then tried another series of connections. Disgusted, Finch slammed out the door and went below to the engine room to find that both D.C. motor and A.C. generator were well out of the water. With a tight grin of satisfaction he raced across the slanting deck to the radio shack—if only he could get juice to the motor!

Finally, after many hours, Finch succeeded in starting the dynamo going—a signal triumph of sheer persistence! Passengers and crew members risked their lives on the slippery decks, clinging to the door and parts of the radio shack, to see what Finch was doing. So engrossed was he in trying combinations of circuits and flipping switches that he ignored the curious company. Dusk was settling down on the doomed *Tashmoo* and soon he would be working blindly in the dark. Suddenly the D.C.

side of the panel began to register voltage and a low murmur of approval came from those who watched.

"So ya got it goin'—huh?" came the half-questioning remark of a grimy oiler.

"Yeah, it's going," Finch explained patiently, "but it could stop at any minute. Besides, it doesn't register even a half a volt on the A.C. side of the panel—so the transmitter's just as dead as ever!"

"Maybe you have the wires on the panel crossed," suggested an elderly passenger. "I once studied electricity in college, and if a dynamo turns up so many revolutions a minute, it's bound to generate power."

"Perhaps you'd care to take over, sir," Finch answered flatly.

The forlorn spectators drifted away silently. It was fast getting dark in the shack and Finch went below to borrow Third Mate Foley's flashlight. On the way back to the radio shack he saw Captain Brieland and the first mate on the bridge preparing to fire rockets into the gloomy cloud-studded sky. A knot of passengers and a few crew members stood by looking up at the bridge.

"So it's that bad?" asked Finch of one of the engineers.

"Yeah, we're tryin' rockets," was the tight answer, "but I doubt they'll do any good. Too wet."

Brieland touched off the fuses of two or three rockets. The sputtering balls of light dropped out with a faint hiss and fizzled out on the deck below. An eerie moan went up from the weary watchers.

"See what I mean," said the engineer disgustedly. "How're ya comin' with the radio, Finch?"

"Just like the damn'd rockets," murmured Finch grimly, "dead!"

Finch found the first engineer in the darkening radio shack. He was jabbering excitedly.

"How did ya get it goin', boy?" he beamed. "What did ya do to it? I was down in the engine room when th' motor started a few minutes ago. It's still goin'! Keep it goin', boy, keep it goin'. We're really in a bad way now! We gotta get an S O S out, but quick!"

"Slow down, Chief," warned Finch, "I got the generator goin', yes—but there's still plenty wrong with th' damn'd set, 'cause I can't get a test on the A.C., and if we don't get that, we're licked!"

At that moment Brieland rushed into the shack. He had a four-day stubby beard; he looked thinner and his cheeks were hollowed, but in his eyes shined a glazy light of hope.

"Well, Finch, you finally got it going!" he said in an elated voice, slapping Finch on the back. Then he fished in a pocket and handed Finch a piece of paper.

"What's this, sir?" questioned Finch, studying the paper with a puzzled look.

"Why, it's the call letters of the *Tashmoo*," answered Captain Brieland with a grin. "Know international code don't you, Finch?"

"Enough to get it on the air—*if we can*," answered Finch.

"Well, let's not delay, my boy," spluttered Brieland. "We've no time to waste!"

"Please, listen, Captain," spoke Finch slowly.

"The set is not working! When the transmitter is working I should get a buzz when I test the key. All I get is a dull metallic click."

"Are you sure, Finch?" Captain Brieland's shoulders sagged with his voice. "Th' generator's goin'."

"But we're not getting juice enough to light a flashlight bulb, Captain," insisted Finch. "How in hell can we send a message!"

"Your life, my life—everybody's life on this ship depends on that S O S!" pleaded Brieland as he slouched toward the door of the shack. Then he turned with the slowness of a heavy fatigue. "F'r God's sake, Finch, try—just try!"

Finch sighed resignedly, clapped on the earphones, and sat on the stool in front of the operator's table. Automatically he glanced at his watch—it was now nearly midnight. Captain Brieland leaned over Finch's shoulder as he started pounding the key . . . S O S . . . KOXD . . . over and over. . . .

"Y' see, Captain," shrugged Finch, "the damn'd thing's dead."

Brieland shook his head. A groan of despair went up from those who clung to the shack's doorway and the rail outside—listening, and hoping against hope, with the spray of heavy seas soaking them to the skin. The *Tashmoo* tossed and pitched, seas broke over her, and the list to starb'rd was worse. Captain Brieland, gray with worry, lurched out of the shack, a beaten man. The chief engineer left and went below. One by one the discouraged ship's company drifted away. Finch was alone. He glumly stuffed the paper with the *Tashmoo's* call number on it into his pocket and silently cussed the day he went to sea. But he wouldn't give up. After a while he rigged wires to an electric socket, screwed in a bulb that threw a dim, yellow glow around the shack. Then Finch picked up the third mate's flashlight and wearily stepped out on deck to find Foley and give it back to him.

Out on the *Tashmoo's* careening deck Finch heard a terrific crash up forward—then a woman's scream. A moment later Finch met Foley and handed him the flashlight.

"What h a p p e n e d , for'ard?" he asked Foley. "Heard a crash, then some woman p a s s e n g e r screamed."

"The skipper had another sea anchor set up to help steady this tub," answered Foley caustically, "but the damn'd thing went over the side in a hurry when heavy seas struck. Boy, we're really in a bad way, Finch! How are you making out in the radio shack?"

"No dice," answered Finch glumly, "the set's dead an' I'm beat up! Think I'll get some shut-eye for a few hours."

"Ya gotta hold on a little longer, Finch," advised the third mate in a grim tone. "Things are bad!"

"How bad, Foley?" questioned Finch sharply. "I mean—how long does Brieland figure th' ship can take this pounding from the storm?"

"Well, it's this bad, Finch," continued Foley. "If there's no help by eight t'morrow morning Brieland's having the first mate take a picked crew an' try t' reach th' shippin' lanes—that gives ya an idea of th' situation!"

"That's enough for me!" nodded Finch. "I'll

stick out as long as I can. I'll try anything on that damn'd set t' get it goin'. Only don't bank too much on an S O S gettin' out!"

The *Tashmoo* lurched sickeningly to starb'rd as Finch slithered aft on the slippery decks. A yellowish glow from the shack's port told him he still had power. When he struggled into the shack he found the steward there.

"Here, grab this," yelled the steward, handing Finch a steaming mug of coffee. "An' I made a few sandwiches for ya—over there on the table."

"Thanks, steward," grinned Finch, "I sure can use 'em!"

"How's it comin'?" asked the steward from the doorway.

"Not too good," answered Finch, "but this coffee'll keep me awake 'til I find out why. Thanks again."

"Luck t' ya, Finch!" And the steward was out the door and gone.

Sipping from the mug he held in one hand, Finch systematically rechecked every wire connection from the generator to the transmitter. Frantically he pressed the key, hoping for some signs of life. Still all he got was that same metallic deadness. He put down the empty mug and for a solid hour he tinkered with wires, finagled with connections, and tested switches. Desperately he checked the voltometer hookup. Again he pounded the key. It was still dead.

Finch, red-eyed with fatigue, slowly munched a sandwich as he pondered the maze of wires behind the panel. He must somehow get in back of that panel and find the trouble; but fifteen inches is a terribly narrow space, between the wall and the panel board, for a man to get into. Finch gingerly squeezed himself up behind the panel, with live contacts ready to pin-point him with a jolting shock if he made a mismove! Tense and sweating, Finch tested the A.C. current to a set of magnets at the bottom of the panel. Then he checked fuses and connections. A sudden lurch of the *Tashmoo* at this point might well send hundreds of electric volts through his body!

The gray daylight of Monday morning sifted through the door and parts of the radio shack as Finch eased himself from behind the panel board. The deck of the *Tashmoo* canted to starb'rd at a crazy angle and he had to cling to the operator's table to save himself from being catapulted across the shack. But in his bloodshot eyes was the look of satisfaction—Finch felt he had the A.C. transmitter trouble licked.

Captain Olav Brieland stumbled into the shack, his face as gray as death. Finch looked up with a faint grin, but it faded fast when he saw Brieland's expression.

"Mate's takin' th' Number 1 boat f'r th' ship lanes at eight o'clock," mumbled Brieland like a man in a trance. "May have to abandon ship soon! Can you do nothing, Finch?"

"Possibility, Captain," answered Finch flatly, "but don't count too much on it. I've traced th' trouble to the magnets behind that panel, an' if I can get some help I maybe could push that juice through t' th' A.C. transmitter."

"That's good, Finch," smiled Brieland wryly, "but

make it fast, or we'll be under th' sea b'fore it *does* any good!"

"There's also the possibility of fire when I trip those magnets," warned Finch tightly, "two men should do this job——"

"Don't make much difference now, Finch!" said Brieland grimly. "Go all out!"

The passenger who had warned Finch of the danger the day before stuck his head in the door of the shack.

"How are you making it, Finch?" he called, then stepped gingerly into the cabin.

"Give me a hand!" ordered Finch, "I'm gettin' behind that panel an' when I give you certain signals I want you to——"

"Not me," cried the passenger in dire alarm. "I'm not gettin' myself electrocuted for you or anybody else!"

"You're helpin' Mr. Finch!" roared Brieland, suddenly alive. "That's an order from me!"

"But, Captain, I ——" stammered the passenger.

The *Tashmoo* heeled over nearly on her beam's end. Water sloshed threateningly around their feet and the man's face went white with fear.

"I'm throwing in all switches in the main panel, an' on th' table," said Finch sharply, "an' when I give the signal, push that white button over there on the wall."

"But you'll kill yourself, Finch, if you get behind that board!" screamed the passenger. "Those are naked, live contacts back there."

"Shut up, an' do what I say!" retorted Finch angrily, rolling up a magazine. "If you see a blue flash of fire push the *black* button. I'll jam these magnets with this magazine!"

Finch again squeezed himself gingerly behind the panel. Brieland and the passenger watched him tensely. The passenger moved uncertainly over to the wall buttons and put a shaking finger on the white one.

"Ready!" shouted Finch. The passenger jammed his finger against the white button. Finch jammed the magazine against the magnets at the bottom of the panel. There was a metallic rattle as the automatic starter clicked and Finch could hear the whir of the generator below. Suddenly the voltometer came to life and began to swing on the panel!

"Okay!" yelled Finch from behind the panel. "Now, go over to th' table and press the key!"

The passenger pressed the key and there was a loud buzzing. Finch slid carefully from behind the panel board, traded places with the passenger, and started tapping out code.

"Good enough," he grinned at Brieland, while the passenger sat on the wet deck and kept the magnets pressed in with the magazine.

"Better let me get our corrected position, Finch," Captain Brieland flung over his shoulder as he bolted out the door. A few moments before nine o'clock Brieland reappeared and handed Finch a scrap of paper. "Here you are, Finch!"

Finch began sending with a short spark gap, gradually increasing its width. He plugged in first on one tuning coil band and then on another . . . 300 meters . . . 800 . . . Finch tried them all. Then back again to the 600-band. Sometimes the antenna was grounded—sometimes he had no antenna at all! But still he went through the same routine ...S O S... KOXD, 12° N, 95° 5′ W, S O S!

Finch was numb, beat up and out on his feet, but he kept pounding the brass in earnest—braced against the table and the side of the radio shack. Several times the *Tashmoo* keeled over dangerously on her beam's end. Finch took a tighter grip on the table and tapped out her signal of distress, her call number, and her position. He glanced at his watch—10:15 A.M.—the appointed time for the "general alert"—the silent period when all ships' radiomen listen for distress calls!

The *Tashmoo's* signals were picked up by the Japanese freighter *Ginyo Maru*, the *President Hayes*, the *Point Sur*, and the tanker *Hadnot*. The *Hadnot* was closest to the stricken *Tashmoo*. The tanker's skipper changed course fifty-five degrees and shortly after the *Tashmoo* was seen nearly dead ahead.

The radioman on the *Hadnot* wondered what kind of a screwball the operator of the *Tashmoo* was. Here his ship was practically alongside the *Tashmoo*, and still the fool kept transmitting code and didn't have the courtesy to answer any questions—and with a signal so weak you'd think he was on the other side of the globe. But when Arthur Finch caught sight of the tanker he quietly withdrew from the radio shack and went below to the pantry for further orders.

With a heavy sea still running dangerously high, the tanker, after several futile attempts, finally got a line aboard the *Tashmoo*. Later in the day the long haul to Salina Cruz, on the Mexican coast, got underway. Finch, himself, stood the bow watch throughout the dark night, exchanging blinker signals between the *Tashmoo* and the *Hadnot* and relaying to the bridge. At thirty cents a month, Finch was, indeed, a handy man to have around!

After a four-day struggle through heavy seas and blinding rain squalls, the two ships finally reached the Salina Cruz breakwater on May 10.

Then came the most ironic twist of all! Once the *Tashmoo* was safely docked and her owners apprised of the close call that she, her crew, and passengers had had with Davy Jones's locker, they immediately sent out an amazing barrage of chicanery to this effect: That the *Tashmoo* was in every way a sound and most seaworthy vessel; that at no time could she have possibly been in very great danger; that she in all probability could have made port under her own power, etc., etc. They castigated the skipper of the *Hadnot* for having the audacity to tow her into Salina Cruz, and then claim salvage!

In utter disgust Finch quit the *Tashmoo* at Balboa and secured passage on another vessel bound for New York. Through the Panama Canal and all the way up the Atlantic coast, Arthur Finch nursed a "slow burn" he felt against the ship's owners back in Seattle. By the time his ship reached quarantine and finally docked in New York, Finch was boiling mad!

On the strength of his feelings, Finch sued the owners of the *Tashmoo* in the Admiralty Court, United States District Court, Eastern District of New York, at Brooklyn, for a share in the salvage award.

He filed his libel on July 12, 1928, and the case was tried before Judge Marcus B. Campbell, October 3 and 8, 1930, in Federal Court.

Finch was denied any compensation for his services. The Court wholeheartedly agreed that the action of the assistant steward had, without a doubt, saved the lives of passengers and crew aboard the *Tashmoo,* as well as the ship and her valuable cargo. *But* here's where the irregular contract licked Finch—because of that contract and the munificent salary of thirty cents a month, Finch was barred from collecting his share of the *Tashmoo's* salvage! It was all quite simple, he was told: He was a crew member of the *Tashmoo* and, as such, he could not sue for salvage award.

Arthur Finch took the decision in stride—in fact he accepted it with unusually good grace, under the circumstances. Later he enrolled in a school for radio operators, passed the exams with flying colors, and became a first-class marine radioman. There is nothing to indicate where he later sailed, or under which flag—but there is scant reason to believe he ever forgot the tramp freighter *Tashmoo,* his first message, or the anxious days in the Gulf of Tehuantepec!

SOURCES OF FACTUAL MATERIAL

Material for this story came from the transcript of the case of *Arthur Finch* vs. *S.S. "Tashmoo"* and her cargo, Admiralty No. 11084. The record shows that the libel was filed on July 12, 1928, and the case was tried before Judge Campbell in the United States District Court, Eastern District of New York, on October 3 and 8, 1930. The decree dismissing the libel was entered December 19, 1930.

VIII

GAMBLE AGAINST THE SEA

THOMAS HOGAN & SONS, stevedores, swung the last two hundred tons of cargo aboard the 495-foot, 10,000-ton British-owned S.S. *Vestris,* tied up at Pier 14, over on the Hoboken water front. It was nearly 3:00 P.M., Saturday, November 10, 1928. At 3:30 P.M. the Lamport & Holt cargo-passenger liner was scheduled to cast off and clear for South American ports, by way of the Barbados.

Late-comers scurried up the gangplanks, bag and baggage. A few score relatives and friends had gathered on the pierhead to watch the final loading of the British vessel, and to bid Godspeed to many of her 128 passengers lining the promenade deck rail.

High above them, Captain William J. Carey, fifty-nine-year-old master of the *Vestris,* slowly paced the bridge. Briefly he paused to watch the ship's noisy little steam winch snaking aboard the last of the deckload—three autocars, with a gross weight of nine tons—easing them down on the Number 1 cargo hatch top, just abaft the fo'c'sle, where fast-working longshoremen lashed them securely. Unhappy thoughts ran through Captain Carey's mind as he watched. He was uneasy about that last two hundred tons of cargo, wondering how far below her winter draft line those "extra" tons would send the *Vestris*. But he had no choice in the matter now—the decision had been made for him that morning at the final "loading conference" in the company's Hoboken office. Only that morning he himself had gotten back to New York from a holiday—too late to be in on the meeting at Hoboken.

They gave Carey the decision to load the extra two hundred tons when he finally arrived at the office. Somewhere between Pier 14 and Ambrose Lightship—where he'd drop the pilot—he knew that they'd expect him to pump the 290 tons of water from Number 2 ballast tank to compensate for the extra tonnage aboard the *Vestris,* bringing her back to her proper winter draft line of 26 feet, $3\frac{1}{4}$ inches, forward, and 27 feet, $2\frac{1}{4}$ inches, aft—plus an allowable four inches at sea.

Lamport & Holt had put him in a terribly tough spot, thought Carey grimly. If he pumped out Number 2 tank it might seriously affect the ratio of the ship's stability and trim. There was the new system of loading coal to be reckoned with, too— it put a total of eighty tons in the forward and aft trunkways on deck, *high* in the ship—then there was that last two hundred tons of cargo, *high* in the hold—plus the weight and height of the superstructure of a shelter-deck cargo-passenger vessel such as the *Vestris*. For a few moments Captain Carey pondered the problem. Should he unload the 290-ton ballast now, or gamble on fair weather to the Barbados and forget about pumping out Number 2 tank? He knew that, generally speaking, enough tonnage would be unloaded there to legitimately raise the draft line to a point of safe navigating—then, if foul weather set in, his ship would have more buoyancy. It was a tricky decision either way.

Below on the main deck, forward, Second Officer Leslie Watson handed the ship's clearance papers to a young clerk from the Lamport & Holt office.

"Here you are, son," nodded Watson. "Tell 'em back at the office that the draft line an' cargo weight are both signed in blank because the loading's not completed—they'll know what to do."

Captain Carey spotted the second officer from the bridge as the clerk left the ship and called to him to come up. A few moments later Carey met him in the chartroom.

"All the cargo aboard, Mr. Watson?"

"Aye, sir. They're securing the deckload now. Third Officer Welland will bring up the cargo weight shortly."

"Better get the draft reading, then—as soon as you can."

"Aye, sir."

It took the second officer only a matter of minutes on the pier to take off the draft figures, bow and stern. As he returned aboard the *Vestris* he met Chief Officer Frank Johnson at the forward gangway. He showed Johnson the slip of paper on which he had written the figures—26 feet, 6 inches, forward, and 27 feet, 11 inches, aft.

"It struck me she was getting too deep," was Johnson's only comment after he read the figures.

"Wonder what the Old Man will say?" observed Watson.

"What can he say," shrugged Johnson. "It's too

late now, but figuring about fifty-eight tons to the inch, this ship's mean average is $5\frac{1}{4}$ inches below her winter draft line—so she's somewhere about 290 tons overloaded, the capacity of Number 2 tank!"

With some misgivings in his mind the second officer went up to the chartroom and handed Captain Carey the slip of paper. When the captain saw the figures, Watson was surprised to hear him say, "That's all right. The office will fill in the draft."

Then Carey turned to the second officer.

"As you know, I've just returned from my annual holiday, so I wasn't around to check the stowing of the cargo. Who checked it in my absence?"

"First Officer Bolger and Third Officer Welland, sir. They checked all cargo hatches on their watches."

"Thank you, Mr. Watson—that's all."

Watson left the chartroom to give Third Officer Herbert Welland the draft figures to enter in the "scrap-log."

At 3:45 P.M. the deep-throated siren of the *Vestris* blasted out the warning, "All ashore that's going ashore!" After a few moments of breathless leave-takings between passengers and kin, the Lamport & Holt liner backed out into the waters of New York harbor and headed for the open roadstead under the guidance of the pilot. But Captain Carey issued no orders to pump the water from Number 2 tank—he had made his decision to gamble on fair weather to the Barbados!

Toward six o'clock they dropped the pilot at Ambrose Lightship and set a course S 15 E by the

standard compass—S 18 E by the wheelhouse compass—with a light wind from the northeast and a
smooth sea. By eight o'clock the weather closed
in; the northeast wind freshened, and the sea became choppy.

When Second Officer Watson came on duty at
midnight he caught scraps of conversation between
Carey and the Chief Officer Johnson on the bridge.
Watson was in the chartroom, checking the course.

"How are things on the weather deck, Mr. Johnson?" Watson heard Captain Carey ask Johnson.

"I've made the rounds, sir, and everything is secure," answered Johnson. Then he asked, "You
saw the draft figures this afternoon, didn't you?"

"Yes, Mr. Johnson—and be careful now about
how you put your draft in the log!"

The chief officer left the bridge and Captain
Carey was checking the clinometer when Watson
took over.

"Well, the clinometer shows no list at present,
Mr. Watson, but call me if there's any serious change
in the weather—I'll be in my cabin."

"Aye, sir."

The first real inkling of trouble aboard the *Vestris*
began at 2:00 A.M., Sunday. The seas were making
up rougher and the weather was getting worse. Captain Carey was lying fully dressed on a settee in
his quarters when Second Officer Watson called him.

"Heavy spray is coming over the foredeck, sir,
and the wind is stronger out of the nor'east—thought
you'd best know."

Carey jumped off the settee and both officers went
on the bridge. The clinometer showed a list of

4° to starboard. Captain Carey calmly peered out through the window, then turned to the second officer.

"Better make a tour of the weather deck and see if everything is secure, Mr. Watson. Report back to me."

"Aye, sir."

Watson found the wind blowing a half gale and the *Vestris* rolled to starboard as it struck her, showering him with heavy spray as he made his way along the slippery deck. So far he had found nothing wrong—all gear was shipshape, and the deckload was riding snugly. But as Watson continued his rounds, topside, the storm howled louder through the rigging, and the wireless antenna hummed ominously. A squall of driving rain hissed across the deck. The second officer turned up his collar against the shrieking wind and slanting rain, and he felt each blast careen the *Vestris* heavily to starboard as he beat his way back to the bridge companionway.

Drenched to the skin, Watson finally came onto the bridge and reported to Captain Carey.

"All's secure on the weather deck, sir—but the gale's increasing, with heavy rain."

"Thank you, Mr. Watson—you'd best turn in as soon as you're relieved and get some sleep—I'm afraid none of us will get much from now on!"

"Aye, sir."

All night the *Vestris* took a beating from the sea. By seven thirty Sunday morning the wind was roaring a near full gale out of the northeast. She was almost on her beam's end with every agonizing roll to starboard—and each time she was slower righting herself. The clinometer showed a variable 5° to 7° starboard list—and sometimes the needle touched 10°!

Meanwhile, Third Officer Herbert Welland, unable to sleep on his off watch, prepared to relieve Chief Officer Johnson and take over the eight to twelve noon watch. For nearly three hours Welland had watched the ship's action in the gale. Each time she rolled he became more and more apprehensive of the situation. Unable to stand the uncertainty any longer, the third officer went up to the wireless shack and handed Chief Operator Mike O'Loughlin a radio message to the weather bureau at Washington.

"Don't look so good for us, does it, Herb?" said O'Loughlin glumly as he pounded the key.

"There're a helluva lot of places where I'd rather be right now!" Welland grinned wryly.

Minutes later an answer crackled in from the Washington weather bureau: "HEAVY NE GALE —FORCE 7 ON BEAUFORT SCALE!"

"This is it, Mike!" was the third officer's laconic comment. He left hurriedly to relieve Johnson.

At nine o'clock Sunday morning, Chief Engineer James Adams was checking to see how the coal was running from the bunkers on the upper deck. As he started along the cross alleyway, he found water pouring in from the port half door (where coal had been loaded before the *Vestris* left Hoboken). It was sloshing about a foot deep across the alleyway, from port to starboard. Adams rushed down to the engine room to see if the water was coming through. When he got below, the fourth engineer ran up to him.

"Trouble with the starboard ash ejector, Chief!" said the fourth engineer breathlessly. "Won't eject ashes—and it's shooting in a helluva lot of sea water!"

Adams followed the fourth engineer and found the bilges full of water and overflowing onto the engine-room floor. The chief engineer tried to eject ashes, but instead water poured back from the sea. Then he gave orders to close off the ash ejector, and no fires were cleaned out after this was done. Adams then had the door to the coaling chute closed to prevent coal washing through. The main engines were running at full speed at this time, and he took steps to pump out the stokehold and engine-room bilges by bringing into use the general service pump, which normally had a capacity of ninety tons an hour, but on this occasion was reduced to forty tons. The chief engineer managed to get the level of the water down for a time, but it began to increase soon afterwards.

A haggard Captain Carey came on the bridge about twelve noon.

"How is it going, Mr. Welland?"

"Not too good, sir. Washington reports Force 7 gale, nor'east, and the ship won't answer her helm, either. We've kept her hard-a-port, sir, but her head keeps veering to port! I had 'em check the telemotor steering gear—they report nothing's wrong with it!"

"Signal the engine room to go half speed on the starb'rd engines—maybe that'll give her a better chance of staying on course."

"Aye, sir!"

Still the *Vestris* kept yawing off course to port like some derelict windjammer without a helm.

"What do you make of it, Mr. Welland?" asked Carey grimly.

"Could be the pressure of the gale against the port side of the ship, sir—and the high superstructure."

"Or too damn'd much top weight!" exploded Captain Carey sharply. "What th' hell's th' use of kidding ourselves! In our own minds we all know what's wrong—this ship's overloaded, Welland—two hundred tons overloaded! An' th' company didn't tell me 'til it was too late to fight against it! Now I must gamble *our* lives—and the lives of a hundred an' twenty-eight passengers—against this sea!"

The third officer and the helmsman, Quartermaster Lionel Licorice, stared curiously at Carey as he finished his hot tirade against conditions aboard the *Vestris*. He well knew what they must be thinking—of his disloyalty to the company!

"Sorry, gentlemen—I'm afraid I let things get away from me just then," said Carey with a weak smile, adding gruffly, "but see to it that my outburst of temper goes no further—that's an order!"

"Aye, aye, sir!" they nodded meekly.

Seconds later Second Officer Watson came on the bridge to relieve Welland. Quartermaster Licorice was still fighting the wheel to keep the *Vestris* on any sort of a course. Captain Carey peered through a bridge window as the ship took a heavy sea over the foredeck, flinging gray water and spray onto the deckload of automobiles on Number 1 cargo hatch, and along the weather deck, amidship. The gusty force of the hurricane on the port quarter rolled the *Vestris* heavily, and she wallowed with a 5° to 10° list to starboard. She never came back upright—the clinometer needle holding at 7°.

Between squalls Captain Carey was able to head her into the wind to ease her starboard list—only to have her fall off by the head when another squall hit her. Suddenly Carey turned to Watson.

"Stop the engines, Mr. Watson!" ordered Carey. "We'll let her go into the trough of the sea, hove to, and see what effect that'll have on her!"

Even then the *Vestris* didn't come fully upright, and she labored hard in the rough waters around her—and the clinometer needle still hovered between 8° and 10°!

Off watch at 4:00 P.M., Watson met Chief Officer Johnson on his way to relieve him. There was a grim look on Johnson's face.

"She's leaking water pretty badly through the starboard coal port into the cross alleyway, Watson," he said tightly. "Better get the carpenter to deal with it before it gets worse!"

"Aye, sir—immediately!"

For two solid hours the raging sea played with the *Vestris*—as a cat might toy with a dying mouse. It tossed and wallowed the 10,000-ton Lamport & Holt vessel in its boiling waters . . . it rolled the ship so that the starboard beam of the mooring deck was awash . . . it smashed in a window of Cabin F on the starboard quarter, drenching the cabin with several inches of water and chasing the occupants to a drier cabin on the port quarter. Not satisfied with its handiwork, the sea momentarily buried the ship's stern under tons of water and flooded the second-class galley about six o'clock —putting out the galley-stove fire and sending scared cooks and galley hands scurrying to safety.

Third Officer Welland rushed aft to learn what had happened and found the second-class galley in a sodden shambles. Most of the water had sloshed through the scuppers, but Welland was grimly aware that the foot or two that remained would never get away while the ship's 8° list to starboard held. This thing was getting serious.

"Bail out an' clean up as best you can!" was all the third officer could advise the galley staff. Then he added a significant warning. "An' for God's sake don't alarm the passengers!"

But the angry sea soon tired of playing with the *Vestris*—as the cat tires of bedeviling the poor mouse. It moved in, now, with terrible swiftness, massing a series of gigantic forty-to-fifty-foot combers — whipped up by the increasing fury of the North Atlantic hurricane — relentlessly smashing them against the ship's port quarter with fiendish relish.

The first great wave struck the *Vestris* amidship at seven thirty that Sunday evening—just as the diners were settling down to their "fish course" in the First Cabin dining saloon. With the tremendous force of its massed attack, the forty-foot wave bodily pushed the 495-foot vessel over to starboard. Diners, stewards, waiters, furniture, and crockery—all went by the board, stumbling and reeling, sliding and crashing down across the heavily slanted deck of the dining saloon. Second Officer Watson—who had taken this time to eat—had barely regained his footing when a lesser mass of water lurched the *Vestris* again—and again she went on her beam's end! Then she settled further to starboard, never fully recovering from the giant sledge-hammer-like blows of a treacherous sea.

Miraculously, no one was killed. Still more miraculous, none was seriously injured! There was no panic. Silently, passengers picked themselves up and stumbled to their cabins, stunned by the cruel power of the sea. Silently, the waiters and stewards began clearing the dining saloon. Many, hailing from the Barbados, prayed to their voodoo gods for protection.

Up forward on the slanting deck of the *Vestris* tons of sea water cascaded over the deckload of autocars and tumbled across the cargo-hatch tops, colliding with the swirling seas that rushed inboard on the starboard beam. The ship's massive cargo derricks swung in crazy arcs as the seventy-five-mile-an-hour gale whipped through the whining guy lines, and the steel beams creaked and groaned in their chocks. A lashing on the deckload snapped with a sharp pistol-like report—a sudden pitch of the *Vestris,* as a heavy sea came over the foredeck, sent one of the autocars headlong through the fo'c'sle bulkhead with a splintering crash. . . .

"Th' bloody deckload's busted loose!" yelled a sailor, jumping free of his bunk in the fo'c'sle. " 'It th' nails f'r y'r lives, boys—th' sea's comin' in!"

For a brief moment heavy seas swirled up to

the bridge as Quartermaster Elton Clarke, a burly
Barbados Negro, clung to the wheel, fighting to
keep it hard-a-starboard. Third Officer Welland,
on the eight-to-twelve midnight watch, saw part
of the forward port rail carry away, tearing two
lifeboats from their chocks and smashing them into
the boiling waters. At the moment the *Vestris*
wallowed helplessly in the trough of the sea, heading southeast, with a northeast gale increasing to
Force 10. The clinometer needle gyrated from a
10° to a 15° list to starboard. At every roll the
Vestris put her mooring deck under water, and
Captain Carey ordered half speed on both the port
and starboard engines with the hope that the *Vestris*
could gain a little seaway in the storm and head
into the seas.

Down in the stokehold of the engine room all
hell broke loose when the two waves struck the port
quarter and staggered the ship. Caught by surprise,
several firemen were hurled into the coal bunker.
Others fought to keep the boilers fired and the
steam up to two hundred pounds pressure. It was
a terrific struggle. Many of the stokers secured themselves with lines to prevent the dangerous possibility of hurtling into the starboard bunkers when
the ship rolled. When the *Vestris* had lurched
heavily, the pressure of the sea had torn away the
seal from the disabled starboard ash-ejector opening—shooting water ten to twelve feet in the air
and filling the engine room to a depth of several
feet. Water streamed down from the port side,
from badly strained hull plates. The carpenter with

a gang managed to seal off the ash ejector again, though water still seeped through.

Grimly Chief Engineer Adams and his ten assistant engineers realized the dire emergency of the situation down there in the "black hole"! At all costs the engines and the dynamos must be kept going! By ten o'clock Adams had all three pumps working at full pressure, drawing water from the bilges and the engine room, and reducing the level about two feet. But it was a losing battle at best and the *Vestris* still continued her heavy list to starboard!

At midnight Second Officer Watson came on the bridge to relieve Welland. He automatically glanced at the clinometer—the needle now pointed to a 15° list! A gray-faced, haggard-looking Captain Carey was talking earnestly to Welland when Watson took over.

"As soon as you're off watch, Mr. Welland," he was saying, "check all possible parts of the ship for incoming water! Particularly the cross alleyway —we're in a very serious position!"

"Aye, sir!"

An hour later Welland reported to Carey on the bridge. There was a grave look on the third officer's face.

"There's four or five feet of water in the alleyway, sir!" His words held an ominous meaning.

"Then for God's sake muster all hands an' bail out the alleyway!" ordered Carey.

"Aye, sir!"

For an awful moment Carey peered helplessly out through the bridge window, supporting himself against a rail of the careening bridge. Dimly he saw the havoc done by the boarding seas and the howling, relentless hurricane—now a full gale, Force 10 on the Beaufort's scale! Salt spray spun against the windows. The clinometer wavered between 15° to 20° at every roaring gust! Slowly the weary captain turned to Second Officer Watson.

"If those pumps are working, Mr. Watson, why isn't the ship coming back to her proper keel?"

"Shifting coal t' starb'rd, perhaps," ventured the second officer.

"More likely the top-weight cargo that never should have been aboard!" corrected Carey acidly.

By four o'clock Monday morning the *Vestris* had increased her list to 20°—reducing her freeboard on the starboard quarter by ten feet! The wind went down between squalls, and Captain Carey again tried to get her head around to the seas. But though the wind went down, the sea did not—and the *Vestris* never headed into the gale. In disgust Carey ordered the engines stopped, and let her lay there —a "dead" ship that wouldn't answer her helm, wallowing in the trough of an angry, malicious sea.

Several times during the night Captain Carey had had Watson go below to the engine room to check with Chief Engineer Adams as to how the pumps were working. At 4:00 A.M. the second officer reported back to Carey that the pumps were holding the water in the engine room and bilges, and that it had even gone down a foot or two.

"Well, if the water's going down, then what in hell's increasing our list?" blazed Carey. "I'm seeing Adams myself, Mr. Watson—carry on up here until you're relieved!"

"Aye, sir!"

Captain Carey was stunned by the conditions he found down in the engine room, but he managed to control himself.

"Just how bad are things down here, Adams?"

"Pretty bad, Captain!"

The chief engineer then showed Carey the water coming into the engine room from the bulkhead and deckhead.

"And what's more, Captain, I'm going to have to shut off the starboard boiler!"

"Why is that?" asked Carey sharply.

"Because, see—" Adams showed the captain where the plates had lifted on the starboard side of the ship, "—it's the pressure of the water that makes 'em lift—and it'll be next to impossible to fire the starboard furnaces!"

Then the captain pointed out a place on the starboard side where water poured down from an unknown source hidden by the coal bunkers above them.

"Where's this water coming from, Adams?"

"Rooms above, I guess, Captain."

"Can't you do something about clearing it out?"

"Comes in faster than it can be pumped out!"

"Just what is up there that would cause all this water?"

"Could be the main lavatory waste pipe, broken —or it might come from a broken scupper pipe!"

"Then for God's sake, Adams, order the carpenter to find the break an' seal it up!" blasted Carey.

"And another thing—start pumping out the Number 2 ballast tank! I purposely left it full, thinking it might help the ship's stability an' trim—but it didn't —so we've got a 20° list right now, and with 290 tons of ballast out of the ship it might help matters! We're in a bad way, Adams!"

A vicious sea plunged and rolled the *Vestris* as it moved in for the "kill." The lifeless ship—like a drifting waterlogged spar—recovered slowly from each onslaught of the massive waves that deluged her port quarter. An eighty-mile-an-hour Force 10 gale, teamed up with the angry sea in a howling roar out of the northeast, combined forces to anni- hilate this steel hulk built by man—like a pair of jungle beasts setting upon a common prey.

Dawn grayed the tumbling waters as Captain Carey grimly watched his helpless ship being ham- mered by the merciless sea and wind—saw her fore- deck dip deep under that sea, rising slower each time, heavy with tons of gray-green water. Im- patiently he swung the engine-room control lever to half speed on both engines . . . hoping against hope!

Around seven thirty Monday morning, Chief Engineer Adams climbed wearily up to the bridge —since eight o'clock Sunday morning he and his ten assistant engineers had been on continuous duty. For that matter, so had Captain Carey and his offi- cers. Carey faced the chief engineer.

"Well?"

"Number 2 tank's pumped out, Captain, but she doesn't seem to come up any!"

"I'm afraid she hasn't, Adams. "What about the steam?"

"Up to four o'clock it was at full pressure—two hundred pounds. It's under 180 now, but if we can keep her there we can keep the engines turning, an' mebbe we can save th' ship—*if we can keep the steam up!*"

"Keep going, Adams—and keep that steam going, too. You can see for yourself what we're up against —and we're going t' need those dynamos, too!"

Things came to a head that Monday morning when Third Officer Welland reported to Captain Carey on the bridge at eight—and, as misfortune after misfortune piled up, it began to look as if Lamport & Holt, Captain Carey—and the *Vestris*— were destined to lose their gamble against the sea!

"How is the bailing coming along in the alleyway, Mr. Welland?" asked Carey sharply.

"Sixty men have been bailing since four o'clock, sir, and up to now they haven't made a dent—the water still holds between four an' five feet!" was Welland's stunning answer.

"Where in hell is it all coming from!" demanded Carey. "Have you made a complete check of all possible sources of inflow?"

"Aye, sir! The half door of the starboard coal port still leaks, but not that much. I couldn't get down the hatches as they were full, but I listened carefully and there was no sound of water there. I checked all the holds and still couldn't hear any sound of water!"

Captain Carey leaned wearily against the wheelhouse door—there was no one at the helm in the wheelhouse, and the wheel had been lashed in a stationary position during the night. Carey rubbed a moist hand across his forehead.

"God of love!" he murmured desperately. Then, suddenly alert, he turned to the third officer. "Mr. Welland, try to get our position by wireless so I can send out a 'Stand by' signal to all vessels near us! Order all lifeboats prepared for lowering! Hurry!"

"Aye, sir!"

Up in the wireless shack Welland found James MacDonald, second operator, on duty.

"We're in a helluva tough spot, Jim! Skipper says t' get our position by radio—we sure can't get it by takin' sights."

"Only possible chance is Tutterton station in Jersey, Herb—I'll try t' buzz 'em, short wave. Our long-wave set went haywire last night—salt spray got into the insulators an' she's blotto!"

Hanging onto the table in the crazily tilted wireless shack, MacDonald pounded away on the key. Both he and Welland prayed that the signal would get through. Eternity seemed to pass in those few minutes before an answer crackled back: "You are Approximately 275 Miles East of the Virginia Capes —Good Luck!"

Welland quickly scribbled the ship's bearings on a scrap of paper and hurried back to the bridge. Back in the chartroom the third officer pin-pointed their approximate position on the chart as First Officer Bolger came through the door. As navigating officer, Bolger studied the chart with Welland.

"Here's our position, Mr. Bolger—radioed from

Tutterton. Best we could get on short wave. Couldn't get any other confirmations! Makes our approximate position in latitude 37° 35′ North and our longitude 71° 8′ West. That's th' best we can do!"

"That's okay. Thanks!"

Captain Carey s t e p p e d into the chartroom, glanced hurriedly at the chart—then turned to Bolger.

"Try to get a message over to all ships in th' vicinity to stand by in case of necessity—the ship's got a 25° list right now! If Adams can't hold steam in the boilers we're going to need help, and fast!"

Bolger flew out of the chartroom on a dead run for the wireless shack. Welland started to follow him. Carey put a hand on his shoulder.

"Mr. Welland, get a gang together and jettison those meat chains on the starboard side—that'll be at least ten or fifteen tons we'll be rid of—then get those cars on Number 1 hatch over the side!"

"Aye, sir!" and the third officer swung out of the chartroom on the run.

The wind had moderated, but the sea still rolled the *Vestris* heavily—and water swept the decks as Welland's gang managed to heave the massive meat chains overside. It killed another hour to get one of the motorcars over the starboard rail—the second car stuck on the rail and hung there. Meanwhile, a number of other seamen—under the bo'sun's direction—were uncovering the lifeboats, checking their equipment, and readying them for lowering —if and when the order came!

Below, passengers were still in their cabins—many

of them there since the crucial lurch Sunday night. Serving regular meals was out of the question— all galleys had been flooded the night before, and the galley-stove fires were cold. Stewards managed coffee and sandwiches—nothing more!

Under First Officer Bolger's orders, Chief Operator Mike O'Loughlin pounded out the C Q stand-by signal—that was 8:30 A.M. But Carey delayed the S O S, hoping against hope that Adams could keep up the steam pressure in the boilers, get the engines started, and save the ship. It was just another losing gamble against the sea, because up on the bridge the clinometer needle was already swinging between a 25° to 30° list to starboard! In desperation, Carey got word to O'Loughlin to put an S O S on the air in a hurry! But precious time had been lost—it was now 9:55 A.M.

Down in the engine room, steam pressure had dropped to ninety pounds. About ten o'clock a dozen stokers scurried off the job and scrambled up the steel ladders to the decks above.

"Where in hell d' y' think you're going?" roared Chief Engineer Adams after them.

"Y' can't stand on y'r head t' fire them boilers, Mr. Adams!" one stoker yelled back. "This damn'd tub's sinkin', an' you know it! We're gettin' t' hell out!"

"But th' dynamos, you fools!" railed Adams. "Without steam there'll be no electric power—an' without power there'll be no wireless to summon rescue ships t' save your own stinkin' hides! Think o' that before y' turn tail!"

The last three or four stokers turned back sheepishly and joined the chief engineer and his assistants. These ten engineers had already stripped to their waists and were firing the careening boilers in a valiant attempt to keep the dynamos going!

At 10:40 A.M. a message from Lamport & Holt crackled through to Carey: "Wire us immediately your trouble!" From Carey to Lamport at 11:00 A.M.: "Hove to from noon yesterday (Sunday), during night developed 32° list, starboard decks under water, lying on beam ends, impossible proceed anywhere, sea moderately rough."

O'Loughlin repeated the S O S at 11:04 A.M.—following it with this additional message: "Please come at once—we need immediate assistance!"

Acknowledgments filled the air in rapid order! The *Yankee Arrow* would arrive at 8:00 P.M. . . . The *Giorgio Ohlson* said she was thirty-five miles away . . . the *San Juan* said she'd get there by 4:30 P.M. . . . the *Santa Barbara* expected to be with the *Vestris* at 7:00 P.M. . . . the French tanker *Miriam*, 4:30 A.M. . . . *American Shipper* would be there at 7:30 P.M. . . . the *Berlin* at 10:00 P.M. . . . the *Ohio Maru* would be due at 4:00 P.M. . . . and the U.S.S. *Wyoming* reported she'd be there at 2:00 A.M. Tuesday! Lamport to *Vestris,* at 11:27 A.M.: "US DESTROYER *DAVIS* PROCEEDING TO YOUR ASSISTANCE."

A half an hour later O'Loughlin sent out the last tense message: "Abandoning ship!" As he tapped out the last word an electronic engineer rushed breathlessly into the water-soaked wireless shack.

"Power's out, Mike!" he yelled. "Engine room's flooded! Better get outa here!"

The last hours of the *Vestris* were bitter ones for Captain Carey. By midday the bridge clinometer showed nearly a 35° list, and as she rolled Carey saw the water come onto the forward well deck. He called Second Officer Watson who was in the chartroom with First Officer Bolger, checking the positions of the various rescue ships that had picked up O'Loughlin's distress calls. Watson steadied himself along the bridge railing as he reported to the captain. Both men's faces were grim with the dire seriousness of the situation.

"Have the port boats lowered immediately, Mr. Watson!" ordered Carey. "See to it that every last passenger is gotten on deck, and is equipped with a life jacket! Follow the rule, 'Women and children first,' though God knows there are plenty of life-boats for all! Carry on!"

"Aye, sir!"

Left alone on the bridge, Carey could almost feel his ship slipping from under him. Bitter thoughts gripped him. Why had the company made him fight a losing gamble against the sea? Why had they overloaded the *Vestris* so that there was no buoyancy left in her? Why did Lamport & Holt captains always have to lie about the true draft lines of their ships—or stop between Pier 14 and Ambrose Lightship to pump out ballast tanks until draft lines were at the proper marks? Had he, personally, been partially guilty for this gamble against the sea? Had he been too late sending out an S O S, hoping—or gambling—that in the end he could save his ship by his own skill—and the skill of his officers? One last voyage—*this voyage*—

and he was to have become Commodore of the line! A hard, bitter laugh escaped his lips . . . *this voyage*—to end an honorable lifetime of service at sea in tragic disaster!

Like a man thrust into an unbelievably horrible nightmare, Captain Carey moved with trancelike precision down from the bridge to the boat deck. Outwardly steel-nerved and calm, Carey was inwardly stunned by the sudden worsening conditions aboard the careening *Vestris*. Instinctively he issued orders, cooly standing by to see them carried out. Mechanically he watched Second Officer Watson's men launching the port lifeboats. He saw them lower boats 4, 6, 8, and 10 . . . saw the Barbados Negro stewards gamely sticking by their duty—guiding passengers up on deck from below . . . saw them adjust life jackets and explain to each passenger how to reach his assigned boat . . . saw women and children being led up over the port rail and down ladders along the slippery side of the ship to the boats.

Carey felt his ship quiver and heel over at a steeper angle. Number 8 boat went down by the falls for a bit, then fetched up on the rivet-studded side of the port quarter. A haze of tears blinded Carey momentarily as he saw nearly a dozen women and children with life jackets in the half-capsized boat. The captain rushed to the second officer's side, helping him to free the stuck lifeboat—trying to lower it further, trying to clear the slanting side of the ship. One fall caught up, one loosened too soon, upending Number 8! The screaming women and children jumped into the sea, but one or two boats in the vicinity picked them up. Carey and the second officer breathed a sigh of relief.

"Mr. Watson, give Mr. Johnson a hand with the starboard boats!" ordered Carey.

Watson climbed up the side of the ship, then followed the grab lines that had been rigged across the heavily slanted deck, slipping and stumbling along with difficulty. Johnson was launching Number 9 boat.

"Get th' plug in th' boat, Mr. Watson!" yelled the chief officer as Watson came alongside him. "I think we can safely get her into the water, but it's going to be tough to get passengers over here from the port side—and time's running out!"

Again pulling on the grab lines, Watson made it back to the port side just as Second Steward Duncan was struggling to help three women to the starboard boats.

"Give me a hand with these ladies, here, Mr. Watson!" pleaded the steward. "Maybe you can convince 'em their chances are better if they get t' th' starb'rd boats—I can't!"

"Come, now, ladies!" cajoled the second officer. "The steward's right—see—all the starboard boats are safely in the water—and with a lot o' people in 'em!"

"But the water, sir!" cried one. "I—I'm afraid!"

"I won't jump into that water!" screamed the second belligerently.

"I—I think we'd better go back!" whined the third.

It took Watson and the steward twenty precious minutes to get the three badly scared women back up the grab line to the port rail. By then it was nearly too late. There were dull rumblings from the engine room, below—black smoke, white steam, and fiery sparks belched out of the ship's stack.

"Get those women down here, Mr. Watson!" shouted Carey. "There's no time to lose!"

"Aye, sir!"

Captain Carey balanced himself against the canting ship's side and the tilted lifeboat, his long black officer's coat belted tightly around him, and his iron-gray hair blowing in the wind. He wore no life jacket—he'd been too busy to bother with one, Carey watched Watson and Second Steward Duncan maneuvering the three women down one of the Jacob's-ladders hanging over the ship's side, to the Number 8 boat. As they came closer Carey forced a thin smile.

"You are brave women!" he said quietly. "We'll help you into this boat, and you'll be safely away from the ship!"

The two officers and the steward managed to get the scared, trembling women into the lifeboat.

"You, steward, will row off the instant Mr. Watson and I slide the boat free," said Carey in an undertone—adding grimly, "I see a number of bobbing heads out there—pick up as many people as you can!"

The second steward nodded, nimbly climbing into Number 8. For a brief moment the *Vestris* lay still in the sea. With the davit lines free, the two officers pushed and shoved the boat. It moved slowly, teetered briefly, then freed itself and slid into the water—clear of the doomed ship.

But the sea wasn't through with the *Vestris*—yet! Slowly she settled deeper—the water washing deeper over her slanting side. A sudden heavy roll to starboard sent the ship's list to 45° . . . then 70°! For a split second the port side of the *Vestris* was nearly flush with the pounding waves. Carey and the second mate clung to each other for support. The sea swirled around their legs. Tears coursed down Carey's care-lined cheeks.

"My God, my God, I'm not to blame for this!"

Suddenly the *Vestris* again rolled heavily . . . this time to 90° . . . started down by the head.

"Jump for it, Watson!" ordered Carey. "She's going fast!"

"But you have no life jacket. . . ."

"Never mind me!" roared Carey angrily. "Jump! That's an order!"

The *Vestris* gave a tremendous lurch and both officers were thrown into the sea. Watson surfaced quickly in his life jacket. But when he had cleared his eyes of salt water, the *Vestris*—and Captain Carey —were gone. Only an angry swirl of water marked their going.

For a time the second officer swam through floating wreckage in a vain search for Carey. Then, with a sudden sickening realization, he knew that Carey had successfully carried out a plan he must have formulated during those last terrible hours of the *Vestris*—choosing, rather, to go down with his ship! Still sick at heart Watson continued to swim around, occasionally clinging to bits of wreckage to look out for struggling passengers who needed help. Close by he spied a woman clutching a hatch grill. Pushing pieces of debris ahead of him, Watson helped bolster up the woman until Number 11 boat finally picked them from the water.

Darkness spread over the rough sea. The dozen tiny lifeboats pitched and rolled. Sudden cries of anguish cut sharply through the night's blackness from a swamped boat whose survivors battled against death! The terrible night became predawn morning before the searchlight of the first-arrived rescue ship raked the stormy skies. The lights of the French tanker *Miriam* beamed warmly across a dreary wind-swept sea at 4:30 A.M., Tuesday, November 13. After her came the United States Shipping Board's *American Shipper* . . . the North German Lloyd liner *Berlin* . . . and the U.S.S. *Wyoming!*

Rescue operations were swift and sure as dawn finally broke. Out of 328 passengers, officers, and crew of the ship's company that sailed with the *Vestris* from Hoboken that bright Saturday afternoon of November 10, 1928, the four rescue ships found only 213 survivors—60 passengers and 153 officers and crew! Only 10 of 33 women survived —no children were saved!

A great gamble against the deep had been lost . . . and the capricious sea had collected its "winnings"!

SOURCES OF FACTUAL MATERIAL

This story was written from the vivid testimony at the (British) Board of Trade inquiry into the loss of Lamport & Holt's passenger-freighter *Vestris* off the Virginia capes, November 12, 1928. *The Journal of Commerce* (Liverpool) published the Board of Trade report, August, 1929.

IX

WHALER BOUND FOR HELL

AN EARLY-MORNING, marrow-chilling mist settled in over Edgartown harbor that gray day of December 15, 1822, and wreathed a thin, wispy shroud around the whaler *Globe* as she tugged impatiently at the lines holding her close to her pierhead. This was to be her big day! This was her sailing day—and that of her twenty-seven officers and men—bound out for a three-year whaling expedition to the South Seas! And there were even wistful dreams of a twenty- or twenty-five-hundred-barrel haul of sperm oil!

Infamous as many of the whalers were in those days, the *Globe* was far from the worst. She was a sturdy three-boat whaling ship, well found and Nantucket-owned from keel to truck. Her owners, all merchants of Nantucket Island and Martha's Vineyard, had heavy stakes in her and they saw to it that she was Nantucket-manned. Every man jack of her officers and crew were "native-born"—from her master, the sea-wise veteran, thirty-eight-year-old, Captain Thomas Worth, down to the last young apprentice.

Seasoned seamen and raw lads scampered up shroud lines to royal and t'gallant yards. Old hands and apprentices scurried over the decks, getting gear shipshape. The last cask of fresh water was hoisted aboard and lashed in place on deck. Coopers' supplies were shipped on board and stowed below—stave shooks and iron hoops and wooden heads for those dreamed-of twenty-five hundred barrels!

Captain Worth stood atop the roundhouse, aft, buttoned to his chin in a dark blue greatcoat, glancing sharply aloft as men and boys broke out canvas on her yards.

Slowly the half-frozen t'gallants and royals unreefed and fluttered, ghostlike, against the dead gray of a winter fog as they were sheeted home by many hands purple with cold.

At just the right moment, Captain Worth's bull voice bellowed through cupped hands to his first mate, William Beetle, who stood abaft the tryworks in the waist of the ship.

"Cast off your lines, Mr. Beetle!" boomed the *Globe's* master.

"Aye, sir!" responded the mate as he leaned over the starboard rail and gave the command that loosed taut lines and sent them with a whipping splash into the water, while young deckhands, fore and aft, went a-scrambling to haul them aboard.

The narrow cobblestone lane leading to the pierhead should have been lined with the people of Edgartown, down to see their kinfolk off. There should have been roaring "hurrahs" for these home-town boys—many of them, young fellows hardly out of their teens—getting their first taste of an honest-to-God whaler's voyage—there should have been a gala throng on hand wishing 'em, "Greasy Luck!"

But there wasn't!

Guarded whisperings had been heard about town the past fortnight—ugly rumors that all was not well with the *Globe's* present venture! Broad hints had been dropped in the port's square that spars and rigging weren't as sound as they should be for a three-year voyage! Townspeople were rankled by the owners' alleged laxity and vented their displeasure by cancelling farewell ceremonies.

A handful of old salts stood by on the pierhead as the *Globe's* lines were cast off—hands deep in pockets, mufflers tightened against the raw, gray morning. They stood there, puffing stubby black pipes—clacking old tongues and solemnly shaking white heads. With watery eyes they watched green youngsters scramble uncertainly up and down slippery rigging. Perhaps memories were jogged back to their own apprentice days—perhaps a few remembered time served on "Old Ironsides"!

Moments later the *Globe* swung free of the pierhead and out into the harbor as steady air out of the nor'west bellied her t'gallants and royals with a noise like the cracking of a dozen dueling pistols, sending her on her way to South Pacific whaling grounds.

No shouted farewells, nor words of Godspeed, came over the water that December day as the *Globe* slid silently beyond the harbor into the thinning fog. The boys felt the emptiness of that silence, too. There was something ominous in it. Even the officers felt it!

"Sally'd have come," complained Second Mate John Lumbard to Nathaniel Fisher, the *Globe's* third mate, as they stood in the waist of the ship,

" 'cept her ma 'n' pa were dead set against it—all because of some damn'd rumor monger!"

Hardly had the hands aloft set the top mains'l and mains'l sheets when the ominous sound of splitting canvas and splintering wood rent the air—a badly cracked mizzen crossjack let go and came tumbling down, bringing with it the mizzen sail amid a tangle of gear and rigging and narrowly missing several seamen! Lumbard and Fisher ducked under the deck of the tryhouse.

"Mr. Beetle!" roared Captain Worth from atop the roundhouse. "Change course immediately! Turn about an' put back t' port!"

"Don't like th' looks o' this!" murmured Stephen Kidder to his brother Peter as they balanced themselves astride the mains'l yard.

"Aye, nor me neither!" agreed his brother.

Old hands glanced askance at the tangled debris dangling crazily against the mizzenmast, then they looked at each other and shook their heads bewilderedly. Was this why their own townspeople—aye, their own flesh and blood—cancelled the send-off? Was this a portentous evil omen? Another of those ill-starred ventures, perhaps? Were those old wives' tales they'd heard around town more than just rumor? A hell of a fine start, this—was the grim thought in their sailor minds—a fine start, indeed!

Back in port, it took nearly four days to fashion a new crossjack, refit a new sail, and hoist 'em both to the mizzenmast. On the dawn tide of December 19, the *Globe* cleared Edgartown, then dropped anchor at Holmes' Hole that same afternoon for want of favorable winds. During the night a fresh breeze sprung from the northwest. At dawn Captain Worth ordered the anchor up and the *Globe* moved out slowly under royals and t'gallants—then squared away to sea under a full spread of canvas.

A strained tautness had built up among the crew during the hours the *Globe* laid in at Holmes' Hole, partly fostered by the ever-present superstitious lore of sailors, the dour significance of the smashed crossjack, and the gloomy fact that no kinfolk were on hand to see them off! Grumblings and mutterings among certain of the fo'c'sle hands made for an edgy tension and an almost occult fear of the unknown!

A full gale roared out of the northwest, bent on celebrating New Year's, 1823, by spanking the *Globe* through heavy seas and clearing the webs of superstition out of the sailors' minds.

"All hands turn to!" barked Third Mate Fisher, officer of the first watch, bobbing his head in at the fo'c'sle hatch. "Gotta reef sail! Look lively, now!"

Half asleep, the second and third watch men stumbled up the fo'c'sle companionway ladder and tumbled out onto the slippery deck. A cold rain fell desolately. Already Fisher's first watch gang were in the mainmast rigging, bending main royal and t'gallants and clewing them to the yards.

Samuel Comstock and Gilbert Smith, the two boat steerers—ratings comparable to naval c.p.o.'s —raced forward from the captain's companionway, aft, and took charge of their respective watches.

"Up into th' for'm'st riggin' y' lan'lubbin' bastuds o' th' second watch!" bellowed Comstock in an ugly mood. "Look lively—y' cow-eyed sons o' Sat'n! Reef in th' fore royal an' foretops'l!"

"Th' Dev'ls aboard 'n' hell's a-raisin'!" loudly mocked seaman Holden Henman as he scampered up the forem'st ratlines.

"Stow y'r lip, y' goddam'd scupper scum!" raged Comstock. "An' git t' hell up that riggin'!"

"Mister Comstock!" blasted Captain Worth, catching the boat steerer's last bit of blasphemy as he came on deck, "B'lay that kind o' talk on this vessel —'t ain't necessary—y' understand!"

"Aye, sir!" snapped Comstock in a surly tone, though he continued to berate his men bitterly.

The wild wind slammed against sharp-cracking canvas and screamed angrily through vibrant shroud lines. The whaler heeled, then slapped her blunt nose headlong into black mountains of heavy water, cascading luminous spray over her bows and forepeak as her bowsprit slashed at sizzling combers.

"Mister Fisher—trim more canvas!" roared Captain Worth through cupped hands. "Keep her a-fore th' wind, under close reef'd main tops'l an' fores'l!"

"Aye, aye, sir!" roared back the third mate against the howling gale. Then to the third watch officer he said, "Mister Smith—send y'r boys aloft an' lend a hand t' Comstock's men—lively now!"

The *Globe* scudded well before the shrieking storm. The wind was fair and while seas threatened to board her at times, her helmsman manfully held her before it. Forty-eight hours later the *Globe* rode out the gale. On the ninth of January, 1823, she made the Cape Verde Islands, bearing southwest, twenty-five miles distant, and crossed the Equator the seventeenth.

Samuel Comstock's bitter blasting of his second watch men the night of the gale had not gone unnoticed.

For days the crew went about routine duties with mixed emotions. Feelings between Sam Comstock and the fo'c'sle hands were pretty much known. The older hands wanted no part of him. He had none of the "makings" of a good officer, neither was he one of them! The younger lads were afraid of him. Beetle, Lumbard, and Fisher shunned him like the plague, except when duty demanded. Captain Worth treated him with austere civility. Gilbert Smith, second boat steerer, who *had* to live with Comstock in their tiny cramped steerage quarters, along with the three harpooners, played it smart and maintained friendly relations of a sort with him.

That's the way matters stood aboard the *Globe* early on the morning of January 29, when they sighted their first whale!

"Whale-ho!" cried the lookout, high aloft in the crow's-nest. "Thar' she blo-o-ows—off th' lee bow!"

In a second all was hurry-scurry aboard the *Globe!* Hands swarmed up out of the fo'c'sle hatch and scrambled on deck. Captain Worth and First Mate Beetle suddenly appeared aft by the roundhouse. Lumbard and Fisher, Comstock and Smith were hard on the captain's heels. The three harpooners raced forward to the tryhouse, grabbed their lances from the rack overhead, and stood by their respective longboats awaiting the lowering.

"How many?" boomed Captain Worth to the lookout, aloft. "Where away?"

"Three 'r four!" shouted the man in the "hoops." "Off th' lee bow—'bout a half league's distance!"

"Mister Beetle!" roared Worth. "Tell off th' crews an' lower th' boats!"

"Aye, sir!" answered the first mate, racing toward the waist of the ship, bawling commands as he ran. "Look lively, lads! Boat steerers, ship y'r crews an' lower away!"

Seconds later, all three longboats, fully provisioned and equipped, were in the water and pulling away under jury sails in the direction of the sighted whales—each boat manned by six men, a harpooner, and a mate. The chase for whales was on!

In a four-hour struggle with a huge "spermer," Fisher's crew made the only "kill" of the hunt! Comstock's boat was nearly broached by a mad whale. A fouled harpoon line gave Smith's boys a "Nantucket sleigh ride." Then they had to cut line or capsize!

When all boats were in and aboard, Comstock groused bitterly about how his crew hadn't followed orders—how his harpoon had missed the whale because First Mate Beetle waited too long in getting the boat to the whale, and let the mammal turn on them! Comstock raged and cursed his men roundly and added pointedly that if it hadn't been *his* superior handling of the longboat they'd have all been whale bait by now! The rest of the crew stared glumly at Comstock as they rigged the huge block and tackle high out over the starboard rail, then hoisted up Fisher's mammoth "spermer" to strip it of blubber!

Thick, belching smoke from the tryworks fires and the acrid stench of sizzling whale fat in the boiling kettles hung like a heavy pall over the whole vessel, mingling with the fetid rankness of a sweating crew, whose feverish intent was to get the blubber boiled down and barreled in spite of a merciless sun burning down on them! Half a dozen men and boys slithered along the catwalk of a king-size scaffold surrounding the whale and "cut in the blanket piece" with razor-sharp boarding knives. Others hauled the blubber on deck with long-handled boarding hooks, then "bible leafed" it into smaller pieces and fed it to the hot, bubbling try kettles.

'Tween decks, below, Cyrus Hussey and Rowland Coffin, the two ship's coopers, stood stripped to the waist in a stifling hell, hammering together barrels for the whale oil cooling in the huge iron cooling tank, abaft the fo'c'sle and just forward of the main hatch. By the middle of the night watch Captain Worth and First Mate Beetle had double tallied the seventy-fifth and last barrel of whale oil as it was lowered into the hold!

With no more whales sighted, the *Globe* beat her way south'ard through the roarin' forties—passed the Falklands February 23—doubled the Horn about March 15—then stood to the north'ard!

An ominous unrest stirred in the fo'c'sle the next few weeks. All hands were touchy and uneasy. Signs of scurvy were apparent in many, for lack of "greens." Others felt the sting of the rope's end for disobedience. Once, before the *Globe* closed with the Sandwich Islands, whales were sighted, but disappeared as night fell. Low murmurings of mutiny were now whispered in the dark recesses of the hold!

In the early morning haze of May 1, 1823, land-fall was made by the lookout of the low, ragged outline of the Sandwich Islands. While the *Globe* was drawing in with the island of Hawaii about four o'clock that afternoon, a flotilla of large native canoes was spotted, loaded to the gun'ls with fresh vegetables, fruit, and fish. Later, amply supplied with fruit, fish, and vegetables, the *Globe* squared away for Oahu, arriving the following day. Immediately, Captain Worth granted the crew a twelve-hour shore liberty.

"Wonder if th' Old Man's wise t' y'r brother?" questioned seaman Joseph Prass as he and young George Comstock prepared to go overside to the waiting "liberty" boat.

" 'T ain't likely," shrugged the younger Comstock, warily. "Wish t' God I knew, though. 'Fraid Sam's bound f'r trouble, but y' can't reason with him!"

"Been some talk," hinted Prass, "that y'r brother was seen down in th' hold a few weeks back, a-talkin' low t' certain dissatisfied coves in th' crew!"

"So I've heard tell," nodded young Comstock gravely.

"Been talk, too, that y'r brother's got friends here in Oahu," suggested Prass.

"Could be," granted George Comstock readily. "Sam's been out here a-fore."

"Wouldn't wanta put two 'n' two t'gether, would

y', George?" asked Joseph Prass with a sly smile as he slung a leg over the port rail and started down the Jacob's-ladder. Young Comstock had no ready answer for that one, but his mind was a mite uneasy as he thought of the evil implication in the sailor's words. He followed Prass glumly to the boat below.

Next afternoon, the *Globe,* in company with the whalers *Palladium* of Boston and the *Pocahontas* of Falmouth, cleared Oahu and set course for the Sea of Japan. Two days later the three vessels parted company. For several months the *Globe* cruised Japanese waters, boiling down 550 barrels of whale oil during that time. Lack of "greens" again forced Captain Worth to return to the Sandwich Islands for fresh provisions.

While the *Globe* laid in at Oahu, taking on fresh supplies, six of her crew deserted ship! In the dead of a black night they swam ashore and escaped. First Mate Beetle put off in a longboat when the mass desertion was discovered and posted a shore patrol around Oahu. Two of the six deserters were recaptured and put in irons aboard the *Globe,* but the two prisoners were so poorly secured that both fled the ship for the second time and were never recovered. Knowing glances passed between certain fo'c'sle hands!

This left Captain Worth shorthanded and posed an urgent problem. He at once called a council of his officers, including the two boat steerers.

"Gentlemen," he began without wasting words, "who knows Oahu well enough to pick me up about five or six good, all-around seamen?"

Captain Worth glanced about the circle of officers. For a moment no one spoke. Then Samuel Comstock took a step forward from the group.

"Well, Mister Comstock?" questioned Worth.

"Think mebbe I can find you five or six such men," said Comstock simply.

"Very well, Mister Comstock," answered the captain with relief. "Pick a crew and take one of the longboats—but make it lively—I want to sail on tonight's tide."

"Aye, sir," nodded Comstock and went forward to the fo'c'sle to get him a crew.

About sunset Comstock climbed aboard the *Globe* and herded the new men aft. They were a tough-looking lot, bearded and unkempt, but they were rugged and could pull their weight in a longboat. The men dropped their gear by the port rail and followed Comstock down the aft companionway to the captain's quarters. A moment later they stood before Captain Worth.

"That was quick work, Mister Comstock," grinned Worth.

"Aye, sir," answered the boat steerer in a flat tone.

"All right—the first man there," continued the captain crisply, pulling the ship's roster out of his desk drawer. "What's your name?"

"Silas Payne, sir."

"Your home port?"

"Let's jus' say—Rhode Island," answered the sailor warily.

"Any papers?"

"Third mate's—but I lost 'em in. . . ." Payne stopped abruptly. ". . . I lost 'em!"

Captain Worth looked sharply at Payne, shrugged, then made a notation on the ship's papers. Samuel Comstock gave Payne a slow wink as he passed him on the way to the captain's desk.

"Here, Payne—sign the roster," said Worth quickly. Payne complied. "All right—next man!"

"John Oliver—Shields, England—got m' bloody A.B. papers 'ere, sir!"

"Very well—sign up! Next!"

"Thomas Liliston—Virginia—A.B. seaman!"

"Sign here. Next man!"

"William Humphries — Philadelphia — an' I'se a cook 'n' steward, suh, if y' all need 'un!"

"Unbleached Irishman, eh!" commented Worth with a faint smile. The Negro grinned. Some of the men snickered. "All right, sign here! Next!"

"Anthony Hanson — Barnstable, Massachusetts — ord'nary seaman, sir!"

"Sign here! Next man!"

"Joseph Brown—San'ich I'land'r—harpoon'r!"

"Very good—we can always use one! Sign right here! Next!"

Comstock pushed a burly-looking fellow in his twenties toward Captain Worth, who looked at him quizzically.

"Who's this fellow, Comstock?" he questioned.

"Name's Joseph Thomas," Comstock told the captain. "He's from Connecticut—wants to work passage back. Found him in th' longboat when I was about t' shove off. Says he wants no share, jus' wants t' get back to th' States!"

Captain Worth hesitated a moment and rubbed his chin thoughtfully, "We-e-ll, all right—a bit irregular, though—we'll put him down as a working passenger. Won't sign him on as crew, nor will he stand watch—but he can bunk in the fo'c'sle. That all, now?"

"Aye, sir," nodded Comstock.

"Very well, Mister Comstock, take the men for' ard." Then he added pointedly, turning to the new crew members, "I'll expect you men to give good accounts of yourselves on the voyage back—y' understand?"

There were a few halfhearted, "aye, aye, sirs" as Comstock led them up the companionway to get their gear and assign them bunk space. There were also a few grumblings from the older hands in the fo'c'sle when the Johnny-come-latelys came below.

After clearing Oahu the *Globe* ran south before fair winds below the Equator, cruising unsuccessfully for whales. Captain Worth then set a course for Fanning Island, lying in latitude 3° 49′ N. and longitude 158° 29′ W. But the *Globe* never made a landfall there!

Too late, Captain Worth discovered to his disgust that Samuel Comstock had systematically "picked up" the scum of Oahu—water front riffraff, beachcombing no-good, the flotsom of many ports—castoffs that no self-respecting shipmaster would give bilge room to. They caused no end of trouble. More frequently than not they'd get blistering reprimands from the officers. Once Captain Worth himself had to give Joseph Thomas a much-deserved flogging with the end of a buntline for his open defiance and stinking insolence.

Then the thing struck with unexpected fury and swiftness, borne on the middle night stillness of Sunday, January 25, 1824—a stillness broken fitfully by creaking yards and a soft wind sighing through the rigging. The mutineers had timed their diabolic plan well, concealing its element of surprise during the weeks since the *Globe* cleared Oahu.

Sixteen-year-old George Comstock, at the helm, was just raising the "rattle" to sound the end of his brother Sam's middle night watch. It was 2:00 A.M. and he suddenly remembered the light! Earlier last evening, Captain Joy, skipper of the whaler *Lyra,* of New Bedford, sailing in company with the *Globe,* had returned to his vessel after spending a good part of the day gamming with Captain Worth. During the visit of the two shipmasters, the young helmsman overheard them agree to set a light at 2:00 A.M. as a signal for tacking. He thought to set the light now and show 'em he "was on the job." But, at the outset of his trick at the wheel, the younger Comstock had been warned in no uncertain terms by his brother to "keep the ship a good full," that she was too nigh the wind. This warning had had an ominous ring to it that left young Comstock with an uneasy mind. Hesitating, he laid the lamp aside, unlighted.

As young Comstock again raised the rattle to shake it, dim figures closed around him in the faint light of the binnacle. Suddenly, out of the darkness Samuel Comstock swooped down on his brother and grabbed his arm in mid-air.

"If you make th' least damn'd bit o' noise," he hissed in his ear, "I'll send y' t' hell!"

Startled by his brother's sudden appearance, he dropped the rattle to the deck and stared aghast at the older Comstock's dire threats. Brushing him roughly aside, his brother then lighted the lamp and started toward the aft companionway. Trembling nervously, George Comstock grabbed up the rattle to sound an alarm, but his brother turned sharply and knocked it out of his hand.

"Lis'n, goddam ya," rasped his brother, brandishing a boarding knife over the youth's head, "if y' so much as touch that thing again, I'll—I'll kill ya!"

"But, Sam, . . ." pleaded the confused boy.

"Stow y'r lip an' mind th' wheel!" Comstock croaked angrily. Then he turned to one of the figures in the outer ring of darkness. "C'm' on, Payne!"

Comstock laid the heavy knife on a small bench by the companionway and started down the stairs, the lamp held high above his head. Payne came directly behind him. Oliver, Humphries, and Liliston crept stealthily out of the shadows toward the companionway. Liliston, suddenly scared, fled forward to the fo'c'sle hatch as the other two followed the ringleaders down the stairs.

Comstock stopped below, just outside the captain's open door, shadowing the lamp with his hand. He turned to Payne.

"Y' got it?" he whispered hoarsely.

"Right here!"

"Give it t' me, an' hold th' lamp!"

Silently Comstock entered the captain's cabin, a heavy axe in his hands. Oliver and Humphries stopped short in the doorway. Captain Worth was asleep in a hammock, slung across the cabin to catch any cross breezes in the sultry tropic night air. Pace by pace Comstock neared the sleeping skipper and slowly raised the ugly-looking broad-axe. With a quick, downward stroke, the axe struck Worth's head with the sound of a popping water-melon, nearly cleaving it in two. Crimson blood spurted over Comstock and spattered thickly over the cabin deck and sides. Payne's face blanched in the flickering light and his hand shook so that the lamp nearly went out. Oliver and Humphries beat a hasty retreat up the companionway. Comstock ran to Payne.

"Where's th' boardin' knife?"

Payne recoiled and stared glassy eyed at Comstock's bloody appearance.

"Y'—y' left it on deck. . . ."

"Gimme th' lamp an' go get it! We've more bloody work t' do!"

Payne stumbled up the dim companionway, fumbled for the boarding knife, then returned below with it. Comstock led the way grimly through the doorway to the captain's office and dining room, then he flung open the unlocked door of the first mate's stateroom on the port side. Beetle raised himself on his elbows while Comstock held the lamp over his head and Payne raised the boarding knife to within inches of the first mate's heart.

"What—what is this!" cried Beetle in anguish, as he suddenly realized the spot he was in. "Oh,

Payne—Comstock! F'r C'ris' sake don't kill me—don't! Haven't I always. . . ."

"Y've always been a goddamn'd rascal!" interrupted Comstock, pushing by Payne.

"But haven't I. . . ."

"Tell lies about me out o' th' ship, will ya!" growled Comstock, menacing him with the axe. "It's a damn'd good time t' beg—but y'r too late!"

Comstock relaxed for an instant. Beetle leapt at him, grabbing him by the throat.

"Why, you low-down bastard!" snarled the furious Beetle, tightening a death grip on the bloody man's throat, "I'll throttle you!"

In the scuffle, Comstock's lamp was knocked out and the axe fell from his hand. Despite his position, Comstock made known to Payne that he had lost the axe. Fumbling in the dark, Payne grasped the weapon just as Humphries, the steward, came aft from the fo'c'sle holding a lamp over his head. Behind him came Oliver. Comstock grabbed the axe from Payne, smashing it against Beetle's head. Beetle reeled across the cabin and fell into the pantry, bleeding from a fractured skull. Oliver went to finish him off with the boarding knife.

The other two mates, John Lumbard and Nathaniel Fisher, were locked in their stateroom next to Beetle's. Lying in a cold sweat in their berth, they listened—fearful of uttering a word.

"God almighty!" breathed Lumbard. "They've mutinied!"

"Aye," whispered Fisher softly, "we must be quiet! God knows how strong they be—best t' wait awhile, an mebbe we'll be spared!"

Leaving Payne as a watch at the second mate's door, Comstock ran up on deck to check matters there. Relighting the lamp that had blown out at the binnacle, he found his younger brother in hysterical tears.

"Are y' goin' t' hurt Smith?" cried George. "Are y', Sam!"

"If I get m' hands on him—yes!" snarled Comstock. "An' what th' hell are y' cryin' about?"

"I—I'm afraid," sobbed young Comstock, "afraid they'll hurt me!"

"Well, dammit, I'll hurt you," snapped his brother, "if y' keep on talkin' in that manner!"

Rushing below with the lighted lamp in his hand, Comstock located a couple of muskets with fixed bayonets in the captain's stateroom. Hastily loading them, he stood in front of Lumbard's door and handed the lamp to Humphries, then fired one of the muskets through the panel, judging as close as possible where the mates would be.

"Who did I hit?" he asked sharply.

"Me!" groaned Fisher in pain. "Y'—shot me in th' mouth!"

"Good!" cried the mad Comstock. "Next time I'll blow y'r damn'd head off!"

"Are you going to kill me, too?" asked Lumbard in a steady voice.

"Oh, no, I guess not," answered Comstock casually.

Then Comstock smashed open the door with the butt of the musket. He made a lunge for Lumbard and missed, sprawling headlong to the deck. Fisher quickly collered him, while Lumbard grabbed the musket and pressed the point of the bayonet at his heart. For a split second the mates had the mutiny in their hands to end!

"Now, now, lads," purred Comstock craftily. "Hand over that musket and you'll live!"

Foolishly, Lumbard let go the weapon and Comstock ran him through several times. Then he turned sharply on Fisher.

"You, y' bastud! You gotta die, too!" Comstock croaked hoarsely. "Y' remember th' scrape y' got me into when I was in company with th' *Enterprise* out o' Nantucket?"

"Why — er — I wrestled you once," stammered Fisher.

"Y' goddam well right did!" roared Comstock. "An y' hamm'r'd my head on th' deck!"

"But you struck me," insisted Fisher, "because y' lost your temper!"

"An' I'll strike y' again!" raged the boat steerer. "An' this time, b'gad, y'll stay struck!"

Comstock angrily grabbed up the other loaded musket, put it to Fisher's head and fired before Fisher knew what was happening. Lumbard, terribly wounded, begged for mercy.

"I'm a bloody man!" bellowed Comstock, turning on the second mate. "I've a bloody hand, 'n' I'll be revenged!"

"F'r God's sake," cried Lumbard in anguish, "give me some water!"

"I'll give y' water!" roared Comstock, plunging the bayonet point into Lumbard. "Right through th' guts!"

With singlehanded bloodiness and maniacal fury,

Samuel B. Comstock, number one boat steerer of the whaler *Globe,* had gone on a wild skull-splitting spree that, in less than a half hour's watch, had resulted in the cold-blooded murder of Captain Thomas Worth; the bludgeoning to death of First Mate William Beetle; the running through of Second Mate John Lumbard with a bayonet and, finally, his blowing out the brains of Nathaniel Fisher, third mate!

Brutal sounds of Comstock's mutinous attack on the *Globe's* officers drifted through to Gilbert Smith's consciousness like a weird and unreal nightmare. Up in steerage, just forward of the second's quarters, he and the harpooners awoke with a terrible start as Comstock screamed, "I'm a bloody man, an' I'll have my revenge!"

"I want no part o' this!" whispered one of the harpooners, opening the door quietly and ducking forward to the comparative safety of the fo'c'sle. The other two harpooners followed him hastily.

Trembling inside with fear, Smith put on a bold front and strode aft.

"What th' hell's goin' on back here?" he demanded.

"Y'r throwin' in with us ain't y', Smith?" questioned Comstock, as he threw his bloody arms around the second boatsteerer's neck. Smith took in the appalling situation at a horrified glance and played his bluff through.

"I'm with you," he answered boldly. "I'll do anything y' want!"

Shortly after, all hands were turned out at Comstock's command. All reefs were turned out, t'gallants set, and every stitch of canvas was made to catch the light airs. A light was soon set as a signal for the *Lyra* to tack, while the *Globe* held her course. Soon the two ships separated.

The mutineers tossed Captain Worth's mutilated body overboard, but not before Joseph Thomas plunged a boarding knife into his bowels and drove it in with an axe 'til the point came out his throat.

"There, b' jeezes!" shouted Thomas in gleeful madness, "that'll l'arn y' not t' take th' rope's end t' Joseph Thomas!"

Beetle, the first mate, was still breathing, but he, too, was thrown over the side. Fisher's limp body was hauled up on deck by a rope around his neck. A double turn of rope around his feet brought the still living Lumbard to deck. As he was hurled over the lee rail he caught on the plank-sheer and begged Comstock to save his life as he had promised. With a sneer Comstock rapped his fingers with the flat of the broad knife and poor Lumbard fell into the sea. But as the second mate still struggled to swim, Comstock, fearing the *Lyra* might chance to pick him up, ordered a boat lowered to finish him off! However, another fear that his own murderous renegades might desert caused Comstock to countermand his orders.

Whither they were bound no one aboard the *Globe* knew, save Comstock. For two days they held a westerly course on an easterly wind. The scene of bloody human destruction in the captain's cabin was scrubbed up and Comstock moved in. His rule as skipper was at once hard and brutal. Silas Payne became mate—though ever suspicious of Comstock. Humphries, the black man, was advanced to the newly created post of purser; young George Comstock took over as steward.

Comstock tipped his hand as to the questionable future of the vessel the day he ordered the fifteen muskets on board to be cleaned and polished. Then he ordered the crew to make up cartridge boxes. Now they knew! Whaling was out—the *Globe* had turned pirate!

Comstock and Payne then drew a set of "Articles," forcing each and every man to sign—at point of death! They were short, but full of terrible meaning:

> "If anyone sees a sail and does not report
> it immediately he shall be put to death.
> If anyone refuses to fight a ship he shall
> also be put to death. Manner of death, this:
> He shall be bound hand and foot and boiled
> in the try-pots of boiling oil."

A surface calm prevailed aboard the *Globe,* though underneath she was a ship divided. There were those who sought to save their own skins by toadying to the mutinous, high-riding Comstock; there were others of the crew who looked mutely to Gilbert Smith for guidance and salvation.

Matters began to head up one night when George Comstock came unexpectedly upon William Humphries in the cabin, loading a pistol!

"What are you doing that for?" young Comstock demanded.

"I've hear'd certain things an' I'm gettin' ready," replied the Negro mysteriously.

"Just what things have you heard, Humphries?" persisted the y o u n g e r Comstock. Humphries shrugged evasively. Sensing this as a veiled threat against himself, George Comstock immediately contacted his brother.

White with rage, Samuel Comstock dashed to the cabin with Payne by his side. They found Humphries, pistol still in hand.

"What th' hell's th' meaning o' this!" raged Comstock. " 'T ain't anybody I c'n trust! Come on, now—talk—or I'll cut y' down!"

Humphries eyed the two renegade officers nervously, then moistened his lips.

"I—I hear'd, . . ." he began, then stopped abruptly.

"Come on—out with it!" rasped Comstock impatiently. "What did y' hear?"

"I—I hear'd that Gilbert and Smith an' Peter Kidder was fixin' t' take th' ship back!" blurted out the Negro, shaking with fear. "S' help me, suh, I—I was so 'fraid I—I started t' load this yere pistol!"

"That's a helluva likely story, Humphries," hissed Comstock. "But t' keep y' honest I'll get Smith an' Kidder in here, now—then, b' jeezes, we'll soon find out if y' th' damn'd lyin' bastud I think y' are!"

Comstock summoned Kidder and Smith and tossed the damaging charges into their laps. Both men hotly denied the charges and denounced Humphries as a lying lunatic! Comstock then ordered a trial for the morrow.

Next morning, "court" was convened. Comstock himself acted as the "chief justice." Smith, Kidder, and Humphries sat on an arms chest during the "trial," surrounded by armed guards. Two seamen served as a "jury." All three were put through a barrage of bizarre and irrelevant questions that elicited nothing of value. But Humphries was so frightened by the proceedings that he was literally speechless—the very effect that Comstock was striving for — a complete admission of guilt through silence!

"It appears that William Humphries," began Comstock in a booming, august tone, using a smattering of quasi-legal terms, "has been accused guilty of a treacherous and base act in loading a pistol for the purpose of shooting Mister Payne and myself!"

Poor Humphries cowered under the impact of the mutineer-captain's words—his black face literally paling. But still he couldn't find words to defend himself. Comstock gave him a sardonic sneer.

"Having been tried," continued Comstock, lashing out his words, "the jury will now give their verdict—whether guilty or not guilty!"

Humphries turned to the two seamen-jurors and besought them with pleading, tearful eyes. But they would have none of him.

"If guilty," rapped out Comstock, "he shall be hanged to a stuns'le boom, rigged out eight feet upon the foreyard—but if found not guilty, Smith and Kidder shall be hanged upon the aforementioned gallows!"

This legalistic flourish of Comstock's greatly impressed the unlettered seamen. It also sealed Humphries' doom. His fate had been fully decided the night before by Comstock and Payne and kept a secret from the rest of the ship's company. Today's trial was a sorry mockery of justice. The two jurors had been dourly warned that a verdict of other than guilty would be very bad for their own health. Judgment came speedily—with the obvious verdict: *"Guilty!"*

Humphries' jaw went slack and he nearly passed out.

Preparations were hastily made for his execution. First, his watch was snatched from him, then he was brutally kicked forward and forced to sit on the lee rail. A cap was drawn over his face and a running bowline slipped loosely around his neck. Every man jack of the crew was ordered to tail onto the execution rope—ready to run up Humphries when Comstock struck the ship's bell!

"Humphries!" rasped Comstock pulling out his watch, "if y' got anything t' say, y' got just fourteen seconds t' say it in! One—two—three. . . ."

"How little did I think I was a-born t' come t' this," he moaned in desperation. But Comstock was an impatient man!

Clang! Humphries' body catapulted into the air! As it was cut down the rope snagged in the rigging and the body was towed 'longside. In the eyes of the superstitious seamen this was still another bad omen come to join the others that had dogged the *Globe* ever since her voyage began! It had a visible effect that shown on drawn faces. Quickly a line was bent on a runner hook and the hang rope was raised and cut away. Humphries' body sank in the sea.

So—having ended Humphries' earthly affairs with speed and dispatch, Comstock returned to matters at hand and roared orders to bear a sharp eye for approaching land.

On February 7, 1824, the *Globe* passed the Kingsmill Islands and on the following day nosed into the channel between the Marshall and Gilbert islands. During this investigative period of "island hopping," Comstock and Payne were constantly topside. Smith took advantage of this situation to contact Peter Kidder, 'tween deck, on the pretext of relaying orders to him.

Smith came forward to the semidarkness 'tween decks, near the main hatch. He peered around cautiously in the dim light to make sure he hadn't been followed.

"Kidder," called Smith in a low whisper, "you down here?"

"Aye, Smith," Kidder answered softly, "over here —for'ard o' th' coolin' tank—starb'rd side."

"Alone?"

"Aye."

Gilbert Smith crossed silently to Peter Kidder, still cautious.

"Comstock's got it into his head t' land at one o' these islands," whispered Smith. "Mebbe it's th' chance we've been hopin' for—mebbe we can retake th' ship with no more bloodshed! Keep y'r eyes sharp, Peter, an' y'r ears open—one day soon, we may sail home—shed o' that devil!"

"Aye, Gilbert—you can rely on me!"

Smith retraced his steps as quickly and cautiously as he had come. On the following day his prophecy began to bear fruit.

Comstock selected a small inhabited island in the

Marshalls, luffed to and sent out a boat in charge of
Gilbert Smith to investigate a good anchorage.

Unfriendly natives swam out to the longboat, trying to steal from it. A canoe full of spearmen
guarded the marauding swimmers. Unarmed, Smith
tried to make it plain to the natives that he wanted
to trade with them for fruit, fresh vegetables, and
coconuts.

He was just getting to an understanding with
them when Comstock suddenly ordered a volley
fired from the deck of the *Globe!* The roar of
musketry was deafening. The sea around Smith's
boat went crimson as a number of native swimmers
writhed in pain and death. Quickly Smith un-
shipped oars and his crew pulled lustily for the
Globe. Spears, hurled by the natives in the canoe,
grazed the gun'ls of the longboat. Another blast
from the Globe sank the canoe and sent its paddlers
and spearmen, scattering and squirming, into the
water. This rare opportunity to test muskets and
marksmanship came as a sheer delight to those
aboard the *Globe* and they roared with pleasure
as "hits" were registered on a tally sheet!

Gilbert Smith was fit to be tied as he and his
crew scrambled aboard and hauled up the longboat.

" 'T weren't a very smart move, Sam!" bellowed
Smith at Comstock. "Firin' at th' natives in that
fashion!"

"Why the stinkin' bastuds woulda 'bible leaf'd'
ya if I hadn't ordered fire!" defended Comstock
angrily.

"I had 'em comin' around," continued Smith in
a hard voice. "I'd a-been tradin' in another few

minutes an' we'd a-got sorely needed fresh provisions aboard!"

"Hell," snapped Comstock, "y'd all been dead men a-fore then!"

" 'Nother thing," countered the still angry Smith, "you'll have t' do a heap o' sailin' 'fore y' find a safe island t' land on, too!"

"How y' figure that?" demanded the mutineer-skipper.

" 'Cause these Kanakas can lay down a fast signal to islands f'r a hundred miles around!" answered Smith sharply. "An' that plainly means any white man venturing on these shores could be slaughter'd as soon as he hit the beach—all in revenge f'r what y'r doin' right now! You should have known that, Comstock!"

So they bore away, easterly, still searching for a suitable base of operations among friendly natives.

On the afternoon of February 13, Comstock finally selected a long, narrow coral atoll in the Mulgrave Islands (now Majuro Island, lying midway between the Marshall and Gilbert groups). Night fell as the *Globe* drew in toward the rocky isle.

"Twelve fathoms!" shouted 'Lumbus Worth, down in the chains taking soundings. Then he warned abruptly, "Ease away—no bottom!" Finally he sang out with the next cast of lead, "Seven fathoms—drop anchor!"

With shore some five rods away, the *Globe* anchored and set a kedge astern to keep her off shore should the wind shift during the night. All hands scrambled aloft and furled sail. Then the crew turned in, save for the anchor watch.

Gilbert Smith sought out Peter Kidder below deck.

"Time's gettin' close!" he advised tautly. "Keep y'r eyes an' ears peel'd, Peter, an' have the right boys ready."

"Aye, Gilbert!" came the soft answer. The two separated and silently faded into the darkness 'tween decks.

In the morning the mutineers faced a sea too rough to risk a landing and Comstock ordered a raft built of spare spars. Next day, Sunday, February 15, they commenced to strip the *Globe*. Payne supervised loading the lighter, while Comstock took charge ashore. Gilbert Smith and Peter Kidder worked, too, watchfully biding their time.

Under the lashing tongue of Silas Payne the crew struggled against time, the threatening weather, and the immense stores aboard the *Globe*. Raft loads of ship's gear, great bundles of spare sail, and huge hogsheads of pork, salt beef, and molasses were hauled up on the beach. Delicacies from the officers' provisions were unloaded—flour, vinegar, apples, tea, and pickles. All were carefully guarded from resentful, sweating, crew members who were angered at the sight of them.

By Monday morning the *Globe* was considerably unrigged. So much so that Smith and Kidder looked at each other in partial dismay. Would there be canvas enough aboard to take her to sea? Nor was Silas Payne too happy as he watched Comstock liberally giving away the undivided plunder to the natives in an all-out effort to build up "good will" among them.

"By jeezes, Comstock!" roared Payne angrily from the *Globe's* rail, "if y' don't change y'r tactics about giving that stuff away a-fore it's divided amongst us, I'm quittin' th' ship an' comin' ashore—y' understand!"

"What th' hell y' mean y'r comin' ashore!" bellowed back Comstock. "I'm orderin' y' ashore—now—y' hear!"

The two mutineers faced each other in an improvised tent set up on the beach from a spare mains'l. Angry words flew hot and heavy between the two.

"Lis'n, goddam ya," raged Comstock, "I helped t' take th' ship, an' I navigated her to this place! I've also helped get her riggin' an' supplies ashore! From now on y' c'n do what th' hell y' want with her! But if any bastud wants anything o' *me,* then b' gad I'll take a musket with him!"

"That's just what I want—a showdown!" Payne replied hotly. "An' b' jeezes, I'm ready right now!"

Payne's quick challenge to a musket duel called Comstock's bluff and threw him off balance. He suddenly backed down from his highhanded talk, as Payne knew he would.

"I'll go on board once more," he answered meekly. "Then, b' gad, y' can do what y' damn well please with her—I'm through!"

Once aboard, Comstock hurried aft to the cabin and grabbed up the paper recording the "Articles" he and Payne had jammed down the scared crew's throat. Angrily he tore the thing to bits, then tossed the scraps of fluttering paper overside. Halfheartedly he challenged all aboard to fight him. But the crew had heard him come off second best with Payne and they stood silently by, staring at him contemptuously.

"I'm leavin' you damn'd bastuds f'r th' last time!" he hissed angrily as he climbed over the rail to the raft below—then shoving off from the ship he flung at them, "Look out f'r y'rselves!"

Ashore, Comstock entered Payne's tent, sheathed a cutlass, hooked the scabbard to his belt, picked up a small knife, a half dozen hooks and lines, and strode out. Payne followed him suspiciously to the tent's entrance. Comstock turned sharply on Payne and patted the cutlass by his side.

"This," he exclaimed sullenly, "will stand by me as long as I live."

"Take care how y' use it!" warned Payne.

At dusk, Comstock passed by Payne's tent accompanied by about fifty natives, headed in the direction of their village. Apprehensive of Comstock's motives, Payne came aboard the *Globe*.

"I suspicion Comstock'll try t' p'rsuade these Kanakas t' murder us all!" Payne observed grimly to those on deck.

"What's best t' be done, Payne?" questioned Smith with quiet wariness.

" 'T would be wise t' set up a guard, ashore," advised Payne. "That fool's up t' no good!"

Musket-armed guards posted themselves around the tent and supplies. A common countersign was agreed on and orders issued to shoot on sight anyone failing to give the proper password. Payne, Smith, and several others remained aboard the *Globe*. Night passed without incident. Early next morning

Comstock was seen at some distance, stalking toward Payne's tent. Payne immediately alerted Gilbert Smith, summoning him on deck.

"You're a tol'able shot, Smith," greeted Payne. "S'pose you pick off Comstock a-fore he gets t' th' tent!"

"He's your man, Payne," countered Smith with a wry grin, determined to remain neutral in the mutineers' quarrel. "You'd best be the man t' draw a bead on him!"

Armed with a pair of loaded muskets, Payne and Oliver hurried ashore. Concealing themselves just inside the tent, they awaited Comstock's approach. When he was within a few yards of the tent, Comstock drew his cutlass and moved quickly toward Payne, who stood alone in front of the tent. Suddenly, at a sign from Payne, the man in the tent came forward, leveling his musket at Comstock. Comstock stopped short, raising his arms above his head.

"Don't shoot!" he pleaded. "Don't shoot me! I'll not hurt you!"

Payne laid down his musket and picked up an axe—the prearranged command to his men! Four muskets cracked in the morning stillness—Comstock dropped in the sand, bleeding badly! Wary that Comstock might be "playin' possum," Payne rushed him and with one blow of the axe nearly severed his head. But Comstock was already dead.

A hasty burial was ordered by Payne. While some of the sailors sewed Comstock's body in canvas, others of the *Globe's* company dug a grave five feet deep in the soft sand. The whole service took on

the same nightmarish atmosphere that had marked
the entire ill-famed voyage of the *Globe!* Everything belonging to Comstock, except his watch, was
buried with him—his cutlass, his axe, musket and
pistol—all were tossed in after him as the diggers
shoveled in the sand! Payne, in mock reverence,
read a passage from the Bible, and Oliver, to complete the mockery, fired a single musket shot over
the grave.

Gilbert Smith, Peter Kidder, and several of the
non-mutinous members of the *Globe's* crew leaned
over the port rail watching Comstock's sudden execution and burial.

"Blasted into eternity with all his sins — an'
shovel'd under th' sands o' Mulgrave without a
tear," eulogized Kidder wryly.

"Aye, Peter," answered Smith with a grim smile,
"an' in scarcely longer time than it takes t' blink
an eye!"

"Here comes Payne, now," muttered Kidder,
nudging Smith, as the mutineer mate crossed in the
raft and climbed aboard the *Globe* with six of the
shore crew.

"Brought these boys over t' help y', Smith," announced Payne. "Want y' to take full charge o' th'
ship."

Deep down inside, Smith and Kidder felt a surge
of elation at Payne's words. But they kept their feelings well guarded. No time now to betray themselves with escape a matter of hours away!

"Aye, Payne," answered Smith, his face expres-
sionless. "Anything special y' want done aboard?"

"Clear up this mess o' gear on deck," ordered

Payne, "then see to it th' binnacle compasses come ashore."

"Aye," nodded Smith curtly.

Quickly Payne surveyed the confusion on deck, then started overside for shore. He hesitated with a leg over the rail, turning toward Smith.

"Make sure o' them compasses, Smith!" he flung over his shoulder, then disappeared down the ladder.

Time was at hand!

Shortly after Payne departed, Smith substituted the hanging compass in the captain's cabin for one of the binnacle compasses—securing the compasses in a piece of sailcloth, tying it tightly with marlin cord. He then detailed a trusted crew member to take the bundle ashore, with special instructions to "hide" it in Payne's tent, thoroughly concealing it under some of the other loot.

At seven o'clock that night, as Gilbert Smith and Peter Kidder quietly set about putting into operation their long-planned scheme of escape, the "exchange" had not been discovered. Smith went below and checked weapons against a chance attack by Payne and his crew. A musket, three bayonets, and a few whale lances were laid out in readiness for any emergency. Boarding knives were distributed at strategic points at port and starboard rails to fend off a boarding assault. Meanwhile, Peter Kidder supervised clearing the running rigging, a duty left to last to allay possible suspicion ashore.

As night darkened, Gilbert Smith took Stephen Kidder aloft with him to the fore-tops'l-yard, loosing the buntlines and turning out the reefs. George Comstock—somewhat saddened by his notorious brother's death, though knowing full well he got what was coming to him—went aloft with Anthony Hanson and loosed the main-tops'l and mains'l. Below, on deck, Smith saw to it that a well-greased handsaw was on the windlass, for'ard, to saw the bow cable. Likewise, the only hatchet aboard was laid by the mizzenmast to cut the stern moorings when the ship should be sufficiently swung away at the bow.

A rising moon made delay doubly dangerous—a touch-and-go situation for all! The slightest slip-up could mean bitter defeat and death!

"I'm goin' 'shore!" shouted Joseph Thomas, suddenly, breaking the stillness of the night.

"Shut up, y' damn'd bastud!" hissed Peter Kidder, catching the troublemaking Connecticut sailor flush on the jaw with a well-swung right. Kidder dragged the limp Thomas below, shackling him in irons down in the lazarette.

Thomas' shouting had done the damage he intended it to!

Figures stirred in the moonlight around Payne's tent and Gilbert Smith was having his hand forced to a quick decision! But Smith had made his plans carefully. Already there were two men aloft—one on the foreyard—another on the fore-tops'l-yard—awaiting orders to let fall the loosened sails. George Comstock was at the helm and two other men at the foretack.

"Let fall y'r sheets!" called Smith to the men aloft—at the same time sawing the bow mooring cable. Two minutes later the cable slid into the water and the ship paid off quickly. When her

head was off the land and the stern cable cut, figures
raced toward the beach head with great shouts.

"Th' ship's sailin'! Th' ship's sailin'!"

With a fair offshore breeze, men scurried aloft
to crack on every stitch of canvas available! Dim
figures on the hazy, moonlit beach of Mulgrave
Island fell astern and a mighty roar went up from
the *Globe's* crew for their successful getaway! Faint
"hurrahs" wafted across the water from the tiny
figures on the beach—from those who now realized
the *Globe's* escape might well be the means of their
own ultimate deliverance!

After a long, rough, and boisterous passage —
during which Joseph Thomas had to be confined
in irons—the *Globe* finally arrived at Valparaiso.
Michael Hogan, American consul there, took immediate possession of her—and all her crew, including Gilbert Smith and Peter Kidder, were put in
irons until a full investigation and examination was
completed.

On June 15, 1824, at the United States Consulate,
Gilbert Smith was thoroughly examined, under oath,
by Michael Hogan. After a three-day testimony
he was satisfied by Smith's answers and with those
of the rest of the *Globe's* crew, who concurred with
Smith. All agreed, however, that Joseph Thomas
was privy to the intention of mutiny and to murder
the officers.

The American consul then ordered the *Globe*
released from his custody. Completely rerigged, the
Globe sailed from Valparaiso under the command
of a Captain King and arrived at Nantucket Island,

Sunday, November 21, 1824—two years, lacking a month, since she cleared Edgartown!

On April 22, 1826, the U.S.S. *United States* sailed into misty New York Harbor. Aboard her were Cyrus M. Hussey, ship's cooper of the *Globe,* and Seaman William Lay, sole survivors of a native uprising and massacre that had horribly slaughtered Silas Payne and the rest of the *Globe's* company left on Mulgrave Island!

For two years Hussey and Lay had lived as captives of the Mulgrave Islanders until they were picked up by Lieutenant Hyram Paulding of the sloop of war *Dolphin,* sent, on orders of the American consul at Valparaiso, to find the *Globe's* stranded sailors and close the records on the grisliest mutiny of them all!

Sources of Factual Material

The material for this story was researched from the eyewitness account written by two members of the *Globe's* crew—Cooper's Mate Cyrus Hussey and Seaman William Lay—of the bloody mutiny aboard the Nantucket whaler *Globe* in the South Pacific in 1823. The Hussey-Lay account was reprinted by *The Town Crier,* Nantucket, Massachusetts.

X

THE GRIM ORDEAL OF THE
DUMARU MEN

"SHIP WILL LAY IN at 'Frisco to pick up cargo . . . ship to be delivered at Manila . . . crew to stand by until cargo is discharged," droned the weary voice of the United States Shipping Commissioner for the Portland, Oregon, area, aboard the S.S. *Dumaru* (doo-may-roo), that sultry afternoon of August 23, 1918.

The Commissioner was in the process of signing on a polyglot crew for the newest of the government-built wooden "Liberty" ships and he was having a bad time of it. As the *Dumaru* swung at anchor in midstream off the Willamette River, still reeking of fresh paint and green Douglas fir timber, the Commissioner sat at a table in her bare saloon, outstaring the hostile glares of the thirty-six nondescript men who crowded around him. Hard cases, all of them!

Then he snapped impatiently, "Transportation back to Pacific coast via passenger vessel—sign here!"

Then the Commissioner sat back in his chair, chewed on the ragged end of a dead cigar, and shoved the ship's articles toward the sneering, smirking men. A couple of self-styled sea lawyers in the ragtag crew-to-be leaned over the table and quickly scanned the articles, then shook their heads.

"Wot g'ar'antee we got that we'll git passage back from Manila?" snarled one of them.

"Yeah—an' f'r that matter," rasped the other, "how th' hell d' we know we'll even git t' 'Frisco in this floatin' crate. Never mind Manila!"

"Damn'd seams in these wooden coffins open up soon's they hit th' tropics!" piped a voice in the rear.

"Cranky as hell in a blow, too!" volunteered another. "Ain't nothin' but jerry-built packin' boxes wid coal-fired b'ilers an' top-heavy sup'rstructures! Gov'ment turned out nigh on t' a hund'rd right here in Portlan' an' they all act up th' same!"

"Pickin' up a cargo o' explosives, ain'cha!" bristled a wiry little guy standing in front of the Commissioner. "Y' ain't told us 'bout dat yet, huh?"

"No sailor man wu'th his salt'll ship in dese dynamite scows!" bellowed a giant in the rear. "So dey git poor bastuds like us t' sail 'em! It's th' damn' gov'ment 'system,' dat's wot it is!"

"That'll be enough of that I.W.W. talk!" bristled the Commissioner. "I'm too damn'd busy t' listen to it. Besides, there's a war on! You wobblies have your choice—either sign up in the Army like men an' fight in the trenches of Flanders—or sign these articles an' go t' Manila! Now, then, which is it?"

One by one, with sullen grumblings, the thirty-six draft dodgers, derelicts, erstwhile lumberjacks and farm hands, signed the articles as crew of the *Dumaru*. Those who couldn't write made their crosses.

August Waywood, who had signed on as first mate earlier in the week, was in command of the *Dumaru* until they picked up her skipper, Captain Ole Borrensen, at 'Frisco. Waywood was a solidly built guy of about fifty, with cold, piercing blue eyes that didn't miss a trick. Standing in a far corner of the *Dumaru's* saloon, unnoticed, he sized up each man and pulled thoughtfully at his red, walrus-like mustache. He had an abiding hatred for all slackers and incompetent seamen.

Once, up in Astoria, Oregon, he'd killed a boardinghouse crimp for getting him just such a ragtag crew as this. He was presented a gold watch by the mayor. He was that kind of a man. Waywood pushed through the crowd and faced his crew for the first time. At once he commanded respect.

"All right, you men!" he ordered sharply. "Pick up y'r dunnage an' go up for'rd. I'll be there shortly to assign duties and watches!"

The two self-styled sea lawyers started to argue, thought better of it, swung their sea bags to their shoulders and pushed out with the rest. The Commissioner mopped his forehead and shook his head.

"My God, Mr. Waywood!" he reflected. "Never did I see a greater bunch of misfits signed on one ship!"

"Don't worry too much about it, Commissioner," answered the first mate in a gravelly voice. "We'll keep 'em in line!"

Next day the *Dumaru* proceeded down the Columbia River, crossed the bar, dropped her pilot, then nosed out into the Pacific for her run to 'Frisco to pick up her skipper and cargo.

On the surface it was a colorless enough beginning—after she crossed the Columbia River bar —though there wasn't a man aboard who didn't feel either misgivings, fear, or smoldering anger at having been "pressed into service." From the bridge to the fire hole a belligerent tenseness reared itself aboard the *Dumaru*. Half-mumbled threats, murderous glances, blasphemous curses—even sharp fist fighting! Each took dour stock of his shipmates and, almost to a man, secretly swore to jump ship at 'Frisco. The I.W.W. "spirit" prevailed from the raising of the anchor.

As the first swells of the Pacific slapped the *Dumaru,* Fred Harmon, twenty-six-year-old first assistant engineer—the guy on whose rugged shoulders fell the responsibility of the engines—quickly sensed what a worthless unit his "black gang" would be. Sounds of pitiful retchings, vile cursing, and mumbled moans from the "sailors" told the two-hundred-pound, six-foot Harmon plainer than words about the rural backgrounds of most of the "crew." That's when he discovered that the ship's only ballast was coal!

"Seam's ar' opening up down in th' fire hole, Harmon!" reported George Olson, hard-bitten little second engineer, grimly.

"Not surprised, Olson," snapped Harmon, studying the diminutive engineer through thick-lensed glasses, "and I just discovered there are no ballast tanks to fill either!"

"What!" exploded Olson. "How in hell are we —what'll we use f'r ballast when we burn the coal b'low an' th' coal on deck's top-heavy!"

"Good question, Olson! Only never mind that now, just get the bilge pumps going!" ordered Harmon. Then, with a thin smile, he added, "Y' know,

Olson, I've a sneakin' suspicion that this tub shouda been named 'You-May-Rue.' Now, get those pumps goin' 'fore she founders off Tillamook Head!"

Olson quickly found he had other troubles. Chips, sawdust, and refuse left by the carpenters choked the pumps and they had to be stopped constantly and cleared. Olson finally got the leaking water under reasonable control—though there were always inches of black, coal-dusty sea water sloshing around underfoot in the *Dumaru's* boiler room.

The first twenty-four-hour watch of the six-hundred-some-odd miles' run down from Astoria to 'Frisco was enough to show the conscientious Harmon that the new, stiff engines needed long, hard, and expert work to break 'em in and get the *Dumaru* to Manila. This meant reducing speed to five knots. It also meant less firing and stoking. The useless black gang quickly made the most of the situation. They loafed, they fought, and they argued. A ringleader shouted dissension talk to a knot of black-hole hands down in the boiler room.

Harmon and Third Engineer Mackey leaned over the railing of a catwalk above the engine and listened, half amused, to the blasphemous bickerings below.

"Who's the guy doing all the ranting, Mac?" questioned Harmon.

"They call him 'George the Greek,'" answered the third engineer. "Name's Nokaladis."

"Sounds I.W.W. by his lingo," observed Harmon.

"Best damn'd stoker in the gang," grinned Mackey, "but a tough cookie all the way!"

"That scar looks like a streak o' lightning hit him in the face!" commented the first engineer.

"They say it's a sabre slash he got in th' Balkan Wars," volunteered Mackey, "and they tell of the time he fired ship for hours, in the Indian Ocean, singlehanded, when the Lascar stok'rs dropped like flies in the 130° heat o' th' engine room!!"

"Good guy t' have around," mused Harmon.

Up on the bridge at dawn next morning, Third Mate Andy Nolan was relieving Albert Staats, second mate. They grabbed a few minutes for a quick smoke together, leaning over the starboard rail of the bridge. Staats was the intellectual type—tall, easygoing, considerate of others, and avidly given to book study. His stateroom was a pocket-size library. Nolan, on the other hand, was Staats' opposite— young and good-looking, smart, apt, and wholly selfish—constantly "on the make," usually at the expense of others.

"Why in hell you've always got your nose in a book, Al, is beyond me." Nolan took a long drag on his cigarette, exhaling slowly and shaking his head. "You're a mystery, Staats. *You* should have a professorship—not a 'Liberty' ship."

"Do a bit of book work yourself, don't you?" Staats smiled tolerantly.

"World of difference," Nolan grinned back. "I study to get ahead. Someday I'll get my master's ticket—someday I'll have my own ship!"

"I read books to improve my mind and understand people, Andy," pointed out the second mate.

"Waste of time," snorted Nolan. "It's every man for himself in this world, Staats. What the hell do

the people you want to understand care about you?
Why, even this crazy crew are making cracks about
your reading so much. They already hate your guts
'cause most of 'em can't read. They're jealous and
suspicious of you! No, sir, if this scow started t'
sink this minute, I'd let the crummy bastards drown
an' grab me th' first lifeboat."

Suddenly a series of sharp explosions echoed
through the ship from the galley below deck, followed by a crash of pots and pans. "Graveyard"
Shaw, the Jamaican Negro cook, bounded angrily
on deck, abaft the bridge wielding a meat cleaver
menacingly.

"Whar's th' goddam son-of-a-bitch wot t'rew live
ca'tridges in m' cook stove!" he raged.

"What seems to be the matter, Shaw?" barked
Staats from the bridge.

Before Shaw could rip out a blasphemous answer,
a roar of unholy laughter broke forth up forward
as seamen poured from the fo'c'sle. Shaw raced forward along the port rail, blood in his eyes and swinging the heavy cleaver wildly above his head. Graveyard Shaw had always hated white men. This morning he hated them more than ever!

"Which one o' you barstuds put dem ca'tridges
in th' cook stove?" he screamed. "I don't hafta
take dat— I ain't no damn' white man's slave!"

With an ugly growl, Big Karl Linns broke from
the rest of the topside hands and stalked toward
Shaw, his huge hands clenched into hamlike fists.
The Russian-Finn had the body of a Goliath and
the stubbornness of a mule. Towering six foot four,
with immense shoulders, apelike arms, and a short,

thick bull neck, Karl Linns strode closer to Shaw
—his tread slow, even, and full of determination.
The big Russian-Finn's bushy black beard jutted
from an outthrust chin—his restless, slate-blue eyes
never once leaving the Jamaican cook. Still closer
came Linns.

Fascinated, Staats and Nolan watched the scene
from the bridge.

"Like th' mate said," snarled the giant, "wot seems
t' be th' matt'r, Graveyard?"

There was a split-second hesitation in Shaw's forward motion—but he still swung the cleaver de-
fiantly.

"If'n I kin catch th' stinkin' barstud wot put dem
ca'tridges in m' stove," he rumbled, "I'll split his
damn' skull wide open!"

"S'pose I done it!" roared Linns with an ugly grin.

"Why, y' goddam son-uv-a ———" raged the livid
cook, raising the cleaver still higher.

For a big man, Karl Linns moved in with the
swiftness of a panther. He caught Shaw's forearm
just above the wrist, twisting it sharply. The cleaver
clattered harmlessly to the deck.

As a roar went up from the fo'c'sle gang, Mike
Sutse, the wise, wiry little bo's'n of the *Dumaru*
elbowed his way through the crowd—pushing aside
men with his great gnarled hands that had known
the feel of the marlinspike. Squat old Sutse, Cape
Horn hard case and last of the old school of hard-
driving bo's'ns, was a thick-set Russian, wrinkled
and tanned a deep saddle brown. Sutse was dominat-
ing, but no bully—gruff, stern, and a stickler for
seamanlike methods, same as Waywood. Signed on

to keep this ragtag crew in line, he was just the
guy to do it!

"That'll be enough, you two!" he barked. "Back
t' y' galley, Shaw, an' start dishin' mornin' mess!
Linns! An' th' rest o' you, y've had y'r fun—now
git b'low an' fill y'r bellies—y'r holystonin' decks
this mornin'!"

The two mates on the bridge nodded approval
as the fo'c'sle men turned and went below. Shaw
faced about sullenly and went back to his galley
with foul-mouthed mumblings.

"Men like Sutse are hard to come by," reflected
Staats.

"Men like Sutse *understand* men like that,"
needled Nolan, "without *reading up* on 'em!"

Staats winced, but said nothing.

Off the California coast Harmon had the *Dumaru's* engine troubles pretty well licked and by
the time she came in at the Golden Gate he had
her doing a spritely ten knots up San Francisco
Bay. But her crew hadn't changed, her seams hadn't
stopped leaking, nor had the pumps kept the fire
hole dry.

When the *Dumaru* warped into her pier at Oak-
land, across the bay from 'Frisco, her skipper, Captain Ole Borrensen, came aboard for the first time.
So did Chief Engineer Howell.

About fifty, Captain Borrensen was tall, quiet,
and had deep-seated religious convictions. A true
seaman in all that that word implies, he'd come
up the hard way in a hundred ships over the seven
seas and had reached the top without the brutality
with which the sea ofttimes marks a man. He rabid-

ly hated blasphemy, though he seldom berated the offender.

Chief Engineer Howell was something else again. Small, rugged, dark, and rather good-looking, the thirty-three-year-old Howell habitually wore a neatly pressed blue uniform—even in the blistering heat of the engine room. Howell was proud of his stripes, though he had a strong smack of cynicism and from the start hated the captain. Aside from a cruise or two on the transport *Thomas*, Howell's sea experience had been confined to a little ferryboat between Los Angeles and Catalina Island. Perversely, Howell held the greatest contempt imaginable toward the sea and those who followed it— while, at the same time, he held his own position inviolate. He could make a fireroom become a living hell!

Hardly were the hawse lines out before the crew hustled off across the bay, bound for 'Frisco's waterfront bars and dives to slop up steamed beer, rotgut, and hogwash, to forget in a brief moment of delirious stupor that the "dam'd ole *Dumaru*" existed! Hours later, they stumbled back to the ship —the one place they'd foresworn—back to their nemesis. As that crusty old pirate, Long John Silver, once philosophized, "Them as dies—aye, they be th' lucky ones!"

On the morrow dawned the day of reckoning! The *Dumaru* was taken over by the United States Navy—lock, stock, and barrel! The Navy ordered her out into the roads of San Francisco Bay to load her cargo—GASOLINE and T.N.T.! Even Captain Borrensen paled at the orders!

Borrensen called a hasty conference of the *Dumaru's* officers in his cabin.

"Gentlemen," he began in a grim voice, "we've our cargo orders from the Navy! High octane gasoline and T.N.T.!"

A disconcerted groan went up from the officers. This could be bad!

"I know, gentlemen," nodded the *Dumaru's* captain with a heavy sigh. "I share your feelings, but"—he shrugged his shoulders—"those are the orders!"

"How soon do we start loading?" Waywood wanted to know.

"As soon as we can cast off and move out into the middle of the bay," answered Borrensen, "and, Mr. Waywood, just what sort of crew have we?"

The officers glanced significantly at each other. Waywood cleared his throat.

"Er—not th' best, sir!" was his far from assuring answer.

"Mr. Howell"—here the captain shot a glance at the chief engineer—"how does the black-hole gang stack up?"

"From my brief observation of 'em, sir," grated the chief, "a pretty damn'd poor breed! But Harmon, here, can give you more—he's worked with 'em down from Portland!"

The captain turned questioningly to Harmon.

"With a little tact and proper pairing up, we can make 'em do," the first engineer pointed out grimly.

"Pamper th' bastards, I s'pose!" snorted Howell.

"That'll do, Mr. Howell," warned Borrensen, quietly. Then turning again to Harmon, "They're green men, I take it?"

"Most of 'em have never been to sea before, sir," answered Harmon, "but we've a couple of old-line stokers who can teach the others. It's the best we can do—and the I.W.W. element aboard is stronger than I'd like to see it, sir!"

"Blasted Bolsheviks all over the ship, sir!" rasped Waywood. "Commissioner up in Portland should have ship'd 'em all to th' Army, but we'll keep 'em in line if we hafta break out the marlinspikes!"

"I don't approve of those methods, Mr. Waywood," said Borrensen pointedly. "Not on my ship!" Waywood shrugged resignedly. Second Mate Albert Staats and Andy Nolan, third mate, held their tongues. Howell's lip twisted into a sneer as he studied the captain. Already he disliked the skipper's consideration for others. Soft in the head, he called him. Olson and Third Engineer Mackey glanced at the chief engineer, then at each other. They knew there'd be hell to pay down in the engine room!

Angry mutterings raced through the fo'c'sle when the half-drunken crew learned of the *Dumaru's* cargo. The mutterings burst into a crescendo of rage when the red warning flag was hoisted on the gaff of the *Dumaru* as she swung at anchor in the middle of the bay!

A bleary-eyed delegation, headed by Big Karl Linns, demanded to be put ashore for a hearing with the United States Shipping Commissioner in 'Frisco. Over Waywood's protests, Captain Borrensen agreed.

"We ain't sailin' on th' *Dumaru!*" they exploded

in the Commissioner's office, as Linns shook his fist under the Commissioner's nose. "No damn'd ship comm'sh'n'r's gonna make us sail a floatin' powder keg!"

The Commissioner heard them out—these red-eyed, scrub-bearded rascals who called themselves "sailors."

"No, you boys don't *have* to go," he answered softly, "but there's a big transport loading at Sausalito for France—for the submarine zone, and for the gas-filled, rat-infested, blood-drinking trenches. You boys have your choice. . . ."

The shabby crew staggered back to the ship's boat and to the *Dumaru*. Though a couple of their number chose the transport to France!

Loading the *Dumaru* from lighters was a tough, time-consuming job—an anxious, tedious, and altogether "touchy" one. An ill-timed move could blow them all sky-high! Captain Borrensen personally supervised the stowage of the volatile cargo and the Navy assigned a lieutenant named Holmes to the *Dumaru* for the dangerous voyage—a voyage that could lead to "the point of no return"!

A silent sigh of relief went up from all hands as the last drum of gasoline came safely over the side and the last case of T.N.T. was delicately stowed below. The hatch battens were down and the *Dumaru* put to sea in fair weather, September 12, 1918, Honolulu bound!

As the *Dumaru* wallowed heavily through the Golden Gate, Chief Engineer Howell finished printing large letters on a huge blackboard down in the engine room: MAKE REVOLUTIONS! THIS CARGO IS NEEDED! Then he whirled around to face his three assistants.

"Olson," he barked, "drive those engines t' th' limit!"

"Do th' best I kin, chief," answered the tight-lipped second engineer with a trace of animosity. "They're new an' they're stiff—y' gotta coax 'em!"

"Don't give a damn how y' do it," Howell shot back at him, "but do it!"

Howell then swung around to Harmon. "You, Harmon, see to it that th' black-hole gang's divided into three watches. Y' hear, drive th' hell out o' 'em —we gotta make knots!"

Harmon and Mackey were adept and ingenious —Olson, competent and aggressive. Among them they set up a "game"—a challenge to each watch to get the most "revolutions" out of the *Dumaru's* erratic engines.

As if by some alchemy of magic, the black gang caught the spirit of the "game" and changed from sullen, surly, drunken sots to fierce, sweating, swearing dynamos! When Harmon saw his gang "hogging" and that Olson's gang was getting out of hand, he shifted George the Greek to Olson's watch. Tension eased and competition was brisker. George Nokaladis shovelled and sweated, inspired with the power of Vulcan!

Then Mackey began to gripe, his Scotch fighting blood aroused. Driving his weaker watch to the limit of endurance, Mackey got nowhere, fast.

"How in Christ's name d' y' expect me t' keep up with you an' Olson," he stormed angrily at

Harmon, "when y' give me th' scum o' these bastards t' work with!"

"All right, Mac," grinned Harmon, seeing the
reasonableness of the third engineer's argument.
"Let's try this—s'pose my gang clears out the fire-
boxes, then your watch'll start clean."

Mackey's "revolutions" came up and there was
peace—but no end of work! All watches were driven
unmercifully! There was brimstone and hellfire in
the boiler room. Heat, enmity, and fatigue got in
their deadly work! Olson, stripped to the waist,
dirty and glistening wet, was the old black-gang
bully; blasting his men and getting blasted back.
In the hell-roaring reflection of the fires, Olson was
the devil himself. Mackey, big and powerful, ruled
by main strength—exhorting his men to greater
work and doing double his own share, toiling as
though his life were in the balance.

Harmon had even a tougher time of it. Only
one man on his watch was competent in any sense
of the word—Wood, an ex-jockey, who had been
passed up by Olson and Mackey because of his short
stature. Powerfully built, Wood learned his job
fast and carried the heavy end in Harmon's watch.
Olson's biggest headache was the bad blood between
George the Greek and a stoker named Banfield.
Always wrangling, always at each other's throats,
always hurling red-hot clinkers and shovelfuls of
fire at each other!

"Cut it out, y' bastards!" Olson would roar, "or
I'll knock y'r damn'd heads t'gether!"

For a week they toiled, fought, and cursed over
the Pacific.

Then the tail end of a nor'wester struck the *Dumaru* and sent her on her beam's end with her butt nose ploughing heavy seas. She began shipping water in a hundred different places as her seams opened. Water rose nearly to her engine crankshafts and the black-hole gang threatened to desert their posts!

A nasty 30° list to port sent men headlong into the bulkheads. Savage driving and fighting, and the fear of drowning, set up a screaming, cursing bedlam! Some of the "weak sisters" in the gang collapsed into the murky, foot-deep, coal-dust-laden water of the fire hole. These had to be carried topside, while green lubbers were sent below as replacements.

Olson was like a man possessed as he struggled over bilge strainers, worried with faulty auxiliary pumps, and labored to hold together his snarling gang!

Things began to get out of hand! The *Dumaru* was rolling—and not coming back! Olson's burnt-out, seamed face, contorted rage!

"Howell! Harmon!" he screamed in a high-pitched voice. "F'r C'ris' sake, find out wot's wrong on deck 'r we'll capsize, sure!"

"What th' hell's th' matter up there?" barked Harmon into the phone to the bridge.

"Coal's shifting on deck!" shouted back Third Mate Nolan. "Get all hands topside t' trim coal!"

"No ballast tanks!" exploded Olson angrily. "Told y' there'd be trouble when th' deck coal got top-heavy!"

Howell piped new bilge lines and it was touch

and go before the water, below, was brought under control; the deck load of coal leveled off and the *Dumaru* came back on an even keel. It had been a close call!

But crisis followed crisis! No sooner had the ship been leveled before a mutiny was in the making —led by a burly, red-bearded stoker known as "Heavy." Shortly after the foundering threat was over, Heavy had been called below for his watch. Backed up by George "the Greek" Nokaladis and others in Olson's watch, Heavy stubbornly refused to go on duty. They flung back an angry ultimatum at the engineering officers.

"Wot th' hell y' mean, 'go below'!" roared Heavy. "Ain't we jus' done an eight-hour watch, trimmin' coal on deck. Ain't we jus' saved this goddam tub from foun'rin'? Like hell we'll go on duty!"

"Mr. Howell, put those two men in irons!" ordered Captain Borrensen from the bridge.

Grabbing slice bars and shovels, Howell, Harmon, and Mackey, backed up by First Mate Waywood, advanced on the ranks of the men in Olson's watch. In the sudden skirmish the officers forced the black-hole gang to give ground, wrenched Heavy and Nokaladis from them, and clamped the two trouble-makers in chains. Then the others meekly gave up and went below to the engine room.

Suddenly Howell turned on the other officers with his characteristic sourness.

"Are you men so stupid that y' can't know wot's going on around here?" he rasped bitterly.

"What d' y' mean, Howell?" asked Waywood, puzzled at the chief's sudden change in manner.

"Get all the officers t'gether in the messroom an' I'll damn' soon tell you!" ordered Howell. "All the officers except Staats—Staats I don't want!"

When the officers of the *Dumaru* assembled in the messroom, Howell faced them as one with authority, burdened with a heavy secret.

"Well, Mr. Howell, what's on your mind?" questioned Captain Borrensen, greatly annoyed by the chief's gall in calling the meeting without his knowledge. Then he added emphatically, "And it better be good!"

Howell fully exploited the moment. His tone was nasty, threatening and ominous.

"Ever since you came aboard at 'Frisco, Borrensen," lashed out the chief engineer, "you've coddled these bastards 'til now y' got a damn'd hornet's nest in y'r cap. Now, b'jeezes, I hope y'r satisfied!"

"Mr. Howell, when you address me, you'll do it civilly!" blasted Borrensen angrily. "Now, then—just what is it you're driving at!"

At this point Howell tossed a bombshell at them.

"There are plans underway t' delay, sabotage, and destroy this ship, its officers, its men, an' its cargo!" Howell's voice was thick with foreboding.

Howell paused dramatically to let his words sink in. For a second, the other officers were too dumbfounded to speak. Waywood, the first mate, glowered at the chief engineer.

"Where in hell did you get that crazy idea?" The first mate shot the question at Howell in his usual gravelly voice.

"Y' think this mutinous resistance by Heavy an' Nokaladis was accidental!" shouted the chief. "Y'

think all those threats by this goddam crew o'
slackers, draft dodgers, an' cutthroats is just hearsay!"

For a moment the officers grappled with Howell's
disquieting questions and all the terrible impli-
cations they held. Borrensen thought of the highly
volatile cargo just under them!

"Who would be so foolhardy as to be responsible
for such a crackpot plan?" asked Captain Borrensen
pointedly. "And why? Why would anybody aboard
want to execute such a diabolical plan? What would
they gain—how would they accomplish it?"

"Ha—that's a joke!" sneered Howell malevolently.
Then, after a brief pause, he leaned toward Borrensen in a semi-confidential pose. "I'll tell you who's
responsible, Captain! Staats! That's who! Staats
—y'r book-lovin' second mate—an Heavy—they're y'r
goddam ringleaders!"

There was a hum of disbelief among the officers.

"An' what's more, I tell y' I know what I'm talkin'
about," rasped the chief engineer sourly. "When
we get t' Honolulu, I'll notify authorities there!"

"Y'r nuts, Howell!" growled Waywood. "Plumb
nuts!"

Howell turned sharply and left, cursing their stu-
pidity. Captain Borrensen, with deeply furrowed
brow, said little. Had Staats not been named,
they might have credited Howell's story. But not
Staats! . . . Enough had been said, however, to
divide the officers on the matter—there was now
bad feeling among *them* as well as among the crew.

The *Dumaru* was now two days to Honolulu—
two days of turmoil and dissension. George the

Greek and Heavy chafed, swore, and lunged in their chains. Graveyard Shaw, in his galley, threatened, vilified, and damned all white men to a sailors' hell. He boasted of the men he'd killed, enlarged on the gruesome details of each murder, and became more arrogantly mutinous and dangerous. Three men had already vowed to kill him—Big Karl Linns; Mike Sutse, the bo's'n; and George the Greek! And though he ranted, openly, deep inside he seemed to sense that his days were numbered.

In a moderate gale, next day, the bearing on a rudder post support cracked and dropped the quadrant till it bound the chains to the steering engine drum. The *Dumaru* was laid to and Mackey rigged a chain hoist from the rudder post to take the weight off the chains. It was a devilish place to get to—working in the narrow confines of the stern of the rolling ship, sucking in the stifling, fetid air of the hold. Even Mackey cursed the day he signed the ship's articles!

Finally, the *Dumaru* made a landfall on Diamond Head and entered Honolulu harbor on the misty morning of September 22. She proceeded directly to the Navy docks where longshoremen waited apprehensively to unload the gasoline and munitions cargo there. Aboard, the sight of land seemed to sooth the half-mutinous crew—they were quiet.

"These bastards are too damn'd quiet," observed Mackey to Harmon. "Something's brewing!"

Mackey wasn't far wrong! With the unloading well underway and the officers gone ashore, the Bolshevik "spirit" began to ferment anew in the idle crew. They crowded around Big Karl Linns on the fo'c'sle head, and he held them spellbound.

"We're quittin'!" he shouted at them. "We're t'rough—we're walkin' off this damn'd ship—we had enough!"

"That's mutiny talk, y' goddam fool!" roared Mike Sutse, the stocky little bo's'n, trying to break up Linns' "rally." "Y'd not get fur if y' went ashore —gov'ment men'll pick y' all up an' ship y' back t' th' States—then b' jeezes y' *will* go on that transport t' France! Th' gov'ment ain't foolin' wid bastuds like you. Dis is war!"

"Mutiny 'r no mutiny!" blasted the big Russian-Finn. "War 'r no war—we're t'rough—d' y' hear!"

Attracted by the shouting of Linns and the bo's'n as he returned to the *Dumaru*, Captain Borrensen acted instantly. Securing all gangways, Borrensen rounded up the would-be mutineers and tried unsuccessfully to reason with them—but their stubborn minds were made up. Then he called in the Department of Justice men. The G men took over, selected about a dozen of those they figured were the "hard cases" — the worst troublemakers — and hustled them off the ship. Those who signed on to take their places were even worse.

But a graver cloud hung over the *Dumaru!* Chief Engineer Howell had made good his threat to "notify the authorities at Honolulu"!

"What's this about a charge of suspected sabotage against Second Mate Staats?" the Justice Department men wanted to know.

No tangible evidence to support his charges could be given by Howell during an hour's talk with the Justice men. Staats and Heavy were searched.

Nothing incriminating was found. Howell raged in exasperation. Staats was grilled unmercifully for a second time. Heavy was given the third degree. Still no evidence to bear out Howell's malevolent accusations! The G men shrugged and went ashore and the matter was dropped. Staats stayed aboard as second mate. Heavy, more resentful than ever, returned as a boss bully down in the fire hole.

For seventeen steaming days the *Dumaru* churned westward, deep in the tropics, her fire hole seldom under 120° and her black gang constantly fighting, snarling, and bullying. But under the iron grips of Harmon, Olson, and Mackey the three watches fed the insatiable fires.

Slopping up huge quantities of water, the black gang quickly became one continuous victim of severe cramps. Lime juice was issued—it helped for a while. Then the small-statured Filipinos shipped at Honolulu soon burned themselves out. Oilers and water tenders had to be pressed into service as stokers. This didn't work too well, and more ill feeling was generated! Only Borrensen and Mackey bore up without flinching. The rest of the officers were at their wit's end!

At long last the *Dumaru* raised Guam, but there was no shore leave for her restless, sullen crew. The entire island was quarantined in the throes of a "flu" epidemic!

There were no docks at Guam and the assigned cargo had to be lightered ashore. The job was tough and slow under the intense heat of a searing tropic sun. The crew was surly to the point of insolence!

A sailor named Barrett suddenly developed a violent swelling in his left hand during the unloading. Captain Borrensen took one look and rushed the man ashore to the naval hospital. Navy medics diagnosed Barrett's condition as the dread tropical disease, elephantiasis!

Through Barrett, the *Dumaru* added her score to the afflictions already besetting the tiny island. At 3:00 P.M., October 16, her consigned cargo unloaded, fresh water and supplies stowed, the *Dumaru* cleared for Manila. She raised anchor, waddled out of the bay into the Pacific—and straightway to tragedy!

Then up cropped an ironic twist. While this man Barrett was informing naval officials back at Guam of a *very real plot* to blow up the *Dumaru*, nature stepped in and took a hand!

Flashing eerily out of the inky black clouds of a sudden tropic squall, great jagged forks of lightning clutched, like giant blue fingers, at the surface of a darkened sea. Rain deluged the *Dumaru* in such torrents that her scuppers couldn't carry it away. Topside sailors waded through knee-deep water to secure movable gear on deck. Time and again twisting tongues of lightning dimmed the ship's lights. Then it struck suddenly, at 5:10 P.M.! There was a terrific, rumbling explosion forward of the bridge!

"Jee-sus! Th' ship's blown up!" bellowed the black-gang hands as coal bunkers toppled and black and bloody stokers struggled to free themselves from tons of coal!

"On deck! All of you!" roared Howell as heavy, acrid smoke eddied into the engine room.

Topside, forward, the *Dumaru* was fast becoming a sea of flame! Captain Borrensen, sensing the terrible possibilities, boomed out a command from the bridge. "Stand by to abandon ship! All hands at lifeboat stations!"

Grimly, young "Sparks," the *Dumaru's* sixteen-year-old wireless operator, stuck to his post in the wireless shack, pounding out an S O S through a half-burned-out transmitter. Ugly tongues of flames licked at the bridge and billowing smoke hid the skipper from view!

Below, in the fire hole, Mackey and Harmon rushed to shut down the engines and open the sea cocks a moment to flood the fires, then raced up the ladder to the boats. There was chaos and confusion everywhere. Never, perhaps, will a ship be abandoned with such speed and savagery!

Third Mate Andy Nolan, living up to his motto, "Every man for himself!" launched a boat with only six men and rowed off in the first few minutes of the holocaust! Those who saw him take off cursed his guts to hell. The lifeboat could have held twenty more!

Flames roared over the bridge—unmindful of the tropical deluge hissing down! Frenzied crewmen, with their lives in the balance, tore at the stiff lifeboat tackle. Searing fire licked at them as they tried to free the new, wet rope that twisted and stuck in the blocks. Cool-headed Waywood and the sea-wise bo's'n, Mike Sutse, finally freed the lines and the boat was launched just when all seemed doomed. Four men rode it down to the mountainous seas, below. Then three dozen fearful men leaped into the water after it — struggling to get aboard as best they could.

It was getting darker, now, and there were still men aboard the *Dumaru*—Captain Borrensen, Second Mate Staats, and several panicky seamen. At each passing second, time ticked away life—a king-size explosion was overdue!

"F'r God's sake, Captain—jump! Quick!" shouted Lieutenant Holmes from the overcrowded lifeboat, bobbing precariously in the waves below. "She's gonna blow any minute!"

High above them the skipper's voice boomed back through cupped hands, "There are too many in the boat already! We'll try t' get a raft launched! Get clear o' here before she explodes!"

Holmes ordered the painter cut, then shouted, "Row for your lives!"

The men in the boat needed little urging. Out into the darkness and storm they rowed, bending to each stroke in frenzied fear that it might be their last! The *Dumaru* was now a raging inferno!

Would the Captain and the other men get away? The thought troubled Jim Ferreter, an old-time seaman, as he bent to his oar! He could scarcely believe that such selfishness and cowardice were possible in the old traditions of the sea! Old Jim had rankled at Nolan's selfish act—and now *they* were deserting the skipper!

Ferreter turned angrily on Lieutenant Holmes. Almost speechless with rage, he croaked, "Return at once for the captain—you can't leave him like this!"

"No!" roared Holmes. "It's impossible—can't y' see the ship's ready to blow up!"

"Why, you yellow-livered bastud!" screamed the old sailor. "So y' call y'rself a Navy man—an' y' leave th' skipper t' be blown up with th' ship! Y' outa be hanged, goddam ya!"

"Pipe down—y' old walrus!" shouted Big Karl Linns, pushing Ferreter to the thwart.

Beside himself with rage, Ferreter freed his hand, grabbed the mast in the center of the lifeboat, and heaved it overside. "There, you sons o' bitches, I hope t' hell y' *all* die!"

They dared not stop to pick up the mast because the *Dumaru* was a roaring pyre and treacherously near, but the incident had terrible repercussions later on!

Bending to the oars again, the survivors sent the boat a good mile distant before a nerve-shocking explosion tore apart the *Dumaru's* superstructure and deck, sending them skyward in a huge fiery shower of blazing embers like a giant skyrocket! Still another ugly danger faced the men in the boat. The sea around them suddenly lit up into a seething sheet of gasoline-fed flame and a strong wind edged it toward the lifeboat with diabolic rapidity!

Again it was another rough race with death. The spent rowers urged the boat clear of the floating, flaming hell! At last, as in a nightmare, they managed to outdistance the fire! But there was little rest. The sea rose in a tumbling series of black, foreboding mountains and the torrential rains came again.

A short "breather" was ordered for all hands,

then a sea anchor was rigged and Holmes, under an oil slicker, laid a course for Guam by using the boat's compass lighted by the smoky glimmer of a lantern. Rigging a makeshift leg-o'-mutton sail on two long oars lashed together, the boat's speed was greatly increased and some of the company even talked of breakfast at Guam.

However, this idea was short-lived as Holmes called a sudden halt for fear of crashing Guam's outer reefs in the inky darkness. There was loud disagreement as to Holmes' overcautious judgment, but they hove to and through that long first night the boat rode with her head into the sea. A hasty shelter was thrown together with the sail set over oars lashed athwart the gun'ls. But it fell far short of its purpose. The deck-hand gang took over. Then the black gang pushed them out.

"Get out o' there, y' deck swabs!" bellowed George Nokaladis. "This here shelter's f'r th' fire-hole gang—get t' hell out!"

Big Karl Linns strode angrily forward from the boat's stern.

"What th' hell y' mean—the fire-hole gang!" he boomed. "Come on, you topside hands—le's clear them bastuds outa here!"

Then a free-for-all broke out amidship—seamen and stokers fighting each other for space under the tiny shelter.

"Belay, back there!" barked Holmes from the bow. "You'll all take turns—watch an' watch, alike!"

Order was restored in the boat and Big Karl Linns stalked grumpily aft, joining Harmon and Ole Heikland, another old-time sailor. Officers were up forward—crew survivors amidships. Astern, Harmon, suffering severe face burns inflamed by the salt water, bore his pain stoically. Linns and Heikland shared their oil slicker with him.

All hands slept fitfully that first night in the lifeboat. At dawn they awoke to take stock of a bad situation, facing up to grim realities!

Thirty-two men overloaded a boat built for twenty-six! All the officers of the black gang were aboard — Howell, Harmon, Olson, and Mackey. Waywood, the first mate, was the only deck officer aboard and just how Lieutenant Holmes claimed full authority to take over was never made clear.

Waywood sensed that the very presence of men like Graveyard Shaw, George "the Greek" Nokaladis, and Big Karl Linns meant potential trouble! He wondered if Holmes sensed it, too. The first mate knew how little law and order were regarded by such men and how the slightest deviation from discipline could throw the entire balance of control into the wrong hands—could literally toss them all into the oblivion of a trackless Pacific!

Grimly Waywood studied the faces of the men in the boat while Holmes explained to them what had to be done. Grimly he drew a mental picture of "who would side with whom" in case of a showdown.

There was the steward, Christiansen, atheist and cynic—he and Shaw cronied together aboard the *Dumaru*. He'd be Shaw's man. What of the messman, Metcalf? Metcalf, the sniveling lady-killer from Portland—he'd follow Shaw and the steward to hell, of course. "Honolulu" Peter? Not to be trusted—

he shipped at Hawaii and was no better or no worse than the "hard case" he had replaced.

Waywood speculated on the black gang. They'd probably stand by George the Greek to a man, come a showdown of strength against command. Topside? It would be a tossup, Waywood thought. They could count on the Jenningses—father and son. Ole Heikland and Pete Wieland, old Jim Ferreter —and there were a few others who might be counted on in a pinch. Then there was Mike Sutse, the bo's'n—he'd help keep 'em in line, if he had to use an oarlock to do it!

Among the officers? Howell and Olson would be no help—they'd antagonize the black gang into starting trouble! Harmon? Mackey? Good men to have around! Holmes? Waywood shrugged—too inexperienced to handle men. Young "Sparks"? Good kid—honest and a worker. Did a yeoman job trying to get an S O S on the air!

Waywood watched dissension, suspicion, and conspiracies erupt aboard the lifeboat as the Dumaru men tried vainly to beat their way back to Guam. He saw morale beginning to disintegrate among them as they fought slowly toward the island, only to have wind and the sea dead against them! Day after day it was the same—the changing trade winds, tides, and crosscurrents ganging up on thirty-two sea-weary men!

The first mate watched it all. He saw irritations grow into arguments, then break out into a rash of knockdown, drag-out fights amidships. He saw Shaw and Honolulu Pete tear into each other with such snarling savagery that they nearly went overside. He noted the look of genuine disappointment among the crew when they didn't! Waywood watched the hangdog expression on haggard faces when the daily rations dropped to a single sea biscuit and a dram of tepid water per man—and the island of Guam leering in their faces, off the port bow!

Howell, up forward, was hoarse from his damning condemnation of Staats.

"It's him that blew her up!" stormed the chief engineer vitriolically. "That dirty bastard, Staats, blew up th' *Dumaru!*"

The clear voice of young "Sparks" rose to refute him.

"You're wrong, Mr. Howell—dead wrong! He didn't do it!"

"Don't argue with me!" roared Howell. "I tell y' Staats did it!"

"I tell you he didn't!" raged back young "Sparks." "I saw the flash that fired the hold—th' same one that got my antenna!"

And so it went—growing dissension and suspicion from all quarters. Waywood made mental notes of the touchy situation and it wasn't a pretty picture. He realized that something serious could develop in the minds of these jokers as the sun seared them by day and the winds chilled them to the marrow by night.

Harmon, the big first engineer, huddled in the aft quarter of the boat, suffering much but saying little. Big Karl Linns poured blasphemous maledictions on all of them for leaving Captain Borrensen stranded on the burning *Dumaru;* for the gross inaptitude in the handling of the boat by Holmes, and for the rascality of Ferreter in pitching the mast overside in a fit of anger!

As the short Pacific twilight of the third day deepened into a bronze dusk, Waywood caught the shifting motions of Shaw and George Nokaladis skulking toward the preciously meager stores of food and water.

"Mackey," he whispered hoarsely, picking up a small hatchet near by, "grab th' other hatchet, quick —Shaw 'n' th' Greek are tryin' t' raid th' stores!"

In a surprise attack the two officers rushed the marauders.

"Belay, there!" ordered Waywood as he and Mackey forced the two back. "What's the big idea!"

"We wuz hungry!" growled Shaw as Waywood shoved him to the bottom of the boat.

"We share 'n' share alike on this boat!" blasted the first mate. "Next time y' try that trick I'll crease y'r thick skull with this hatchet—y' understand!"

Two days later Lieutenant Holmes glanced up at the makeshift sail and studied it disconsolately.

"Take down the sail!" he ordered—then added, "every man will take a thirty-minute turn at the oars and we'll try to close with the island!"

But it was no good. The boat was too heavy and cumbersome—the seas and wind too strong against the weary *Dumaru* men!

"Belay the rowing!" commanded Holmes after several hours at the oars left the lifeboat no nearer Guam. He rationed out a biscuit and a dole of tepid water to the exhausted survivors. The rumble of discontent grew louder.

"Mr. Waywood, sound our water supply," ordered the Navy lieutenant. "It's time we took stock."

Waywood sounded the two water tins with a splinter cut from an oar. "We've just four and a half gallons aboard, for thirty-two men!"

"We ain't got that!" cried Mike Sutse, the bo's'n, pointing to the can they had been using. "She's leakin' out!"

"Oh, Christ!" wailed Holmes as the first mate poured the precious water into the sound can before the eyes of the suffering men. Only the poised hatchets halted a near riot and kept them at a safe distance.

To lessen physical and mental friction, the cramped positions each man had had to assume in the overcrowded lifeboat were ordered rearranged. This move served two purposes—it relieved stiff muscles and bolstered waning discipline.

Harmon, Mackey, "Sparks," Ole Heikland, Big Karl Linns, and Metcalf took over the bow and cockpit. Waywood, Holmes, Howell, and Olson held the stern quarter. Honolulu Pete and three Filipinos were quartered amidship. Just forward of them were George "the Greek" Nokaladis, Graveyard Shaw, and the rest, graded aft in inverse ratio to the swing of an oar and the hatchets by the able Master-of-Arms Mackey, aided by the stout little bo's'n, Mike Sutse.

Endless fighting continued among the Filipinos and night brought on skirmishes for places under the narrow shelter of the sail. When the sea was calm the crowding thinned out with a few lying along the broad gun'ls of the lifeboat. Nokaladis the Greek early adopted the philosophy that the Filipinos and Graveyard Shaw would be better off fed to the sharks. On one occasion he, singlehandedly, tossed the Filipinos overside to prove his point. They were quickly fished out, but not before sharks began snapping at them hungrily.

More dazzling days drifted over the glassy-eyed survivors. The blistering rays of the tropic sun seared them unmercifully. All were suffering from a lack of water and, heedless of the dire consequences, Olson and Howell slopped up quantities of sea water.

"Quit it, you fools!" bellowed Waywood. But it was like taking drugs—insidiously it grew on them —they couldn't stop!

There was never a sight of the captain—or Nolan.

Then one day the *Dumaru* men spied the Guam patrol boat! Hopes were lifted to the skies. They considered themselves well on the way to rescue— but the boat never sighted them and their hopes were dashed into despondency! It had, perhaps, altered its course toward them to clear a reef, then disappeared from sight beyond a jut of land. The incident had its tragic effect — gaunt-faced men peered after it with tearful eyes and the Greek rose and faced Holmes angrily!

"You good-f'r-nothin' bastud, Holmes!" screamed Nokaladis. "Y'r t'rough as command'r—d'y' hear!"

Holmes' face drained white as the shock of the Greek's words struck him, but he held his silence.

"Y' lost y'r chance t' save us th' night we left th' *Dumaru*," stormed the Greek, " 'cause y' didn't have th' guts t' make f'r Guam an' keep goin'.

Sure they's reefs—but we had a goddam good chance!
Now, b' jeezes, I'm callin' f'r a vote t' t'row y' out!
Wot d' y' say, boys!"

"Aye!" roared back voices from all quarters.

"To whom?" asked Holmes, relinquishing his
command as gracefully as circumstances permitted—
knowing his life wasn't worth a nickel in that crowd
of desperate men.

"Waywood, of course! Who else!" boomed Big
Karl.

Waywood, in the stern—cold as steel—assented by
addressing them in general but eyeing the Greek in
particular.

"I take the boat, not because you want me to
—I don't give a good goddam for any of you! I take
it because it's *my* boat and it's *my* place to handle
it. Now that y'r all staring hell square in th' face
y' come t' me. Okay. But when I give an order
I want it carried out!"

His words came evenly, almost confidentially, but
there was deadly import in them and they weren't
wasted on the scarecrows amidships.

"If you think I can sail this scow into Guam or
any other island, with the trades and tides against
us, y'r damnedly mistaken! You're a hell of a long
way from Guam," Waywood continued brusquely,
"only y' don't know it! The passing of that Guam
patrol boat very likely sealed our doom! Our track
will be out of the lanes in spite of all we can do
to prevent it!"

Tensely and in awed silence the survivors hung
onto his words, for they instinctively knew that
their lives were in his hands—good hands, too, for

few seamen knew the Pacific better than Waywood.

"In my opinion, our only chance is to sight fishing boats from the Caroline Islands," he added ominously.

As his words sunk into their dulled minds, the crew's last illusions fled—they knew the worst!

"Now, bend to the oars," ordered the first mate, "and let there be no shirking!"

Through the night they toiled, watch and watch. The sea and wind came up and they struggled to hold what little they had gained. A lantern and two friction flares silhouetted the grotesque shadows of the *Dumaru* men, bending mechanically to the oars like Roman galley slaves! They continued to question Waywood.

"How long we gotta row this goddam tub?" they whined.

"Thirteen hundred t' two thousand sea miles, as I figure it." He gave them the naked truth in a steely voice, then added, "But there may be squalls from the right quarter, at times, that'll help draw us to the Philippines.

"Good Christ!" they moaned. "Le's take another chance at Guam!"

"No good!" snapped Waywood. No one knew better than he how much the cards were stacked against them. Still, he didn't hesitate a moment in turning west from the island.

Waywood was also quick to discern that the brutal labor, with little water and almost no food, would soon finish them! He combined the know-how of Ole Heikland and the ship's carpenter, Frank Ferdette, in an attempt to improve the boat's sailing and spare the men. The situation bettered for a time.

Then came another one of those weird bits of irony—one of those satanic twists that crop up so often in disasters at sea! They sighted a ship that seemed to be hove to! A queer, massive object a mile or two off the starboard beam. Excitement ran high—they changed course, all hands waving wildly! As the lifeboat drew into hailing distance—the "rescue" ship, like kaleidoscopic objects in a nightmare, became the burned-out-hulk of the *Dumaru* —bottom up! A charred, mute token of their present predicament!

"Oh, God," groaned the *Dumaru* men, cursing the day they set eyes on her!

"Stop it!" roared Waywood. "We still might get through to her stores!"

They sought to force an entry into the hull, but with their meager tools it proved hopeless—even dangerous—for at any moment she might settle to the bottom and suck them into the sea with her! With downcast hearts they heaped blasphemies on "th' damn'd old *Dumaru*" and turned away from the loathsome object which had once been their ship. But the sagacious Waywood had correctly surmised from the position of the hulk, the almost insuperable force of wind and tide.

On the lonely wastes of the vast Pacific they drifted, cursed, speculated, and suffered. Sharks followed in their wake forbidding a dip into cooling waters to ease pain and thirst. A few of the more venturesome risked it while mates fended with boat hooks and oars.

The passing days were but somber preludes to blacker days to come! Tongues began to swell. Dehydration left their bodies wizened scarecrows.

Graveyard Shaw's iniquitous curses croaked from a swollen throat. He and Francisco Benedicto, a still vigorous little Filipino, snagged a few small fish by ingeniously opening the inlet valve of the Lundin-type boat, then pumping the water in and out. But the small success was to cost Shaw dearly —the fish added to his thirst and he quenched it momentarily, at a price, by drinking more and more sea water!

Around the thirteenth day, Waywood cautiously announced that they were in the zone of the Caroline fishermen.

"Bear a sharp watch for fishing craft!" he ordered every lookout. But the first mate secretly believed there was only narrow possibility that such craft would be sighted. The Philippines were their last real hope!

Such fitful and erratic winds and tides made steering watches useless in keeping the boat out of the wind's eye. There was meager consolation in the fact that they were nearing a point where the nor'-west monsoon might work in their favor. Hour upon hour, Howell, Holmes, and Sutse argued on these possibilities. It kept them reasonably sane! No charts or instruments were aboard the lifeboat, except the boat's compass, but Waywood's sea lore was sound and sure.

Then another struggle for power began. Holmes was strictly "navy," with a naval rating, and he felt he was being "left out in the cold." Backed by the irascible Howell, plus the pressure of growing dissension aboard, Waywood gave Holmes authority over the priceless waning stores of bread and water. Howell was to be his assistant. "Sparks" and Harmon were to keep the boat clean—Mackey to keep order!

The wind now rose and fell at precisely the same time each day. It became a "clock" for changing watches, the doling of the thimbleful of water and the few crumbs of sea biscuit. The survivors quickly learned to conserve strength. Morning hours were designated for necessary tasks, no matter how trivial. After the "dole" there was nothing to look forward to but another twenty-four hours! Each serving could well be their last, they knew, and this anxiety, alone, was distracting to the point of sullen desperation!

The fifteenth day brought the last pitiful drop of water and then overwhelming thirst! One by one the *Dumaru* men began to break! Olson deteriorated fast—Holmes developed a fiery ulcer—Graveyard Shaw became a dangerous maniac!

Out of a background of engineering know-how, Howell came up with a suggestion to sound the air tanks forming the double bottom of the lifeboat, theorizing that they still held test water sealed in at the shipyard. With energy, fired by desperation and the hope of *water,* Howell adroitly removed the studs securing the manhole cover with the hatchet butt. He slid carefully into the tank and found precious water! Sponging it up with reverent care, Howell passed it topside to Waywood who readily

pronounced it "fresh" water—but contaminated with
particles of red lead.

"So long as it isn't salt!" growled Howell, scoop-
ing up more of it in a small tobacco can. Then he
emerged and resealed the tank.

"Forget it," advised Waywood, "chuck it overside!"

"Drink!" retorted Howell angrily. "Be damn'd
glad t' get it!"

Those who drank were soon to die!

Big Karl Linns, sadist, enjoyed it all. "You bastuds laughed at me an' my yarn of th' boat off Chile!
Now y'r gonna see! Yes, b' jeezes, an' y'r gonna
feel, too!" Then he laughed uproariously.

Holmes, Howell, and "Sparks" tried to filter the
salt from sea water by passing it through a canvas
stocking filled with cork from life jackets and char-
coal from charred boat splinters. It failed miserably.

"Give me wat'r 'r I'll kill y' all!" croaked Shaw,
hour after hour. His far-spent condition belied his
threats. Later, the big Jamaican cook roused up
and began a wild, croaking chant—then he'd pray
in a strange disjointed jargon—a sacrilegious dirge
of sorts that ended in a string of oaths and the pro-
nouncement, "I'm no white man's slave!"

"That's all f'r him!" announced the Greek scornfully.

Shaw died near sunset. It was a terrible sight
and made a grim impression on the rest of the
Dumaru survivors. Bloated and swollen to the point
of bursting, Shaw lay stretched out in the bottom
of the boat, the skin of his face drawn tight like
a mummy's—a grotesque, black tongue protruding

between thick, cracked lips! Linns and the bo's'n heaved him over the side. It was a relief to all, but it marked the first death among them, and with each passing hour they grew more despondent. From then on, sharks never left the wake of the lifeboat!

That night, after Shaw died, a young seaman named Bolin and Second Engineer Olson, who already was in a bad way, began drinking sea water. By evening, next day, they laid in the boat's bottom, raving mad. Both died during the night! Three gone—and despair settled down heavily over the wan survivors!

The sixteenth day passed and with it the last chance of overhauling the Carolines!

What remained of the ship's biscuits went begging—swollen throat membranes refused to swallow them!

About the seventeenth day, Mackey and Holmes —partly to escape going mad—began working on a rather ingenious device to distill water from the sea. They conceived the idea of using a biscuit tin for a boiler, the water tank for a condenser, and the hollow plunger on the bail-out pump as the hookup line to the condenser. The device was to be fired by oars, clothing, shoes—anything that would burn.

With their limited tools and waning strength, Mackey and Holmes set to work. Tedious hours later they produced an evaporator that actually worked! But it was too slow. After nearly everything aboard had been burned, less than a quart of fresh water had been distilled!

Driven to desperation by thirst, Hetinger, another

young seaman, went berserk and made a wild attempt to wreck the evaporator. He had to be forcibly restrained and became the fourth death shortly after. A few words of prayer that someone remembered were said over him—then he was cast into the sea. His clothes were saved for firing the evaporator, but, after getting only a few more thimblefuls of water, Mackey and Holmes temporarily gave up the distilling idea.

Then Big Karl Linns and Louis Samuelson, an oiler and erstwhile film router for Fox Films, set up an agonizing discourse on cold beer and stuffed fowl. But the "gourmets" were doused by a man-made wave. Linns was insulted and roared, "If I find out th' bastud who did that, I'll. . . ." But Big Karl never found out.

The death of young Hetinger was a harbinger for Chief Engineer Howell. Howell went fast—too much sea water and red lead had licked him! In his delirium the chief engineer imagined he was back on the *Dumaru*. "Stop those engines!" he shouted wildly. "Stop 'em, you bastards—y' hear!" Then Howell slipped to the bottom of the boat—dead! The fifth man to go!

As Jennings, the elder—an A.B. seaman—watched Howell gasp his last breath, he began an incoherent gibberish. Day after day, Jennings' fatherly devotion to his son had earned him a warm spot in the hearts of all the *Dumaru* men aboard the hopelessly drifting lifeboat. He had refused water time and again—sacrificing his share that the boy might be better able to pull through this grim ordeal! But such sacrifice had been too much for the senior Jennings, and a horrified son, powerless to help, watched his father slowly "crack up" under the terrible mental and physical strain!

For sheer agony, Pete Wieland, seaman, had suffered the most of any man aboard—and without a whimper! Wieland was one solid ulcer from head to foot—burned by the sun, doused by the salt spray, and racked by the nerve-consuming pain! Youngest and healthiest of the men in the boat, Wieland should have been the last to go—but the ulcers had doomed him and he knew it! Grimly he bore his great burden in stoic silence, neither asking help nor begging favors!

It was in the early evening of this seventeenth day, during a lull after a long, gruelling stint at the oars, that George Nokaladis fell strangely quiet. When most of the men—worked out and semi-delirious—had sunken into a comatose stupor, the Greek, lying back against a gun'l, studied Howell's body through half-closed eyes, then turned them on Mackey. A malevolent grin twisted his scarred face as his vile mind conjured up a sure-fire plan for self preservation.

With the aid of the Filipinos, the Greek suddenly seized the knives and the two hatchets—then defied the rest! Rising up on one of the thwarts, he reeled off a bold speech—all a part of his plan!

"Lis'n—all o' ya!" bellowed Nokaladis, "I'm takin' c'mmand o' this boat! Y'll take y'r orders from me, now, an' I'll save y' all—give me any lip an' I kin kill y' all!"

The men looked at him with unfeigned contempt, too weary to bother with an answer. Mackey was

on the point of charging him, but at a sign from
Waywood, held off. Night came on and most of
the men drowsed back into their nightmarish stupor
—all except the Greek and his gang of Filipinos.
Nokaladis smiled indulgently on his cohorts. The
first phase of his plan was working to perfection,
a plan, not so much for the desire for command but
for the sole possession of the still warm body of
Howell! The men had been so far spent that they
hadn't thrown him overboard!

The whispered words and the huddled forms
around the chief engineer's body caught Harmon's
curiosity. Mackey, too, was quickly alerted to the
macabre inference of the situation. He moved silently to Harmon's side.

"The Greek's all set t' cook up the Chief's body!"
warned Mackey in a whisper to Harmon. "Heard
him spring it on the Filipinos just before dusk.
Must have taken a page outta' Big Karl's book!"

"Why Big Karl?" questioned Harmon, shooting a
puzzled look at Mackey.

"Because Karl's a cannibal himself!" grinned
Mackey grimly. "Y' heard that yarn about the boat
off Chile, didn't ya?"

"Hell, Karl was just pullin' our leg on that one,"
Harmon grinned back.

"Don't kid y'rself, Harmon," Mackey whispered
seriously. "That yarn was th' McCoy all right—an'
I heard Karl tell th' Greek if he could boil that
meat a little in sea water there ain't no salt in it
an' only a little in th' broth—Karl says it would
save some lives!"

Harmon cursed softly.

"Y' know what," Mackey went on, "that damn'd Greek asked me this afternoon if he could use the evaporator! Now, b'gad, I know what for!"

"Does Waywood know?" asked Harmon.

"Sure—but what th' hell can he do?" shrugged Mackey. "Th' Greek's got th' ace!"

Strangely fascinated, the two engineers watched the grisly proceedings. Even to a couple of practical guys like Harmon and Mackey the whole thing seemed incredibly unreal—bizarre—like something out of the *Arabian Nights!*

There, in the wavering yellow glimmer of the lantern, the grinning little Filipinos, huddling closer, began stripping the clothes off Howell's body, while the Greek in the grotesque shadows above them busied himself with the evaporator! Mackey momentarily broke the macabre picture by darting forward and with deadly precision snatched the chief's coat and cap from the hands of a surprised Filipino —then, as quickly, darted aft—nights were cold and clothing was scarce! The Greek said nothing, only grinned.

So hardened had they all become to suffering that they watched with little emotion as the knives cut away flesh from Howell's lean frame. But Harmon turned aside from the gruesome scene when the Greek hacked off the head with a hatchet.

After the biscuit-tin boiler was a little more than half filled with meat, sea water was added and a fire started underneath it. Ironically, Nokaladis kindled the blaze with papers from the chief engineer's pockets! Suddenly Nokaladis was aware he had an audience. He turned on them sharply in a storm of profanity.

"Look, y' chicken-hearted bastuds!" he leered. "Look! An' that, b' jeezes, is all y'll get—a look!"

Meanwhile Holmes and the mate argued pro and con as to the value of such nourishment. Holmes was against it—Waywood was for trying it.

"If we eat," argued the young naval lieutenant, "we'll all die quicker!"

"No—you're wrong, Holmes," refuted Waywood. "It saved Linns' life off Chile, didn't it? I've heard of cases, myself, where such extremes saved lives —and God knows *this* is an extreme case! I'm for tryin' it!"

Shortly after the fire was lighted under the biscuit-tin boiler, the Greek lost control of the boat. In their enthusiasm for "dinner," the Greek and his gang of Filipinos forgot the weapons. Alert to the changes of fortune, Mackey and Sutse seized them without a struggle. George Nokaladis grinned sheepishly, but he knew his plan had worked—he'd won his point—self-preservation! The Greek even thought of himself as a "hero" of sorts—other lives might be saved!

After a time the meat dissolved into broth and the *Dumaru* survivors crowded around the steaming biscuit-tin boiler with cups, tins and bailers— waiting for the "dole out." The salt in the sea water was absorbed by the flesh, leaving a not-unpleasant salt-free broth that gave almost immediate strength to all—but for Pete Wieland and the elder Jennings nourishment came too late—for them the end was only hours away!

That night the survivors suffered little. The improvised sail was drawing from a fair wind, the seas were calm, and the lifeboat steered itself. They slept soundly—all but George the Greek! Nokaladis sneaked back to the pot and selfishly finished it off. But he overplayed his hand on "self-preservation." He went raving mad!

"Th' longboat veal's got him!" was Big Karl's laconic comment.

There was less hardship next day—the survivors' eighteenth in the lifeboat—but it had its events. They counted their first suicide—and they caught their first sizable fish.

The ship's steward, Christiansen, self-styled atheist, small-time snitcher and erstwhile crony of Graveyard Shaw, suddenly decided to give up the struggle! His lot had been a tough one aboard this boat of human wrecks. Christiansen had abandoned ship in the only clothes he had on at the time of the first explosion—a pair of thin shorts. Huge ulcers had eaten into his shoulders and he had long been excluded from the makeshift shelter, amidship. Nobody wanted him!

"Now, I *know* there ain't any God!" he remarked caustically around noon. Then he slid silently overside! There was no effort to save Christiansen—they all knew, only too well, that it was the most merciful way out. He had every right to die the way he had chosen. For a time, the little steward trailed the boat, clutching the grab line with his head submerged. Then he let go and sank from sight—the sixth death!

"That's a helluva way t' do it!" growled Big

Karl contemptuously. "Why didn't th' little bastud
jus' let go 'stead o' holdin' on?"

"Took consid'r'ble guts to do what he just did,"
explained Waywood. "He was afraid o' the pot—
so when he went down, he meant to *stay down!*
Though to my way o' thinkin', it was kinda stupid—
sharks or men—what th' hell's th' difference?"

They could only shrug at the mate's explanation
—but secretly most of them could see the steward's
point.

Waywood, on his watch, fashioned a gigantic gaff
and fishhook from a ⅜-inch steel rod out of the
pump plunger. By heating, hammering and rasp-
ing, he had worked it out, barb and all. He turned
it over to Big Karl, one-time Baltic fisherman, who,
with his tremendous reach, snagged a dolphin on
the first cast and landed it straight into the boat!
For those able to partake, it was a reprieve from
death! On two successive days they had had nourishment and new hopes soared.

On the nineteenth day they caught a quart of
water from a sudden squall—pouring it out of the
sail into an empty turpentine can! Big Karl snagged
another dolphin. They also counted three more
deaths—a young messman, Samson; the senior Jennings; and a Filipino fireman. That brought the
total to nine dead! But this time Big Karl Linns'
"good fishing" worsened their condition. Those
who could eat overate, retched, and ended up weaker
than ever.

The twentieth day saw the *Dumaru* men staring
dull-eyed at the Greek's final convulsion and horrible, writhing death—the tenth! Big Karl celebrat-

ed it by unceremoniously heaving him overboard
with the profane requiem, "Good-by, you son-of-a-
bitch, and don't come back!"

Cracked lips twisted into painful smiles.

Strangely enough, no one recorded the twenty-
first day, but the twenty-second day was a day of
madness, horror, and approaching death!

Ole Heikland, Honolulu Pete, Wood, the ex-
jockey, Jim Ferreter—all of them had slumped to
the bottom of the lifeboat, more dead than alive!
Metcalf, messman and self-styled Romeo, had little
to say of his romantic conquest back in Portland—
his number, too, was rapidly coming up! Time and
again he repeated in a semi-conscious monotone that
he didn't want to die at sea—that he frankly dreaded
the pot and the sharks alike—that a coffin on solid
land was his fondest wish. Always the reprobate,
he now chanted over and over like a litany, "Surely
God cannot let us die like this!"

On the twenty-third day, twenty-two miserable
men lay like so many apparitions about the boat—
gaunt-faced, hollow-eyed—they had reached the apex
of suffering! Waywood, the mate, still sat up,
propped against the stern of the lifeboat—keeping
ceaseless vigil for ships, storms, changes in wind and
current. He sat like a phoenix risen out of the ashes
of hell—determined, inflexible, and unyielding!

Nor was Big Karl Linns ever down for long.
Catching fragments of talk between Honolulu Pete
and Ole Heikland—a jumble of gibberish of the
delirious—Karl crept to their side and tried to solace
them in his own rough way.

"Stick it out, boys—don't give up now!" he said,

pouring out a cascade of cheer—though his own features belied his optimism. "We're hittin' th' beach in a matter o' a couple of days! Think o' it, Ole—wild pig, coconuts, fruit, an' rivers o' water! No more o' this f'r us, Ole—it's a cabin for us, near th' salmon grounds o' Sou'western Alaska! Christ, man, this is nearly over! Brace up, Ole!"

Only a deep, low groan came from Ole Heikland. He was past help. Harmon, "Sparks," and several others came over to Big Karl, looking at him questioningly.

"How can you be so sure, Karl?" asked Harmon at length. "I mean—about the land—coconuts, an' y'r rivers of water!"

"Why—why th' sea birds I seen this mornin'!" answered Big Karl, surprised at Harmon's disbelief. "Th' bo's'n bird 'n' other shore birds, big pieces o' shore growth, weeds, kelp 'n' coconuts!"

"Instead o' soundin' off about y'r pipe dreams," interrupted Mackey dubiously, "you'd better be hustlin' some fuel f'r the evaporator. It's y'r only chance t' see those pretty things you've been paintin'!"

A solemn conference on the grim status of the bleak situation was held by Harmon, Mackey, and the mate. For the first time Mackey himself began to give up hope.

"What are the possibilities of our having skirted the Philippines?" he asked Waywood bluntly. "S'pose we've already passed into the China Sea?"

"Impossible, Mac," answered the mate. "It's a straight course no less than thirteen hundred miles from Guam to th' Philippines, so it's far too soon t' believe we're in th' China Sea!"

"Yeah—but we've been driftin' westward f'r more'n twenty days!" put in Harmon. "Even allowing f'r wind, current, an' calms, we must be gettin' near *some* land!"

Waywood hesitated a moment to make rough calculations—then nodded. "Mebbe y'r not far wrong —mebbe we might reach land any time from now!"

Harmon and Mackey agreed that under these circumstances the evaporator could be started—even though it meant burning the thwarts and other wooden parts of the lifeboat. Harmon called an inventory to find who could work and chop wood. Seven men out of the twenty-two were fit for the task—Mackey, Waywood, Sutse, Big Karl, "Sparks," Samuelson, the oiler, and himself.

Suddenly the mate looked around the boat and asked sharply, "Where th' hell's Holmes?"

Holmes was out—sprawled in the bottom of the lifeboat—burned up by fever, with a fiery ulcer clutching at his throat! Waywood hadn't forgotten how Lieutenant Holmes had taken over his boat the night they abandoned ship—it galled him and he hated Holmes for it! Up to this moment Waywood had controlled his feelings on the matter, now he seized Holmes and dragged him to his feet! But the helpless Holmes "blacked out" and sank limply to the bottom of the boat again, while the mate, between gasps for breath from the exertion, soundly berated him. It was the first real sign that Waywood, too, was beginning to crack!

Feverishly working in pairs to conserve strength,

the eight able-bodied *Dumaru* men chopped away thwarts and solid oak inboard ribs of the boat—anything that would produce fire to distill precious drops of water! The terrific heat of the tropic sun beat down on them unmercifully. They staggered through the day, dripping with the sweat of sheer weakness! The evaporator finally gave off a few sorry thimblefuls of water only enough to make their thirst more torturing!

A couple more of the Filipinos died—the raving in their Tagalog dialect ended! Twelve of the original thirty-two in the boat were now dead!

As sunset slanted across a coppery sea, all hands exhausted themselves luffing sail to catch the erratic "cats-paws" wafting fitfully over the water—only to have the wind puffs haul into the north that night and nearly freeze them!

Wood, Honolulu Pete, and Ole Heikland were obviously dying. Big Karl raised the shapeless semiconscious form of Heikland in his arms and broke into pitiful sobs over his pal. Honolulu Pete died at 10:00 P.M. by the mate's watch—marking the thirteenth death. Clutching Heikland closer to him, Big Karl cried, "F'r C'ri' sake—can't any o' you help me with Ole?"

Dumbly they stared at Linns out of a helpless stupor. Suddenly, Louie Samuelson, the oiler, made his way over to Big Karl and had a few whispered words with him. Linns nodded, his eyes brightening in the weird, yellowish light of the lantern. Samuelson crossed to Honolulu Pete's body.

With Ole Heikland still in his arms, Big Karl murmured directions to Samuelson who grimly

stripped Honolulu Pete, beheaded him, hung the
body over one of the remaining thwarts, and caught
the blood in an empty kerosene can! Trembling
with acute nervousness, Samuelson managed to di-
lute the blood slightly with sea water. He nearly
dropped the can as he passed it to Big Karl. Big
Karl forced the opening of the can between Heikland's lips. Ole downed a few swallows and pleaded
for more!

After Heikland had all that Big Karl thought
was good for him, the can was passed from lip to
lip. Even the mate stumbled forward for a drink,
mumbling thickly, "Give me some—I'm dying!"

What little remained in the can was taken up
forward to Holmes and "Sparks" who both lay nearly
unconscious in the bottom of the boat. Holmes
scorned the drink with a feeble wave of the hand;
"Sparks" drank his share and felt stronger!

Gruesome though the task was, five of the ablest
Dumaru men, led by Big Karl, cut flesh from Honolulu Pete's body, put it down in the biscuit-tin
boiler, half filled with sea water, and started a fire
under it with Pete's clothing—grimly knowing that
the nourishment from the broth would save and
sustain life!

At this point, Holmes roused himself to semi-
consciousness and muttered his last words to
"Sparks," handing him his watch.

"If you get out of this mess, send this to my wife!"
he whispered. Then, balancing himself on the boat's
gun'l, he snarled scornfully at his mates, "I'd rather
die—than live with man-eaters!"

Then he plunged into the sea—and became the fourteenth death!

The gray, clammy dawn of the twenty-fourth day —their last day in the lifeboat—broke over the Pacific and etched a grisly picture deep into the minds of the *Dumaru* men—an image that would remain with them forever! Honolulu Pete, headless and armless—half leaning, half sitting against the starboard gun'l of the lifeboat—confronted the survivors as the dawn's light broadened into day! Beside the unhuman spectre sat a half-crazed Filipino, holding the kinky-haired head in his lap.

Big Karl, at a grim nod from Mackey, lifted the head by the hair and before tossing it overside, studied it a moment in silence—then murmured in gruff tribute, "Y' kept us alive las' night, Pete!"

Old Jim Ferreter, somewhat revived, had just taken the bow watch. He was said to have had the best eyes in the lot, but right now he wondered if they were playing him tricks—there had been too many false sightings of "land" lately—he wanted to be sure this time!

Ferreter looked again, but he swore he'd make no outcry until he *was* sure! Then inwardly trembling with excitement, he spoke almost casually, "There it is, boys! Land ho!"

But after an hour the "land" again faded into a cloud mass on the western horizon. A change came over old Jim and he fell into a stupor—he had believed with all his stout heart and soul that he'd really sighted land. That afternoon he died without regaining consciousness—the fifteenth victim of the grim ordeal!

Then, hardly an hour after Jim Ferreter had died, palm trees along a sandy beach were sighted. Land!

None believed it now . . . just another mirage . . . another disappointment! It couldn't be land— the weary *Dumaru* men shrugged off the thought . . . all land had sunken into the sea! But, slowly . . . like the awakening from a horrible nightmare, they became conscious of it . . . there it was! Land, trees, a coral reef . . . *the Philippines!*

Sunken eyes blinked back tears of joy. . . . Yes, by God, it was true . . . unbelievable, but true! They had reached the island of Samar, near Luzon!

But their troubles were far from over! For a time a terrible inertia seized them . . . they couldn't make themselves move . . . their arms, their legs —even their minds refused to respond! Their reserves were so far spent that they hadn't the energy to pit themselves against the formidable breakers, coral spits, and reefs that must be conquered before they could put their feet on the blessed land once more!

Back and forth along the shore they maneuvered, seeking a favorable spot and moment to come in . . . but in vain! Could it be that they had struggled and suffered those long, weary twenty-four days, only to die on a beach!

Big Karl Linns got the pot boiling again—setting the remains of Honolulu Pete to simmering again with a fire from the last of the friction flares! He alone had energy and foresight. What did land matter? They might beat about like this 'til eternity! Maybe there'd be neither food nor water ashore—but mainly, his thoughts were for Ole Heikland—poor Ole must have nourishment. Maybe he could yet save Ole! To hell with what Mackey or anyone else thought!

Then destiny played its own hand! The life-boat was hurled into the breakers, capsizing and tossing seventeen human scarecrows into a boiling churning surf! Unsung heroism ran high—the stronger rescuing the weaker! But the sea still took its toll—Ole Heikland was torn from the struggling Linns and perished in the combers within feet of safety—Francisco Benedicto and another Filipino were dashed to death against a jagged coral reef!

At last, more dead than alive, fourteen surviving *Dumaru* men sprawled out in a pitiful group on the edge of Samar's sandy shore!

The survivors were found, next day, by a native —a sagacious man who brought them fresh water, allowing them but a sip at a time. He listened to their incredible tale as it was pieced out by the surviving Filipinos in the boat, then he told them of the near-by village of San Jose and of the white settlement at Borongan, a short distance away.

After a brief rest, Big Karl, "Sparks," and Sutse set out for Borongan. Through a wild, primitive jungle they stumbled and up across inhospitable mountains they climbed, but they made it! They were received with open arms at Borongan. Word was flashed out to the Philippine Constabulary that more *Dumaru* survivors had been found! Through the efforts of the friendly natives, American traders, and a kindly padre, the sick and ailing men were moved to the village of Lornette and given much-needed care. They improved rapidly—though there wasn't a single man among them who wouldn't carry the scars of the grim ordeal to his grave!

When they were stronger the *Dumaru* men returned to Borongan where they learned that Nolan, with *all his men,* had made a landing on the island of Masbate, near Manila, on the twenty-fifth day in their boat. At no time, they also learned, had the supply of biscuits and water been short!

"Th' lucky bastuds!" sneered Big Karl laconically.

Later, aboard the American revenue cutter *Polillo,* bound for Manila, they further learned that Captain Borrensen, with two men on his life raft, had been picked up by the United States Transport *Logan* about three hundred miles west of Guam on October 27. Second Mate Albert Staats had died minutes before the captain's raft was sighted! The *Logan* sighted the hulk of the *Dumaru* soon after picking up Borrensen's raft, sinking the derelict by gunfire!

Waywood, when he heard this, felt he erred in his judgment in not standing by the hulk—then, all his men would have been saved!

"But, Mr. Waywood," pointed out the cutter's skipper, "it wasn't in your hands to know that the *Logan* would sight the *Dumaru!*"

It was after they'd arrived in Manila that the real story leaked out! Being wined and dined at the best hotel, most of them, sailorlike, drank too much and tongues were loosened. Especially Big Karl's! One night at the Silver Dollar Bar he enlightened those present with a strange story of cannibalism in an open boat—a wild, weird tale that no one believed at the time. Later, by a Board of In-

quiry, it was found to be all too true—and as grim
a saga as was ever recorded in the long history of
the sea!

SOURCES OF FACTUAL MATERIAL

The facts of the *Dumaru* story were gleaned from
the Navy's Board of Inquiry into the explosion
aboard the wooden Liberty ship *Dumaru,* set off by
lightning during a sudden tropical thunder squall
off the island of Guam, October 16, 1918, and the
subsequent stark testimony of the fourteen emaci-
ated survivors of First Mate August Waywood's lifeboat which drifted nearly two thousand miles in
twenty-four gruelling, mutinous, cannibalistic days
and which finally was cast up on the shores of Samar,
in the Philippines—also, the facts which First Engineer Fred Harmon so vividly recounted to Lowell
Thomas, who retold it in their book, *Wreck of the
Dumaru,* Doubleday, Doran & Company, New York,
1930.

XI

THE MAN WHO SANK THE *ROYAL OAK*

THE CHILL DARKNESS of a mid-October night in 1939 hung somberly over Scapa Flow. Light cruisers, heavy cruisers, destroyers, subchasers, and battle-wagons of the great British Fleet rode silently at anchor, murky waters lapping fitfully against their hulls. The thin stem of a periscope broke water as a slim-hulled medium submarine glided in silence through the east passage along Holm Sound, leaving scarcely a ripple in its wake. Down past the cruisers, the destroyers, the subchasers, and the battlewagons moved the silent *unterseeboot* with brazen deliberateness. In the periscope the vast bulk of the 29,150-ton H.M.S. *Royal Oak* vaguely silhouetted itself against a dim skyline. A split second later twin white wakes marked the course of two deadly torpedoes . . . the submarine veered sharply about, gliding eastward as stealthily as it had come . . . an instant of time seemed suspended in the night air before the terrific double explosions rent the stillness over Scapa Flow. Vivid tongues of angry flame turned the heavily listing *Royal Oak* into a seething, sinking funeral pyre for more than 800 of His Majesty's 1,200 sailors aboard!

Morning headlines blazed forth to a stunned Allied world!

BRITISH BATTLESHIP SUNK! U-BOAT SCORES HIT; 370 RESCUED!

On the heels of such headlines came the somber announcement by the Admiralty: "The Secretary of the Admiralty regrets to announce that His Majesty's ship *Royal Oak* has been sunk, it is believed by U-boat action."

The shock stunned the British people, from Buckingham Palace to humble Lambeth Walk. Words of wondered bewilderment burst from millions of British lips. How could this thing have happened? they questioned. How could this great naval veteran of the battle of Jutland be torpedoed? Wasn't she a "floating fortress"—impregnable to submarine attack? Where was she when she was torpedoed? The Admiralty had remained silent as to the duty the *Royal Oak* was on when she was sunk, where the sinking took place, or where survivors were landed.

But the Axis knew! Hitler plastered the Nazi press in huge block type and ranted fanatically over the Nazi-controlled receiving sets: "WE WILL SINK THE ENGLISH NAVY, SHIP BY SHIP!"

Captain Guenther Prien, thirty-one-year-old commander of the submarine that sank the *Royal Oak*, knew, too! Feted by the jubilant Germans from Kiel to Berlin, Prien told them she was "sunk at her base, within fortified waters and amidst the whole fleet." Then he added significantly, "Through my strong binoculars I saw the effect of my torpedoes after I had already turned the boat, heading out the bay."

Strangely enough, in spite of the tumultuous acclaim that the Nazis accorded Prien and his crew, their enthusiasm was erroneously placed, and the man who *actually* sank the *Royal Oak* was never publically credited.

Alfred Wehring was that man. Officially, he didn't exist. Yet for sixteen long years he had planned thoroughly—and in utter obscurity—to bring about this master stroke against the British Navy! Then he chose to vanish into the oblivion that successful secret service operatives so much desire.

Wehring was in the Imperial German Navy during World War I. He was a well-informed officer —a truly seagoing man-o'-warsman, expert in gunnery, adept in navigation, and an outstanding authority on naval architecture. Wehring knew the *Royal Oak*—he had served against her at Jutland. Much later his carefully laid plans were to sink her. In Spain he served as a naval attaché under Walter Wilhelm Canaris—the crafty, formidable Canaris, soon to head the much-dreaded Nazi secret service.

Canaris had long eyed Alfred Wehring favorably, pigeonholing him in the back of his scheming mind as a man whose knowledge and finesse might one day prove valuable. Nor was the cunning Canaris wrong. In the black days after the Armistice of World War I, Canaris cleverly secured a sizable pension for this ex-naval officer—though not without ulterior motives. The canny Canaris had schemes of vast range and great magnitude—plans which were to encompass all corners of the earth.

Then came 1923 . . . Hitler . . . the *putsch!* The pieces were falling neatly into place for Canaris and his long-range plans. German agents were placed at strategic points in all foreign lands, and, among these, Alfred Wehring was foremost.

Canaris, personally, gave Wehring his assignment and instructions. England was to be his "permanent" assignment—"to keep a close watch on the British fleet" were his instructions! Alfred Wehring smiled grimly at the cold, calculating Canaris. Canaris nodded curtly and dismissed the Kaiser's ex-naval officer.

Wehring laid down his course with his usual Teutonic thoroughness. He must first go to Switzerland — to best serve his *fuehrer* he must have a change of personality, a completely new bckground. Switzerland, to Alfred Wehring, was something more than a country of scenic mountains. There was also the world-renowned Swiss watch. Being a man of strong resolutions, Wehring determined to learn all there was to be learned about watches—from the ground up.

Once inside Switzerland, Wehring played his hand adroitly. He managed to wangle himself a job as a salesman of jewelry and watches—both wholesale and retail. Then he smartly apprenticed himself to one of the best watchmaking schools in Switzerland and, after three years of intensive study, he graduated as an expert watchmaker. But Wehring was not content with a trade alone. He must have a solid "Swiss" background, and a solid "Swiss" name. He chose "Alfred Ortel." A few months later, in 1927, "Alfred Ortel," armed with a newly forged passport, emigrated to England. Without a second glance he was processed through customs, and nothing in his bearing suggested that he had ever trod the bridge of a German battlewagon.

As "Alfred Ortel," Wehring became a man of sincere warmth and friendliness. Friends came easily. He was both witty and cultured—and, above all, he was most careful not to lose the "common touch." He also let it be known that he had a zealous interest in the sea and in the ships that sailed it. That he preferred a seaport town was natural. What better place could Wehring have selected than the Orkney Island coast town of Kirkwall? Situated as it was on Pomona Island, Kirkwall was conveniently near the great British naval base at Scapa Flow—and Wehring *was* interested in ships, the king's fighting ships!

Kirkwall made welcome the "Swiss" watchmaker with his genial smile, his skillful hands, and his inherent love of the sea. Ortel found these simple seafaring people delightful—perhaps it was because he remained a sailor at heart; perhaps for them, too, this great love of the sea explained Ortel's intense interest in the activities at Scapa Flow.

Ortel the watchmaker prospered. Within a few years he became the owner of a well-stocked jewelry and watch shop. He was often consulted by the captains of the larger Kirkwall ships regarding the proper setting of chronometers and watches. He mingled graciously with Kirkwall's best society, while yachting and fishing became two of his leisure-time hobbies—at least as far as his friends could tell.

But the adoption of a country must be complete, and so, in 1932, Alfred Ortel became a British subject under the Crown. There were relatives in Switzerland, Ortel often hinted to friends, then smilingly admitted he couldn't find it in his heart to leave his beloved Kirkwall, even for a visit. So it was that these "relatives" often came to see him. They seemed genteel folk, spoke German in quiet, cultured tones, and were well dressed. Like Ortel, they, too, were accepted by Kirkwall. Regular mail came from an aged "father" in Germany. Ortel explained sadly that the infirmities of the old man kept him constantly bedridden, or in a wheel chair. There were many other letters, too. Old school chums of his, smiled Alfred Ortel blandly, who seemed forever scattering themselves over the face of the earth. Often wished he had had their rare opportunities to travel in far places. Ortel was scrupulously faithful in his correspondence.

The years passed. Hitler ranted at Prime Minister Chamberlain . . . then came Munich . . . and finally Hitler's *blitzkrieg* on Poland in September, 1939!

Alfred Ortel shook his head sadly, spread the Union Jack up over his shop door, and, along with all other good Britishers, dug deep to buy bonds to pay for this fearful war. No longer was he Swiss neutral, he explained tearfully to his many friends in Kirkwall, for he was now a loyal subject of King George! He regretted miserably that his age kept him from taking up arms against this rascal Hitler.

Avidly, Ortel followed the progress of the war. He assimilated reams of the British press. Tirelessly he devoured periodicals, books, and reports. Especially shipping reports. At his modest home he spent long hours with his ears glued to an ancient radio set, listening to the war news.

The roadstead at Scapa Flow, extending east and west some fifteen miles and about eight miles in width, quickly became alive with naval activity. Two very narrow passageways mark its only entrances—Holm Sound at the east end; Hoy Sound at the west. Kirkwall nestles on the coast of Pomona Island, just north of the western entrance, and lies a scant few miles due west of the island's southeast tip. Both passages had been further narrowed by sunken hulks, purposely scuttled at these strategic points. A maze of strong fortifications—mines, steel nets, and sunken piles—protected the British Fleet within Scapa Flow.

The war was scarcely a month old when Alfred Ortel—ever mindful of his *true* purpose of being at Kirkwall, and his instructions personally given to him by Canaris, sixteen years before—had managed to learn that certain obstructions were out of place at the eastern entrance to Scapa Flow. How he acquired such top-secret knowledge is to this day unknown. Few knew of this "chink in the armor." Ortel was one.

Alfred Ortel moved swiftly. Low-scudding clouds, he casually mentioned to his clerks one bleak October day, meant only one thing at this time of year—a storm. Since there probably would be few customers, the clerks were welcome to take the rest of the day off. They thanked him profusely and left. Ortel closed the shutters, locked the door of his shop, and sauntered home. He wanted no appearance of haste. The day was damp and dreary, and a few minutes after arriving home he had a briskly burning fire in the hearth. A copper kettle hanging over the blaze soon bubbled merrily and Ortel, in the true tradition of a Britisher, brewed himself a particularly strong cup of tea.

Leisurely Ortel sipped his steaming tea, calmly contemplating the face of a clock ticking off the seconds on the teakwood mantle. A short time later it struck four, Greenwich mean time. Ortel sprang into immediate action. In a near-by alcove, Ortel drew up a chair in front of his antiquated radio set and flipped a switch. Within the ancient cabinet a high-powered short-wave transmitter and receiver hummed to life. Deftly Ortel dialed a certain frequency and spoke in guarded code, holding a small hand microphone close to his mouth. His voice became rapid and voluble. He poured out the words in sharp, guttural German—then he repeated his message slowly. His listener must make no mistake —there was no margin for error, now.

A Nazi naval attaché in neutral Holland was taking the message; in a heavy German voice he read it back. Ortel nodded approval. Minutes later the message was channeled through to *No. 14 Bendlerstrasse, Berlin, attention of Walter Wilhelm Canaris!*

Canaris acted instantly—his confidence in Wehring's skill was about to pay off—and there were no "tomorrows" in Canaris's timetable! All German U-boats in European waters were alerted in code to stand by for urgent orders. A naval attaché in Holland had coded instructions to radio-contact the Kirkwall operative—a certain watchmaker known as

Ortel. Nazi patrol charts showed clearly that submarine *B-06,* under the command of Captain Guenther Prien, was nearest—in the waters adjacent to Scapa Flow. The orders given him were simple and to the point: "Make the kill tonight!"

Weather played a major role in the success of the operation. Reports to Prien were covered graphically in one word: "Overcast." The course was set. Prien's orders were to proceed to Holm Sound, eastern passage to Scapa Flow, then surface at the southeast tip of Pomona Island, just opposite Kirkwall, keeping a sharp lookout for an on-shore signal light—one long flash—two short—one long. The signaler to be taken aboard would give Captain Prien further detailed instructions. Prien proceeded at half throttle. He didn't want to risk the dangerous error—in precarious waters—of arriving *before* the fixed hour.

The operation was gotten underway smoothly. The *B-06* arrived at the rendezvous point sharply on the hour scheduled. Prien cut her engines, cautiously surfaced, then stood on the steel grating of the conning tower deck. Prien thought he could hear a vague ripple of water against the near-by shore. Uncomfortably close, he muttered as he reached for his powerful night glasses. There was nothing in sight except inky blackness. A thin sigh of wind held the threat of rain and stirred a soft slapping of the North Sea against the hull of the submarine. Prien swept the dim outline of the shore with his glasses—but there was nothing there. Suddenly, off the starboard bow, a tiny light blinked from the shore. A long flash—two shorts—another long flash!

Prien gave a hushed order. A sailor manned a rubber collapsible boat, lowered it, and moved silently toward the flashing light. Minutes later it returned with a grim-faced passenger—Ortel, the watchmaker of Kirkwall. Prien and Ortel silently shook hands, then Prien ordered the boat aboard and they hurried below. Seconds later the *B-06* dipped cautiously beneath the surface of Holm Sound.

No navigating officer in the British fleet knew the waters around Scapa Flow as did Ortel. Hadn't "yachting and fishing" been his "hobby" during the past sixteen years? He had systematically chart-ed the great roadstead, pin-pointing with deadly accuracy the bearings of *all* defenses—from Holm Sound on the east to Hoy Sound on the west. Ortel, with his carefully marked chart before him, took over the wheel of the *B-06,* while Prien concentrated his efforts on the preparations for the "kill." The U-boat moved under half throttle, inching along foot by foot, and twisting by obstructions into the waters of Scapa Flow. Even for Ortel it was touch-and-go maneuvering. It took split-second timing to dodge these cunningly contrived defenses, but Ortel made it. Sometimes with only inches to spare on either port or starboard; sometimes with less than a fathom of water under the keel.

Silently the *B-06* swung into the wider waters of Scapa Flow itself. The U-boat's crew was quietly jubilant. Naval history was being made. Prien and Ortel cautioned them against undue optimism—a false move now could mean sudden death! Ortel further warned them that a measure of luck had favored them, too. Prien ordered the periscope up. The *B-06* still maneuvered under half throttle. Ahead, British warships dimly silhouetted themselves against a dull sky line—the cruisers, destroyers, subchasers, and the battlewagons of huge proportions. Down the line moved the U-boat, while Prien studied the ships at a safe distance.

Still more cruisers, light and heavy. Never before did Prien realize the great magnitude and strength of the British Navy. Now more destroyers. A battleship loomed in the periscope—then another. Prien beckoned to Ortel to confirm what he saw. Ortel peered through the periscope.

"*Ja*, the last one in line," nodded Ortel. "That's the *Royal Oak!*"

Prien ordered the torpedomen to load the forward tubes as he edged the *B-06* into position for the "kill." The great bulk of the *Royal Oak* loomed larger, riding silently at anchor. She was low in the water, massive, solid, with deck armor ranging from one inch to four in thickness, and thirteen-inch-thick "anti-torpedo blisters" along her sides, extending below her water line. Her grim fighting top towered into the night sky. She was the pride of the British Navy—aye, of the whole British people —and her eight death-dealing fifteen-inch guns bristled menacingly from their turrets. Even Prien sensed a strange thrill as he peered intently through the periscope. Then he ordered the engines stopped when the *B-06* was abeam the *Royal Oak's* starboard quarter.

Distance and bearings were carefully checked by Prien. Ortel marveled at Prien's exactness of precision.

"Prepare to fire!" ordered Prien calmly.

The U-boat's commander again peered intently into the sighting lens of the periscope. Slowly his hand raised above his head—a second passed as he waited for the cross hairs to "zero in" on the target —then his hand swept downward.

"Fire one!" came the clipped command.

Number 1 torpedo sped destruction toward the great British battlewagon. Up went Prien's hand again . . . then swished down!

"Fire two!" snapped Prien.

Number 2 torpedo was away a split second after the first had blasted through the *Royal Oak's* thirteen-inch "anti-torpedo" armor with a tremendous underwater explosion . . . the second explosion was even more terrific! Prien checked results through the periscope. Ortel then stole a quick glance. What he saw he would not soon forget!

Prien turned the U-boat sharply about, racing for the east passage under full throttle—mission completed. A slip-up now meant their own destruction, so Ortel again took over at the wheel and worried the *B-06* through tortuous Holm Sound. Out in the open waters of the North Sea the U-boat's crew turned berserk with joy. Nazi discipline went by the board. Prien even broke out his own private stock for his officers and crew. *This was an occasion!*

But the watchmaker from Kirkwall was entirely forgotten. Ortel sat apart, features immobile, a faraway look in his eyes. *His* job was done. His sixteen-year-old mission had been accomplished. Now he was leaving England forever—that was all that mattered.

Alfred Ortel—he was now Wehring again—silently slipped into the roaring crowd at Kiel and disappeared while harbor whistles shrieked and brass bands blared out a triumphant welcome to Captain Guenther Prien and his men. Two days later Wehring was in Berlin, making a personal report to Canaris at No. 14 Bendlerstrasse—a report that embraced sixteen years of his life devoted to the "One Idea." Even as they talked, the sounds of a tumultuous ovation for Prien and his crew came to their ears from the street below. But the two men were not interested in celebrations. It was enough for Alfred Wehring that the tight-lipped Canaris *knew* who sank the *Royal Oak!*

SOURCES OF FACTUAL MATERIAL

The material for this story came from certain confidential sources as well as from material found in the *New York Times,* dated October 14 and 19, 1939, and in the *New York World-Telegram,* dated October 14, 1939.

GLOSSARY OF SEA TERMS

A—Highest classification of vessels registered at Lloyd's, London. Subdivided into "A-1," "A-2," etc.

A'—Contraction of "on" or "in" and constantly used at sea—such as "a'back," "a'board," "a'stern," etc.

A.B.—Initialed form of "able-bodied"—a first-class seaman, commonly known as an able seaman, an "A.B." This contrasts in rating with an "ordinary" seaman who can make himself useful on board, even to going aloft, but who is not as complete a sailor as is an A.B.

ABACK—In a sailing vessel, when a sudden change of wind forces the sails flat against the masts, they are said to be "taken aback."

ABAFT—Toward the stern of the ship. Example: "Abaft the stack," if in a steamship, or, if in a sailing vessel, "Abaft the mainmast."

ABANDON—To "abandon ship." A vessel is said to be "abandoned" when left by her master and crew in an open sea or on a foreign coast. However, it doesn't necessarily follow that the "right" or the "claim" to a vessel and its property or cargo is abandoned, if found and subsequently brought into safety. The case of the *Mary Celeste* is an example in point—the master and crew of the *Dei Gratia* were awarded 20 per cent of the ship's value and cargo value as "salvage pay." On the other hand, Captain Kurt Carlsen of the *Flying Enterprise* did not abandon ship after he sent the ship's crew and passengers away in lifeboats. Instead he held aboard her in a valiant attempt to salvage her and bring her into port. Captain Carlsen abandoned the ship *only after* she began to sink fast.

ABEAM—At right angles with the ship's keel. "Abeam the starboard side," on the starboard beam, or, "abeam the port side," on the port beam.

ABOARD—On or in a vessel.

ABOUT—To "go about," to bring a vessel about in a different direction.

ABOVE—"Above board," above deck. As, "ten feet above board."

ABREAST—Opposite. Example: "The vessels were *abreast* Atlantic City when the accident occurred."

ADRIFT—A vessel is "adrift" when parted from her moorings, as in a storm, and driving about out of control.

AFORE—The main hatch is "afore" the bridge. "The ship was kept *afore* the wind," "afore" being a contraction of "before."

AFT—The captain is "aft," on the quarter-deck ; or, "behind"—nearer the stern.

AGROUND—To "run aground," to run a vessel onto the shore, beach, rocks, etc.

ALEE—Opposite direction from which the wind blows. "Put the helm alee!" is a command to the helmsman to push the rudder-tiller (or wheel) down to the lee side of the ship—which in present practice means to turn the rudder over to the windward (i.e., the back of the rudder blade is to the windward of the stern post, or in the *opposite* direction to the rudder-tiller), which makes the vessel's head turn in the direction of the wind.

ALL HANDS, AHOY!—This command is given by the bo'sun (boatswain) and his mates at the fo'c'sle hatchway to assemble the ship's company. "All hands, on deck!" is the more modern way of putting the same order. "Ahoy!" is used in hailing ships at sea, the same as "hello" is used ashore by a landsman. Example: *"Mary Celeste,* ahoy!" which means, "Hello, *Mary Celeste,* is there anyone aboard?"

ALOFT—Overhead. In the upper rigging, or in the yards, etc.

ALONGSIDE—By the side of; "alongside" the pier, "alongside" another vessel.

AMIDSHIPS—In the middle of the ship.

ANCHOR—To "drag anchor." When the ship pulls the anchor chain, or cable, and into the water so that it may fasten itself on the bottom and hold the ship.

ANCHOR—To "drag anchor." When the ship pulls the anchor with her, either from violent winds or heavy seas.

ANCHORAGE — Ground to anchor in — in this instance "ground" meaning the consistency of the bottom that would best hold the anchor's fluke secure and not allow the ship to "drag anchor."

ANCHORS AWEIGH!—The order to heave up the anchor or anchors by capstan or windlass.

ASHORE—On land; aground. Or, in another sense, "The captain was *ashore*."

ASTERN—Behind the vessel; in her wake.

ATHWART—Across. The rowers' seats in an open boat are "thwarts" because they reach across the boat.

AVAST—The order to stop or pause in a given action aboard ship, as, "Avast heaving!"

AWASH—Under water. Example: "Her decks were *awash*."

AWEATHER—Toward the weather side of a vessel, the side on which the wind is blowing.

AYE—To answer in the affirmative at sea, generally with a repetition, "Aye, aye, sir!" meaning, "I understand and will execute the order!"

BALLAST—A quantity of iron, stone, gravel, or other material placed in the bottom of the hold to give a ship proper stability when she has no cargo.

BAROMETER—A widely known instrument for measuring the weight and pressure of the atmosphere. Whatever tends to increase or diminish this pressure will cause the barometer to rise or fall. In the earlier days a simplified barometer, known as a "glass," was used by sailing vessel captains. Hence the expression, "The glass is falling," or, "The barometer is dropping." Both expressions indicate a low-pressure area and serve as a warning that a violent storm is coming, such as a typhoon or hurricane. On the more modern barometers, anything below twenty-nine inches of pressure means a possibility of gales from seventy-five to ninety miles an hour (hurricane winds).

BARRATRY—Any fraudulent or knowingly illegal action on the part of the ship or cargo owners, or of the master and crew of a vessel, such as a "planned" accident which would result in the loss of the vessel in order to collect insurance on the cargo or vessel, or both.

BATTEN—To "batten down" the hatches, to fasten the edge of the cargo hatch tarpaulins by means of battens, wedges, etc., to the hatchway coamings.

BEAM-ENDS—A vessel is said to be on her "beam-ends" when she is lying so far on her lee side from the force of the wind, or by the shifting of her cargo, as to submerge her lee rail. Example: "The *Vestris* was lying on her *beam-ends*."

BEARING—To ascertain the direction or position of any object by means of a compass.

BEAUFORT'S SCALE—A scale devised by Sir F. Beaufort, R.N., in 1805, in which the strength of the wind is indicated by numbers from 0 to 12.

SCALE NUMBER	MILES PER HOUR
0. Calm	3
1. Light air	8
2. Light breeze	13
3. Gentle breeze	18
4. Moderate breeze	23
5. Fresh breeze	28
6. Strong breeze	34
7. Moderate gale	40
8. Fresh gale	48

BECALMED—A sailing vessel is "becalmed" when, having no wind, or having so little she can make no seaway, she cannot be controlled by her helm.

BEFORE THE MAST—A seaman is said to be "before the mast" when he is lodged in the crew space (or fo'c'sle) and is performing the duties of an "ordinary" sailor.

BELAY—To "belay" means to fasten, to secure, a rope or cable to a bitt, a cleat, or belaying pin, by taking several turns with it around any of them. Sometimes belay is used in the sense of a "stop" command—such as, *"Belay* that kind of talk, mate!"

BELLS—On shipboard, bells express the time, and they are struck by the officer of the watch every half hour. The day of twelve hours is divided into three parts: (1) noon to four o'clock; (2) four o'clock to eight o'clock; and (3) eight o'clock to midnight. The same division of time follows through the night. Thus, in every four hours there will be eight bells: at noon, four o'clock, eight o'clock, and midnight. Example: Noon—eight bells; twelve-thirty—one bell; one o'clock, —two bells; one-thirty—three bells; two o'clock—four bells; two-thirty—five bells; three o'clock—six bells; three-thirty—seven bells; four o'clock—eight bells. But in the dog watches (*see* Watches), these being of only two hours' duration each, there will be only four bells.

BELOW DECK—Under the deck, or under the water.

BEND—1. (relating to rope). The bent portion—the knot —becomes a "bend," and "to bend" becomes a general sea term for fastening anything, as, to *bend* one rope to another, a sail to a yard or gaff, the anchor to its chain or cable, or a cable to a bitt. 2. "To bend," as in a sailing vessel, is to lie over under press of canvas.

BERTH—On shipboard, a cabin. Sometimes a bed, or any space for the "swinging of a hammock," as it is called. A ship's "berth" is the place in which she lies, or is anchored. Also, a "berth" is a position, or employment to be secured, as, a "captain's berth," "engineer's berth," etc.

BETWEEN DECKS—In a vessel of more than one deck, to be between the upper and the lower, generally called " 'tween decks."

BIGHT—1. The double part of a rope when it is "bent" (*see* Bend), in contradistinction to the end of the rope. 2. A small inlet or bay on a seacoast, or in the bank of a river.

BILGE—The "bilge" is the lower part of a vessel upon which she rests when aground. A vessel is said to be "bilged" when damaged in her bottom by grounding on some hard object, such as rocks, etc. "Bilge water" is the stagnant water that lies in the bottom of a vessel's hold.

BINNACLE—The fixed case and stand in which the steering compass in any vessel is set. Located in the wheelhouse on the bridge of a modern steamship, or aft on the poop deck, just forward of the wheel, on a sailing ship.

BITTS—Small metal or timber heads secured through the deck of a vessel, to which mooring cables can be bent —such as "bow bitts" and "stern bitts."

BLOCK—A "block" is a machine made up of several parts, and it may be regarded as being among the most important parts of a vessel's rigging. On shore it is generally referred to as a "pulley," but among seafaring men it is a "block." When two or more blocks are used to move a single weight, they, with their ropes, constitute a "tackle." The "block" is the piece (or "block") of wood which constitutes the main body of the machine. The "shell" is the outside casing, the upper part of which is called the "head." This shell consists of two parts which encase the block and which are bound together, or seized, with a band called the "strop"; and to prevent this strop from slipping off, they have grooves cut in them, above and below. These grooves are called "scores." The scores do not meet at the head of the block, but at the bottom they do, forming a continuous groove. The "sheave" is the wheel of the pulley, and it fits into the "sheave hole" or "swallow," which is the slot cut through the block to receive it. Blocks may be "double sheaved," "triple sheaved," or "fourfold sheaved," according to the number of sheaves they carry. The axle that carries the sheaves has a square head set flush in the shell.

BOAT STEERER—In the old whaling days the "boat steerer" of a whaleboat was an important member of a whaleship's crew. He had to be both able seaman and experienced harpooner, with a rating comparable to that of a naval petty officer. His job was twofold. Once a whaleboat was lowered and the "chase" for the whale was under way, the boat steerer became the harpooner, taking his position in the bows of the boat. The boat crew, under the command of one of the whaleship's mates, sped the boat across the water toward the sighted whale, and when the boat was "on the whale," the harpooner must make the "strike" with skill and precision. Then, after the harpoon was fast in the mammal, the harpooner must again scramble aft and take his place at the tiller while the mate went forward to make the "kill," With his razor-sharp lance he must, at dangerously close range, penetrate some vital spot in the harpooned whale before it could be taken in tow.

BOATSWAIN (bo's'n or bo'sun)—The "boatswain" is an A.B. seaman employed as a noncommissioned officer to superintend the men when occupied in the rigging or in other work aboard ship. A "bo'sun's mate" is an assistant to the bo'sun.

BOOM—A "boom" is a pole extending outboard (i.e., outwards from the vessel). Sail booms take their names from the sails they extend, as the "fore," "main," and "mizzen." On square-rigged ships they are termed "yardarms."

Bow—The "bows" of a ship are the sides at the fore part of a vessel, designated as "starboard bow" (right) and "port bow" (left).

Brig—A vessel with two masts (fore and main), both of them square-rigged, but having a gall mainsail (schooner rigged). A "hermaphrodite brig" is a combination of the brig and schooner rigs, from which comes the modern "brigantine."

Brigantine—A vessel with two masts (fore and main), the foremost brig rigged with square fore course, and the main mast schooner rigged—as was the *Mary Celeste.*

Broach—Used in the phrase "broach to" and referring to a vessel running before the wind. A dangerous situation for a ship to be in in a heavy sea, out of control, and under constant danger of capsizing. The *Antinoe,* the *Vestris,* and the *Flying Enterprise* were in very similar situations.

Bunk—A bed on board ship. The word is used in contradistinction to "hammock." A bunk is *fixed*—built in; a hammock is *swung.*

Bulkhead—"Bulkheads" are partitions in a vessel—like walls in a building ashore. They may be made of any material, as wood, iron, steel, etc. Oftentimes they render a vessel additionally secure by dividing it into watertight compartments.

By—As "by the head"—another way of expressing the phrase "down by the head." The *Titanic* went "down by the head."

Cabin—Living quarters on shipboard, such as the "captain's cabin."

Cable—The rope or chain by which a ship's anchor is held—or the rope and steel cables used for mooring the ship at dockside. For towing purposes, much stronger steel cable is used. As an example, the British tug

Turmoil towed Captain Kurt Carlsen's *Flying Enterprise* with a five-inch steel cable. A cable's length is one tenth of a nautical mile, or approximately one hundred fathoms, two hundred yards.

CALMS—The term given to regions of the various oceans where tranquil conditions usually prevail. 1. "Calms of Cancer"; the horse latitudes. The calms between the northeast trades and the variable winds. 2. "Calms of Capricorn"; horse latitudes of the Antarctic. The calms between the southeast trades and the variable winds. 3. "Doldrums." The calms between the northeast and southeast trades near the equator.

CANT—To lean over. A ship in heavy weather "cants" to leeward by force of the wind against her weather side.

CANVAS—The material from which the sails of a ship are made. But there is another general application at sea of the word "canvas" to all or any of the sails set. For example: the ship has "all canvas spread," or she is under "shortened canvas," or again, "trim more canvas."

CAPSIZE—To turn over completely in the water, often due to shifting cargo in heavy weather, or if a vessel should be "broached to" by heavily breaking seas and cannot be controlled by her helm. Both the *Vestris* and the *Flying Enterprise* were nearly capsized before they finally sank.

CAPSTAN—A large, somewhat concaved, drum-shaped piece of mechanism set upright and strongly secured in the foredeck of a ship. When "capstan bars" are put in the holes of the drumhead and the men walk around and around, the "capstan" revolves, turning up the cable on the drum. Dowels, fastened securely at the bottom of the drum, engage iron stops secured to the deck and hold the drum from turning when the men around the capstan stop moving. Used to heave up the anchor, haul the ship along the wharf, etc.

CAPSTAN BARS—Heavy pieces of timber put into holes in the drumhead of the capstan and secured there by iron pins. The men push against them to revolve the capstan.

CAREEN—To heel or make to lie over on one side. A vessel is said to "careen" when she inclines under press of canvas at sea—or a steamship "careens" when heavy winds blow against her weather side.

CAST—To "cast off lines" from a pier in preparation for sailing. Example: " 'Cast off your lines, Mr. Beetle!' boomed the *Globe's* master."

CHART—Roughly speaking, a chart is a map of the ocean's floor and of the coast projections, made for the use of the navigator.

CHRONOMETER—A "chronometer" is an extremely accurate clock which is suspended in gimbals and stowed in a specially constructed box and used solely for computing distances by time in relation to the number of knots logged by a vessel. Chronometers carry Greenwich mean time, and ships have three chronometers in order to make daily comparisons and keep a constant check for errors. "Hack chronometers" and "sidereal chronometers" are those used to compare with the "standard chronometer" for accuracy. "Sidereal" means pertaining to the stars, and the "sidereal chronometer" is so regulated that it denotes the exact time in reference to the movement of a fixed star. The least reliable of the three chronometers is the hack chronometer, sometimes called a "hack watch." It was a hack watch that the first mate of the *Dei Gratia* took aboard the *Mary Celeste* when he sailed her to Gibraltar.

CLEARANCE—The act of clearing a vessel at the customhouse by presenting the required documents and obtaining her "clearance papers." Example: "The ship had presented her *clearance papers* at Hoboken two days before she sank at sea."

CLINOMETER—A "clinometer" indicates the angle of a vessel's roll or pitch. If a vessel does not come upright after a roll, the clinometer will indicate her angle of list. Example: "The *Vestris* registered a 30° list on her *clinometer*."

CLOSE-REEFED—A sailing vessel is said to be "close-reefed" when, owing to the stress of weather, the principal sails are reduced so as to expose the smallest possible surface for reefing.

CODE SIGNALS—A collection of signs or symbols reduced to an orderly arrangement and made use of by vessels at sea. There are three categories: 1. Flags. For signaling ship to ship when in sight of each other. 2. Long-distance signals, which include radio and Morse code. 3. Call letters of various shipping companies as well as international code letters and signals.

COMPANIONWAY—Steps or ladder leading down into a cabin from the "companionway hatch." The sliding cover over such steps or ladders is called the "companion."

COMPASS—An instrument which, by means of a magnetized bar, indicates the magnetic meridian. The disc or face of the "mariner's compass" consists of a circular card, sometimes transparent, the circumference of which is divided into thirty-two parts, called "points." These points may be again divided into two, each division being a half point, and these again into quarter points. Each point is named and marked on the card with the initials of its name, as N for North, N by E for North by East, N N E for North Northeast, N E for Northeast, and so on around the circular card. The "cardinal points" are North, South, East, and West. These cut the card into four quarters, and each quarter is divided into eight points. Below are listed sixteen points and their opposites:

North	South
North by East	South by West
North Northeast	South Southwest
Northeast by North	Southeast by South
Northeast	Southwest
Northeast by East	Southwest by West

East Northeast	West Southwest
East by North	West by South
East	West
East by South	West by North
East Southeast	West Northwest
Southeast by East	Northwest by West
Southeast	Northwest
Southeast by South	Northwest by North
South Southeast	North Northwest
South by East	North by West
South	North

The repetition of these points, and their opposite equivalents, is called "boxing the compass." Often half points are asked for in examinations. The north point is always distinguished by a large arrow, and the card is fixed to an iron bar or needle laid exactly in line marking North and South. The "North" end of the bar having been previously magnetized, it is then either balanced on a pin or floated in spirit in a semiglobular basin; this basin, by an arrangement of two rings, called "gimbals," set at right angles —one working within the other—is so contrived that whatever position the ship may be in, it keeps the horizontal position. The card revolves, but the case, though horizontal at all times, retains the same position with respect to the keel line of the vessel. On the inside of the basin—and in line with the keel, or in other words in line with the head and stern of the vessel—is made a distinct line or mark, called the "lubber's line," and it is by this line that the vessel is steered. If the vessel is sailing due north, the line will meet the arrowhead on the dial of the compass; if the ship is sailing due east, the lubber's line revolves around the dial until it meets the letter E. In iron ships there is always a counterattraction to be overcome, which means a ship's compass must be tested and corrected before starting a voyage. This variation of a ship's compass from the true magnetic meridian is called the "deviation of the compass," and methods of dealing with this condition form a science in itself.

CON, CONNING—An officer who directs the helmsman of a ship on how to keep her head is said to be "conning" the ship. Hence the name "conning tower" on submarines. Also, on men-o'-war there are conning towers, which are elevated deckhouses containing the compass, and from these a good lookout may be maintained.

COOPER—A "cooper" in the old whaling days was the one who knocked together the barrels for the whale oil. The barrel staves generally came aboard the ship bound together in "shooks," while the "hoops" came on separately. The cooper formed the barrels from the staves, then hooped them, readying them to receive the whale oil from the cooling tank of iron located 'tween decks abaft the fo'c'sle.

COPPER—Copper is recognized as the best material for preserving the bottom of a ship from sea growth, barnacles, etc. When a vessel's bottom is sheathed with it, it is "copper bottomed," or "coppered."

COURSE, COURSES—A "course" is the direction in which a ship travels by compass. For example, the course is N E when she is moving in a northeasterly direction. "Courses" in a square-rigged vessel are those square sails which hang from the lower yards. In a full-rigged ship, the fore, main, and mizzen sails will be the "courses." The bark is without the mizzen course; the brigantine has only the fore course.

COURSE, TRUE—The course which a vessel has really sailed through the water, after correction for leeway, variation, and local attraction, is called the "true course."

CREW—The collective number of persons in service on board a vessel, including the master, officers, engineers, stewards, etc. It should be observed that according to the German law the term *Mannschaft* comprises only officers, seamen, and boys, i.e., the men (exclusive of the master) employed for navigating, steering, and working the ship.

CRIMP—Nickname for one of those unconscientious agents who, before the establishment of sailors' homes, used to take seamen in, board them, find them ships, and then finally rob them of everything. It was one of these that First Mate August Waywood shot to death on a street in Astoria, Oregon. Waywood was the mate aboard the *Dumaru*.

CROSSJACK—In full-rigged ships the "crossjack" (pronounced "kroj′ek") is the lowest yard on the mizzen mast. It was a crossjack on the whaling ship *Globe* that broke and crashed to the deck and caused Captain Worth to return to Edgartown for repairs before starting on a whaling voyage to the South Pacific. The superstitious crew looked upon the incident as an ill omen.

CROW'S-NEST—Lookout station located high on the foremast of modern vessels. It is usually cylindrical in shape and covered for the protection of the lookout men. Aboard the old whaling ships the "crow's-nest" was placed high in the mainmast, and the only protection it afforded the lookout man was the large metal or wooden rings, coming to above the waist. The lookout was sometimes called the "man in the 'hoops.' "

CYCLONIC STORMS—The term given to violent revolving storms usually accompanied by very heavy rains (or snow, hail, and sleet), which differ from ordinary storms not only in their greater force but also in the peculiarity of their compound motion. Both the *Antinoe* and Captain Kurt Carlsen's *Flying Enterprise* were caught in such storms.

DAVIT—A light but strongly constructed crane on a ship's side for lowering and lifting lifeboats.

DAVY JONES—The spirit of the sea.

DAVY JONES'S LOCKER—The bottom of the sea, because it is the recepticle of all things thrown overside. Those

who have been buried at sea are said to have gone
to Davy Jones's locker.

DECK—Generally speaking, the covering of the interior of
the ship, either carried completely over her or only
over a portion. Large sailing ships and steamships
may have various decks, as:

MAIN DECK—The principal and often the only deck in
a vessel.

ANCHOR DECK—A small raised deck in the bows.

BRIDGE DECK—A deck amidships upon which the
"bridge" is built. The bridge itself is a form of
elevated platform which extends from the starboard side of the ship to the port side above the
railings and is used by the officers on duty. This
is called the "navigating" or "upper" bridge.
Under this bridge is the "captain's bridge." On
many vessels the captain's quarters are located on
the captain's bridge.

FORECASTLE DECK—The covering of a "decked" fo'c'sle.

HURRICANE DECK—An upper deck extending across a
vessel amidships (the navigating bridge).

ORLOP DECK—The lowest deck near the bottom of a
ship.

POOP DECK—Deck covering the after part of a vessel.

PROMENADE DECK—On passenger vessels, a deck covering the saloon, usually reserved for first-class passengers.

QUARTER-DECK—That part of a decking at the stern
which covers the officers' quarters; or it may be
a separate deck raised over that portion of the
ship, in which case it is called a "raised quarter-
deck."

DEGREE—The 360th part of a circle's circumference. The
circumference of the earth is divided into 360 degrees
of sixty minutes each.

DERELICT—The term applies to ships from which the crews
have been withdrawn and on which no domestic
animals have been left.

DERRICK—The massive steel crane aboard freighters and

cargo-passenger ships which is used for loading and unloading cargo. It consists of one or more steel booms joined to a steel mast at the base, with whip and tackle which connects to the deck winch for raising and lowering the cargo booms.

DISTRESS—A vessel is said to be "in distress" when, from any cause, it is in a dangerous position requiring assistance.

DONKEY ENGINE—A small, stationary steam engine with a vertical boiler—more often called a "donkey"—used aboard large sailing vessels for hauling cable, raising sails, and working the cargo boom for loading and unloading. On modern vessels, power-driven winches having one or more drums on which cable, chain, or rope can be wound, are used in place of the old-style "donkey." These winches may be powered by steam, or by hydraulic or electric-driven motor.

DRAUGHT—The "draught" of a vessel is the depth of water she draws—the vertical depth from water surface to keel. In other words, the distance of the lowest point of her keel from the surface of the water.

DRIFT—To "drift" is to be carried with a stream or current. With a ship it implies that she is not under the control of the helm.

FORE—The forward part of a vessel—"foredeck," "forecastle" (fo'c'sle), etc.

FORE-AND-AFT—Meaning in the direction of a line drawn from stem to stern of a vessel—that is, from the forward or "fore" to the after or "aft" part; and such sails, or yards and spars, as are set in this direction constituting that which, among seafaring men, is known as "fore-'n'-aft rig." Such sails as yachts and sailing boats carry are "fore-and-aft sails"; and such as are set in the direction *across* the ship are called "square sails," constituting the "square rig" of most of the old sailing merchantmen.

FOUL—Unpleasant—as bilge water might very well be.

When any tackle or line tangles up, it is said to be "fouled." When one has run into anything—such as a pier, a buoy, or another boat—one is said to "foul" or "run foul" of it. And stormy or foggy weather is called "foul" weather.

FOUND—A vessel is said to be "all found" when she has masts, rigging, gear, and all other necessities for starting a voyage, and "well found" when all these things are good.

FOUNDER—When a vessel, either through storm or accident, fills with water or sinks, she is said to have foundered.

FREEBOARD—That portion of a vessel's side which is free of water, that is, not submerged. The extent of "freeboard" is measured from the load water line to the deck where the distance is shortest. In the case of the *Vestris* it was the lack of freeboard on her starboard side, due to her increasing list to starboard, that finally caused her to founder.

FULL-RIGGED SHIP—A ship having three masts with their full complement of sails, or, in other words, having royal masts. Until the introduction of four-masted sailing ships, the "ship" had all the masts, sails, spars, etc., that it was possible to carry.

FUNNEL—The smokestack for carrying off the smoke in steamships is also called the "funnel." There are many designs for the modern funnel and most of them play an important part in creating a more efficient draught for the vessel's furnaces.

GAFF—The spar which extends the "head" (or upper portion) of a fore-and-aft sail, such as the mainsail of a sloop, cutter, or yawl. A sail suspended by a gaff is called a "gaff sail," in contradistinction to a sail suspended by a yard, which is a "square sail." The mizzen sail of the *Mary Celeste* was a gaff sail.

GALE—The term "gale," as used at sea, has a different meaning from that of the word ashore. A gale is a continuous wind, of which there may be several degrees: 1. A "fresh gale." 2. A "strong gale." 3. A "heavy," "hard," or "whole gale." Velocity varies from twenty-eight to fifty-five miles an hour.

GALLANT—"Gallant" comes from the word "garland," which in ancient days was the name of a ring of rope used for moving or "swaying" (hoisting) a heavy mast. When a mast was added to ships, above the topmast, it was called a "garland mast." As the word became corrupted, it eventually resolved itself into "gallant," in writing, but the original pronunciation, "garn," as in "t'garn" for "topgallant," has been preserved among seamen to this day. Hence, when old sailors speak of topgallant sails, they say "t'garns'ls."

GALLEY—1. The cookhouse of a ship. 2. A big, open boat with six or eight oars.

GAM, GAMMING—In the old whaling days it was customary, when two whaling ships met at sea, for the captains to pay each other a visit. These visits were called "gams." When speaking of such a visit, sailors aboard the whaleship being visited would refer to it as, "Captain So-and-So is *gamming* with our captain down in the captain's cabin."

GASKETS—The small cords by which a sail, when furled, is kept bound to a yard, boom, or gaff. There are several—the "bunt gasket," the "quarter gasket," the "yardarm gasket," etc.

GUNWALE—The gunwale (pronounced "gunnel," sometimes abbreviated to "gun'l") is the topside of an open boat. In it, at regular intervals, are holes for the oarlocks or tholes.

HAIL—To call to a ship or person.

HALYARD—A rope or tackle by which a sail, flag, or yard is hoisted—hence the name, "haul yard."

HAMMOCK—A swinging bed, much used at sea.

HAMPER—"Top hamper" is weight aloft, that is, above decks of a vessel. The upper rigging and spars, the topmasts and yards of a ship, constitute her top hamper. If these are too much for her, she is said to have too much "top hamper."

HAND—Term used for members of a crew, as "all hands on deck," "another hand wanted," etc.

HANDLE—To "handle" a boat well is to sail her well, and to work her in a seamanlike manner.

HARD—"Hard," as a nautical term, is often joined to words of command to the helmsman, signifying that the order should be carried out with the utmost energy. "Hard a'port!" means to put the wheel, or tiller, over to the left side of the ship, so that the ship's head will turn to starboard. "Hard a'weather!" is a command to put the wheel of a vessel sharply over to windward. "Hard a'lee!" calls for putting the wheel quickly over to the lee side of the ship.

HARPOON—A long, iron-shanked, and barbed weapon, securely fastened in a wood shaft, which is used in killing whales. To the end of the shaft a line is bent, the balance of the line being coiled and ready for use in the whaleboat's bow.

HATCH, HATCHWAY—A "hatchway" is an opening in the deck of a vessel through which persons or cargo may descend. A "hatch" is the removable cover (or covers) over a hatchway.

HAUL—To "haul" is to pull on a single rope or cable without the assistance of block and tackle.

HEAVE—To pull on a rope with the aid of mechanical means, as distinguished from "hauling."

HELM—The "helm" is the steering apparatus of the ship, i.e., the rudder, with its operative parts, the tiller and the wheel used on large vessels.

HELMSMAN—The man at the helm or wheel, steering the vessel.

HOLD—The inner space of a vessel, below decks, in which the cargo is stowed.

HOLYSTONE—A soft, porous stone (usually white sandstone) used in most ships for the purpose of rubbing or scouring the decks with sand every morning soon after daylight. A large, flat piece is called a "bible" because it is used by men in a kneeling position. A small piece, for getting into the corners, is a "prayer book."

HOUSE FLAG—A square flag displaying the device and colors of a mercantile shipping company, used as a signal in port and when meeting other vessels on the high seas.

HOVE—The past tense of "heave"; for example, "The ship *hove to* during the squall." Or it can be used in the present tense, as, "The ship was *hove to.*" "Hove to" means that a vessel has been brought up head to wind, with sails reefed so that she makes no progress. She is then said to be "hove to" or "lying to."

HURRICANE—A violent tropical storm with cyclonic changes in wind. Winds of seventy-five miles an hour or more are hurricanes, and the velocity often exceeds one hundred miles an hour.

JACOB'S LADDER—A rope ladder having wooden rounds, or rungs, and fitted with hooks on one end. A more substantially constructed ladder is a "jack ladder," with wooden steps connected by double rope sides.

JETTISON—To "jettison" is to cast goods overboard, either to lighten or get a ship on an even keel if she's aground, or, on the high seas, that she may ride more easily when in distress.

JURY—At sea, this word means a substitute or temporary rigging. A temporary mast is a "jury mast." Such masts were used in the old whaleboats to hoist temporary sail and save rowing until the boat was "on the whale." Then the jury mast was unstepped and the rowers pulled the rest of the distance to a point where the harpooner could hurl the harpoon into the whale. The use of jury masts on large sailing vessels was often necessary in cases where storms had dismasted the ship. The jury mast made it possible to spread sail and make port.

KEEL—The "keel" of a vessel is the principal timber, resembling the backbone of the human frame, while the side timbers constitute the ribs.

LANDFALL—Sighting or making land at the end of a sea voyage.

LATITUDE—Distance north or south of the Equator, expressed in degrees.

LAZARETTE—Storage space 'tween decks, aft. The aft hatchway that leads to the lazarette is called the "lazarette hatch."

LEE, LEEWARD—The "lee" side of a vessel is the side opposite to the one on which the wind blows; the other side is the "windward" or "weather" side. "Leeward" (pronounced "lū'erd") means "on the lee side." A vessel "to leeward" would be seen over the lee side. To be "under the lee" of any vessel or shore is to be under its shelter—that is, on the lee side of it.

LIFEBOAT—Built of wood or metal, a "lifeboat" is designed and equipped solely for lifesaving purposes at sea. The boat is usually about thirty feet long and has an eight-foot beam, is nearly flat-bottomed, and has a weighted, heavy keel. It is, generally speaking, propelled by eight or ten oars and rowed double-banked, though it is equipped with mast and sail—and in some instances is powered by a small inboard engine. A boat's buoyancy is increased by watertight air compartments fitted along the sides, inboard, under the side seats, and at the bow and stern. The lifeboat is of the whaleboat type—bow and stern having the same lines. The number of lifeboats carried by merchant ships is governed by the number of passengers the vessel carries. The capacity of airtight compartments is so calculated as to give such buoyancy that, even with the boat completely full of water and with its full complement of people, it cannot sink. Secured to the gun'ls outside the boat is a line that completely encircles it, known as the "grab line," so that persons in the water can catch hold of it. Provided, also, are concentrated provisions and fresh-water tanks. A number of thwarts provide room for the rowers. Lifeboatmen are certificated seamen who are trained in the launching and handling of lifeboats under sail or oars. They, and a coxswain, take complete charge of a lifeboat in a sea disaster. How many lifeboatmen are assigned to a boat varies from one, for boats with twenty-five or less passengers, to five for boats carrying between 86 and 110 passengers.

LIGHTS—
  1. A steamboat under way exposes on the starboard side (right) a *green light;* on the port side (left) a *red light;* on the mast, one *white light.*
  2. A tug, or a steamship towing another vessel: on the mast, two *white lights;* with port and starboard lights the same as above.
  3. A sailing vessel under way, or being towed, has on the starboard side a *green light;* on the port side a *red light;* but *never a mast light* unless at anchor.
  4. All vessels (steam or sailing) at anchor show two *white lights* on the mast not over twenty feet above the hull. These are known as "riding lights" and are shown one over the other.
  5. A ship which is being *overtaken* by another shall show from her stern to the passing vessel a *white light,* or a *flare-up light.*
  6. The *meeting* of vessels, *head on,* will show the port and starboard lights *in reverse,* in appearance.

LLOYD'S—Lloyd's of London has been in existence since 1716. Its name is derived from a coffeehouse kept by one Edward Lloyd, where all interested in shipping matters met. From there it was removed and relocated in the new Royal Exchange. Besides undertaking all matters of insurance through its members, it publishes, periodically, a large-volumed inventory of shipping intelligence, known as *Lloyd's List,* the importance of which, in the mercantile shipping trade, cannot be overrated. Lloyd's was incorporated by act of Parliament in 1871. Risks to ships insured are ac-

cepted by individual members, each one of whom
signs for a specified sum, as an underwriter, for which
he alone is responsible. Before a member can be
elected as a Lloyd's underwriter, he must place with
the corporation a minimum amount of some fifteen
thousand pounds sterling in securities, the amount
determined by the greatness of the member's commit-
ments. Lloyd's membership has six hundred members and two hundred nonunderwriting members.

LOAD WATER LINE—In the lines of a ship, the supposed
line of deepest immersion when loaded. It is, in fact,
the ship's proper displacement, and the water line
corresponds to the maximum draft to which a ship
is permitted to load, either by freeboard regulations,
the conditions of the ship's classifications, or her conditions of service. In 1930 (two years after the overloaded *Vestris* sank) an international convention on
load lines drafted rules to determine the maximum
permissible load line in merchant ships of 150 tons
or more, and engaged in international voyages. The
load lines prescribed by this convention, and adopted
by most maritime countries, are as follows:

Summer load line, marked "S."
Winter load line, marked "W."
Winter North Atlantic load line, marked "WNA."
Tropical load line, marked "T."
Fresh-water load line, marked "F."

A horizontal mark, nine inches long and one inch
wide, indicates each of these lines, and the marks
extend from, and at right angles to, a vertical line
mark twenty-one inches forward of the load line disc.
The load line disc is twelve inches in diameter and
is marked amidships *below* the deck line, intersected
by a horizontal line eighteen inches long and one
inch wide, the upper edge of this line passing through
the center of the disc (which is also called the "Plimsoll mark," for Samuel Plimsoll who originated this
"freeboard mark" and promoted the three shipping
acts which were passed by the British Parliament in

1874-75-76, bringing the freeboard problem to a satisfactory solution).

Log—The most primitive way of calculating a vessel's velocity through the water seems to have been for a sailor to heave the "log" over the bow of the vessel, then run with it until he reached the stern. The speed at which he ran formed the basis upon which the vessel's speed was reckoned; and it is said that unusually accurate results were obtained by this rough method. Until comparatively recent years, the "log" consisted of a piece of wood, usually in the form of a quadrant of a circle about five or six inches in radius and a fourth of an inch thick. This piece of wood was called the "ship" and was so balanced by a lead weight as to float perpendicularly almost submerged in the water. The "ship" was fastened to one end of a long line, called the "log line," the other end being wound on a reel secured to the stern rail of the vessel. When the log or "ship" was "heaved," or thrown into the water, it theoretically kept its place while the log line ran off the reel as the vessel moved, and the length unwinding in a given time indicated the rate of the vessel's sailing speed. This, in turn, was calculated by "knots" made on the line at specific intervals, and by a sandglass which ran out in a certain number of seconds. Thus, in order to avoid unnecessary calculations, the length between these knots was so proportioned to the time of the sandglass that the number of knots unwound while the glass ran down indicated the number of miles the vessel was sailing per hour. The intervals between knots is usually 47 feet 3 inches; hence, the term "knot" means the velocity in nautical miles per hour of a vessel. A nautical mile is 6,080 feet, being, for practical purposes, the length of one minute of arc of a meridian. But the system of logging a vessel's speed, as given above, was subject to considerable contingencies, such as currents, etc., and is now being superseded by various forms of self-registering rotators which give the actual speed of a vessel much more accurately.

Logbook—The "log" being heaved at certain times in each watch, the particulars were entered in the vessel's journal, called the "logbook." In it were recorded the happenings aboard ship—the distance the vessel had made, her position, the weather, etc. It was called being "logged" for a person to be entered in the logbook; and if it were for an offense, it was considered a serious matter.

Longboat—A strong rowing boat, propelled by eight or ten oars, often double-banked; its length is thirty to forty feet, with a beam approximately eight to ten feet. Such boats were carried by merchant sailing vessels and were equipped with masts, sails, and oars, and were handy in transporting stores, water, etc., in open roadsteads where a vessel lay at anchor. A whaleship's longboat had a narrower beam, and its stem and stern were alike.

Longitude—Distance east or west of a given place, expressed in degrees, minutes, and seconds of arc on the Equator between the prime meridian and the meridian passing through the given place.

Lookout—A "lookout" on a watch is the member of that watch whose duty it is to observe, either from the fo'c'sle deck or from the crow's-nest, any dangerous object lying in or near the ship's track.

Overhaul—In the sense of passing—to "overhaul" another vessel.

Peak, Main—The upper end of a gaff, or, more properly, the uppermost corner of the main sail of a schooner-rigged vessel.

Poop—Properly, an extra deck on the after part of a vessel. Also, when a sea comes over the stern of a vessel, it is said to "poop" her.

Port—1. The left-hand side of a vessel. 2. Ports, or port

holes: the round openings in the sides of cabins of a vessel, to let in light, air, etc. 3. A place for the loading and unloading of vessels.

QUADRANT—An instrument once used in navigation, but now long since superseded by the sextant.

QUARTER—The "quarters" are those portions of the sides of a vessel about halfway between beam and stern; and, in their position aft of the beam, they may be said to correspond with the bows, which lie forward of the beam. Hence, "quarter boats" are ship's boats carried on her quarters; the "quarter-deck" is that part of the deck covering the quarters.

QUARTERMASTER—One of the chief petty officers on board a ship.

RATLINES—The name implies a similarity to a "rat's tail" and the word is pronounced "ratlins." These are the small lines crossing the shrouds of a ship and form the steps of the rope ladders.

REEF—To "reef" means to reduce the area of sail spread to the wind. Square sails attached to yards are reefed at the head by men going out on the yards. Gaff sails, such as are used in a schooner-rigged vessel, are reefed at the foot, or from the deck.

REEVE—Generally speaking, to "reeve" means to pass something through a hole. To reeve a tackle is to pass a rope through its blocks.

RIGGING—The system of cordage in a vessel by which masts are supported and sails extended and worked. There are two sorts of rigging: 1. Standing rigging (stationary), which consists of shrouds, stays, etc., and all such ropes, chains, or cables that hold spars in place. 2. Running rigging (movable), which comprises halyards, sheets, clew lines, etc., and all moving ropes connected with sails, flags, etc. The lower rigging is that of the lower masts; the upper rigging is that of the topmasts.

SAIL—

1. Full-rigged ships: Sails take their names from the mast, yard, or stay upon which they are "bent." The principal sail extended upon the main mast is called the "mainsail"; the next above, which stands upon the main topmast, is the "main topsail"; above which is the "main topgallant sail" (t'garns'l); and above all, the "main royal." In the same manner are the "foresail," the "fore-topsail," the "fore-topgallant sail," and the "foreroyal." Similar names are given to the sails supported by the mizzen or after mast. The "main staysail," "main-topmast staysail," etc., are between the main and fore masts; and the "mizzen staysail," "mizzentopmast staysail," etc., are between the main and mizzen masts. These, however, are used only in dead calms. Between the foremast and bowsprit are the "fore staysail" (commonly called the "foresail"), the "jib," and sometimes the "flying jib" and "middle jib"; and the "studding sails" (stuns'ls) are those which are extended upon booms run out beyond the arms of the different yards of the main and foremasts. To the square sails on each mast may be added one more, above all the rest, called respectively the "skysail" and the "moonsail" (moonraker), though, generally speaking, these last two are not too often used.

2. Fore-and-aft rigged: "Fore-and-aft sails" (such as are rigged on schooners, ketches, yawls, racing yachts, etc.) are those set in the direction of the length of the vessel, such as "gaff sails" (see Gaff), "head sails," "flying jib," "trysails" (which means a gaff sail without a boom).

SALVAGE—Property which has been recovered from a wrecked vessel, or even the recovery of the ship itself.

SCUPPERS—Openings in the bulwarks of a ship to carry off deck water.

SCUTTLE—1. To "scuttle" is to cut a hole. Hence, an opening in a vessel's sides or deck, whether to admit light or to allow persons to descend through it, is a "scuttle." 2. To "scuttle" a ship is to cut a hole in her below the water line so as to sink her.

SEA—The term "sea" is derived from the Greek, meaning "to shake," or "tossed-about water," in contradistinction to stagnant or running water.

> The "high seas" are that part of the ocean beyond the (three mile) limit over which the government of a country can claim jurisdiction.
>
> A "heavy sea" indicates the condition of the surface when waves are large.
>
> A "long sea" means that there is a considerable distance between waves.
>
> A "short" or "choppy sea" refers to waves which follow closely upon each other.
>
> A "cross sea" is one in which, in consequence to a change of wind or the run of the tide, the waves meet each other from different directions.
>
> A single wave is often called a "sea," and, in the plural, "seas" may mean the waves.

SEAMAN—A man who has been brought up to or has served a certain number of years at sea. A complete seaman is called "able-bodied" and is rated an "A.B."; one who has served a lesser number of years is known as an "ordinary seaman"; and one who is only beginning his career, a landsman, is equivalent to an ordinary seaman, second class.

SEXTANT—An instrument used at sea for measuring the altitude of the celestial bodies, and thereby determining the position of a ship. This is sometimes called "shooting the sun."

SHEAVE—The wheel in a block (see Block), and sometimes in a spar.

SHEET—1. The rope attached to a sail so that it may be worked. For example, the "main sheet" works the mainsail; the "jib sheets" work the jib, etc. 2. "Head sheets" and "stern sheets" (in open boats), the floor boards covering the space either at the head or the stern of the boat.

SHIP—The term indiscriminately applied to all large vessels. Among seamen, "ship" is restricted to a vessel which is full-rigged.

SHROUDS—Strong ropes literally supporting a mast. They are now mostly wire cable and are named for the spars they support. For example, "main" or "mizzen shrouds," "topmast shrouds," "bowsprit shrouds," etc.

SIGNAL FLAGS—A flag or flags used for signaling between two ships or between ship and shore. The signaling flags for merchant vessels are those agreed upon internationally and use an international code. Flags of the code, in use since 1932, employ twenty-six letters of the alphabet, a code flag, ten numeral pennants, and three substitutes. It is possible to make any kind of a signal, by means of hoisting not more than four flags, from code or spell words not included in the code. Few colors can be quickly discerned at sea. Red, blue, yellow, black, and white are the ones that can be most readily picked up, though these must not be indiscriminately mixed. For best results at a distance such color combinations as red and white, blue and yellow, white and blue, plain red, white, and blue flags should be used.

SKIPPER—The master of a merchant vessel; called, by courtesy, "captain," on shore, and always so at sea.

SOUNDING—Taking depths of water and the quality of the ground by means of the lead and line. Tallow being inserted into the hollow space at the bottom of the lead, this will enable a small quantity of the ground upon which it descends to be brought up. By this means an experienced navigator can judge his whereabouts in foggy weather, and he can also judge the condition of the bottom under him.

SPAR—One of the timber members of a vessel's gear, usually round or nearly so, and formerly made of a solid piece of lumber. A general term for a mast, yard, boom, gaff, or the like.

SQUALL—A sudden gusty wind, or a sudden increase in its force, often accompanied by rain, snow, sleet, or hail.

SQUARE STERN—A "square stern" is a stern cut off square. The *Mary Celeste* had had a square stern.

STABILITY—"Stability" is the tendency in a vessel to keep upright, or to return to an upright position when careened over. This stability was very much lacking in the *Vestris*, due to overloading, thus having too much top weight to come back upright when the wind and waves smashed against her starboard side. Her lack of stability finally caused her to capsize and sink.

STAND—A command to be ready to do something. For example, "Stand by to cast off!" or, "Stand clear of the cable!"

STARBOARD—The right-hand side of a vessel.

STAVE—To break a hole into anything. Also, to fend, or guard off, one object from another. A vessel may be in collision and have bows or side "stove in," or she may be fortunate enough to evade the threatened danger by pushing, or "staving," it off.

STAYS—The strong ropes, or cables, supporting the spars, or more especially the masts. They form part of the standing rigging of a vessel.

STEADY—To keep a vessel "steady" means to keep her on her course without deviation.

STEER—To "steer" is to guide a boat or ship, whether under sail, steam, or oars; and a good helmsman opposes in time the tendency of a ship to deviate from her course by a small motion, which he relaxes as soon as the effect is felt, thus disturbing her sailing as little as possible.

STEERAGE—The "steerage" in a steamship is that part of a vessel offering the poorest accommodations and occupied by the steerage passengers, or by those paying the lowest fare.

STERN POST—The principal member at the after part of a vessel, usually vertical and extending from keel to deck. On it is hung the rudder.

STEVEDORE—A contractor, or company, whose business it is to undertake the stowage of cargo in ships.

STOW—Stowage is the space in a vessel for the cargo, and "to stow the cargo" is to pack it so that it will not shift as the ship rolls.

SUPERCARGO—A person who superintends transactions relating to the vessel's cargo.

SUPERSTRUCTURE—Any structure which extends above the upper or main deck, such as a bridge house or a decked building on the freeboard deck which extends from side to side of the vessel.

TACK—1. "Starboard tack." A vessel is on the starboard tack when the wind blows from the starboard or right side. 2. "Port tack." A vessel is on the port tack when the wind blows from the left-hand side of the vessel.

TAFFRAIL—The sternmost rail of a vessel.

TILLER—One of the component parts of the helm; the handle, or beam, at the head of the rudder by which the rudder is worked.

TON, TONNAGE—The "ton" serves as a measure of a ship's internal dimensions and as a basis for a schedule of dues, fees, etc. "Tonnage" expresses the size of a vessel and the amount of her cargo.

TOPSIDE—On deck, above deck.

TRAMP FREIGHTER—A freighter which does not run on any schedule, but takes a shipper's cargo to the port he desires. Tramp freighters often carry a few passengers.

TRANSOM—In a ship the "transoms" are the transverse timbers or beams bolted across the sternpost to receive the after ends of the decks.

TRAVERSE—"Traverse sailing," in navigation, is sailing in different courses in succession. A "traverse table" is a table or tabulated form employed in reducing the courses made in traverse sailing. Captain Fried, of the *President Roosevelt,* used traverse sailing when trying to locate the *Antinoe.*

TRIM—The "trim" of a vessel is her position in the water with respect to the horizontal. If she is level, she is "in trim"; if she is on an uneven keel, or if she is lying over on one side, she is "out of trim." To "trim sails" is so to dispose the sails of a vessel that she will move to her best advantage.

TRUCK—A wooden cap at the head of a pole or topmast.

TYPHOON—A tropical cyclone occurring near the Philippines or in the China Sea.

WAIST—Actually that part of a vessel between the beam and the quarter. The term, however, applies more particularly to those vessels which have quarter-decks.

WARDROOM—Officers' messroom on board a warship.

WATCHES—A ship's company is divided into two "watches," the "starboard watch" and the "port watch," these names being derived from the situation in which the crew's hammocks are hung. The chief mate commands the port watch and the second mate commands the starboard watch. The two groups divide the time between them, being on and off duty—or, as it is called, "on deck" and "below"—every other four hours. In order to shift the watches each night, so that the same watch need not be on deck the same hours, the watch from 4:00 P.M. to 8:00 P.M. is divided into two halves or "dog watches," one from 4:00 to 8:00 P.M., and the other from 6:00 to 8:00 P.M. By this means the twenty-four hours is divided into seven watches instead of six. This system of watches has changed somewhat since the coming of steamships, upon which the four hours on and four off has given way to four on and eight off, or to day and night watches of twelve hours' duration.

WEIGH—This term must not be confused with "way," as is too often the case. A vessel is "under weigh" from the moment her anchor is "weighed," or off the ground

or as soon as she has cast off her lines at dockside—
even though she may have no "way" on her.

WHALEBOAT—A longboat used in whaling. It is sharp at
both bow and stern, sometimes as much as fifty-six
feet in length, and has a beam of ten feet.

WHALER—A ship employed in the whaling trade.

WHALES—The "sperm whale" and the "right whale" were
the most valued for their oil. Other types of whale
have a less valuable oil.

WHEEL—Referring here to the "wheel" and axle by which
the tiller of a vessel is worked.

WHIP—A rope and single block used in lifting light articles.
A "whip" was used in hanging Spencer, Cromwell, and
Small aboard the brig-o'-war U.S.S. *Somers*.

WINDLASS—The wheel and axle, turned by either hand-
spikes or a crank, by which the chain cable of a vessel
may be hauled in. Unlike the capstan, the "windlass"
lies horizontal with the deck, though it does the same
work.

YARD—A spar suspended to a mast for the purpose of extending a sail in square-rigged vessels, where the
"yards" go athwart the masts.

YAWING—In a sailing vessel, deviation from the true course.

YAWL—A vessel with two masts—main and mizzen, the
mizzen being small and carrying only one sail. A
"yawl" may be of varying size. The one carried aboard
the *Mary Celeste* was said to have been only sixteen
feet.